Country

CRAFTS · COOKING · DECORATING · FLOWERS

Country

CRAFTS · COOKING · DECORATING · FLOWERS

HERMES
HOUSE

This edition published in 1997 by Hermes House

© 1997 Anness Publishing Limited

Hermes House is an imprint of
Anness Publishing Limited
Hermes House, 88–89 Blackfriars Road
London SE1 8HA

ISBN 1 901289 04 4

Publisher: Joanna Lorenz
Project Editor: Christopher Fagg
Editor: Lydia Darbyshire
Designer: Siân Keogh
Photographers: James Duncan, John Freeman, Michelle Garrett, Lucy Mason, Gloria Nicol,
Debbie Patterson, Steve Tanner and Lucy Tizard

Printed and bound in Germany

3 5 7 9 10 8 6 4 2

Material in this book previously appeared in *Glorious Country* by Liz Trigg, Tessa Evelegh and
Stewart and Sally Walton; *Folk Art* by Stewart and Sally Walton; *The Ultimate Quilting and
Patchwork Companion* by Isabel Stanley and Jenny Watson; *The Ultimate Cross Stitch Companion* by
Dorothy Wood; *The New Flower Arranger* by Fiona Barnett and Roger Egerickx; and *The Complete
Book of Herbs* by Andi Clevely and Katherine Richmond.

For all recipes, quantities are given in both metric and imperial measures and, where appropriate,
measures are also given in standard cups and spoons. Follow one set, but not a mixture, because
they are not interchangeable. Size 3 (standard) eggs should be used unless otherwise stated.

FRONTISPIECE: *Make fragrant wreaths and country-style decorated baskets like these, inspired by ideas from
Everlasting Treats (see page 271).*

Contents

COUNTRY STYLE 6

Country Decorating
WALLS AND FLOORS 13

FURNITURE AND FURNISHINGS 35

DETAILS AND ACCESSORIES 55

Country Quilts and Needlework
PATCHWORK AND APPLIQUÉ 99

CROSS STITCH 161

Country Crafts and Flowers
FRESH FROM THE FIELDS 215

EVERLASTING TREATS 271

Country Gifts
TOKENS TO TREASURE 325

GIFTS FROM THE PANTRY 397

Country Cooking
SPRING RECIPES 417

SUMMER RECIPES 439

AUTUMN RECIPES 467

WINTER RECIPES 491

INDEX 506

ACKNOWLEDGEMENTS 512

Country Style

Picture a house in the countryside on a bright autumn day, smoke wafting from the chimney into a brilliant blue sky. There are trees that have turned glorious shades of yellow and orange and there is a chill in the wind. Cats are asleep in shafts of sunlight, ignoring the birds that chatter on the rooftop. On a summer day, the arch over the gate will be covered with roses, and hollyhocks will stretch up the white walls past the open windows from which muslin billows out, caught by the warm breeze. ❧ Step inside the house and smell bread baking in the range; leave your boots on the rack and walk across the cool flagstones. Sink into a comfortable chair by the scrubbed pine table and look around at stencilled patterns, crocheted lace, gleaming copper pans and wooden spoons. This is the country that we see in our dreams, and if our waking hours are passed in a high-speed, high-pressure city environment, these dreams have an added seductive quality. Rosy images of the pastoral are potent symbols of a way of life that seems somehow gentler, less stressful and more natural than the urban routine. As the pressures of late twentieth-century living mount, we want to put some of that country tranquility back into our lives. One of the easiest ways of doing this is to recreate some elements of country style in the home, providing a restful and welcoming environment to come back to. You don't have to live in a cottage to create the cottage look: the look comes as much from a way of thinking as from a way of living. ❧ This book shows you how to get into that way of thinking, and how to channel it into creative projects that will bring something of the dream of country living into your home — whether that is a farmhouse or a flat. But it's not just the end-product of your creativity that you will value; in the process of designing and making country-style artefacts and effects you will find a satisfaction and sense of peace that are the real goals of country style.

BELOW: *The beautiful yet practical nature of patchwork is typical of country style.*

Achieving a Country Look

Country style has many interpretations and all over the world there are towns-people who dream of a calmer way of life in a place where traffic doesn't bustle, food has more flavour and night skies are filled with stars, not neon. This may be an idealized picture, but it has an underlying truth: country life is still governed by seasonal changes, not man-made deadlines. ❧ Country homes are alive, growing and comfortable and country decorating is for living in, not just looking at. Many of the effects that we think of as talismans of country style have an eminently practical function. ❧ Country style may vary a lot, according to nationality and the local climate, but there is a core of recognizable elements. It is a home-made, functional, comfortable style. There is often a big kitchen area, with a large scrubbed pine table and an assortment of comfortable chairs. Country kitchens can be a riot of pattern and colour, where the dresser is stacked with displays of china and the beams are hung with baskets full of drying flowers and herbs. Gleaming copper pots and pans should never be

ABOVE: *Although several motifs are present in this room, the restricted use of colour pulls the whole look together.*

hidden away in cupboards, so use butcher's hooks to display them out of 'head banging' reach. Floors need to be practical, tough and easy to keep clean, so floorboards, flagstones, linoleum or cork tiles are the favourite choices, and they can all be softened with washable cotton dhurries or rag rugs. ❧ The food prepared in the country kitchen is hearty and nourishing, and is prepared from the produce of the season — warming roasts and stews in the winter and light, fresh vegetable flans or fruit tarts in the summer. Locally grown produce — organic, if not from your own garden — will taste immeasurably

better if it is a seasonal treat rather than a year-round staple.   Through-out the home, flower arrangements take their cue from nature and are combined with other organic materials to provide a more casual, spontaneous look than hot-house blooms. A ginger jar that has been in the family for years stands alongside an enamel jug filled with flowers from yesterday's walk. You might choose to float flowerheads on a glass plate, or collect supple twigs to form a heart-shaped wreath wrapped with trailing ivy. The colours of autumn may be represented by gourds, vegetables and dried seedheads.   The country house is not a fashion statement, and its colour schemes should reflect the natural colour in the landscape; these need not be dull, bland and safe; they can be as rich as autumn, with touches of brilliance, or warm as a summer pasture filled with buttercups or a field of ripe corn.   The house responds to personal touches; a painted border may still be there in 50 years, so paint it thoughtfully. Make time in your life to be creative, whether it be with stencilling, floor-painting or embroidery. All home-made crafts add richness to the home and give you a sense of personal achievement that money cannot buy.   There are step-by-step projects here to suit all levels of experience and creative ability. You may feel daunted by embroidery but more confident about making patterns in tin with a hammer and nail; unsure about flower arranging, but able to pop a few dried flowerheads into a terracotta pot.

BELOW: Decorative panels can transform a piece of furniture. If you are not confident about painting free-hand, stencilling is a simpler option.

Whatever you choose, rest assured that all the projects have been designed to give maximum effect for minimum effort. If you want to ring the changes very quickly on your walls, use a colour glaze with a foam-block print or stencilled border. Giving floorboards the limed look requires the hard work of sanding first, but the painting can be done and

ABOVE: *Patchwork cushions soften a wooden chair, and provide a practical use for odd scraps and remnants of fabric.*

dried in an afternoon. If you have considered laying cork tiles, then stain half of them black and make a real impact with a chequer-board floor. ❧ When it comes to choosing materials, or pieces of furniture to decorate, take a tip from the squirrel and start hoarding! There are so many second-hand stores, car boot sales and jumble sales around, and if you buy things that have potential, you will always have something to hand when the creative mood strikes. It can be amazingly difficult to find a wooden tray or a nice tin can when you want one, so have a 'potential' corner in the loft or the shed, and keep it well stocked! ❧ On a very practical note, there has been a major change in materials for home-decorating recently, with the arrival of water-based paint products. There is no longer any need for solvents to clean brushes; they rinse out under the tap. The biggest bonus of this revolution is that decorating time has been cut in half. Water-based products dry very quickly, and this is especially useful when applying many coats of varnish to painted furniture. The rule to remember is not to mix oil and water, so if you tint varnish for an antique effect, mix acrylics with water-based clear varnish or oil colour with traditional varnish. ❧ Whether you go for the total country look for your home, or just a few details, always try to decorate in a way that is sympathetic to the character and age of your house. Use the best features, like an interestingly shaped window, as focal points; be courageous about removing a ghastly fireplace, or disguising oppressively heavy beams. Your home should please you, and country style is about personal touches, natural materials, warmth and comfort. So, follow your instincts and enjoy the charm of country life.

COUNTRY
Decorating

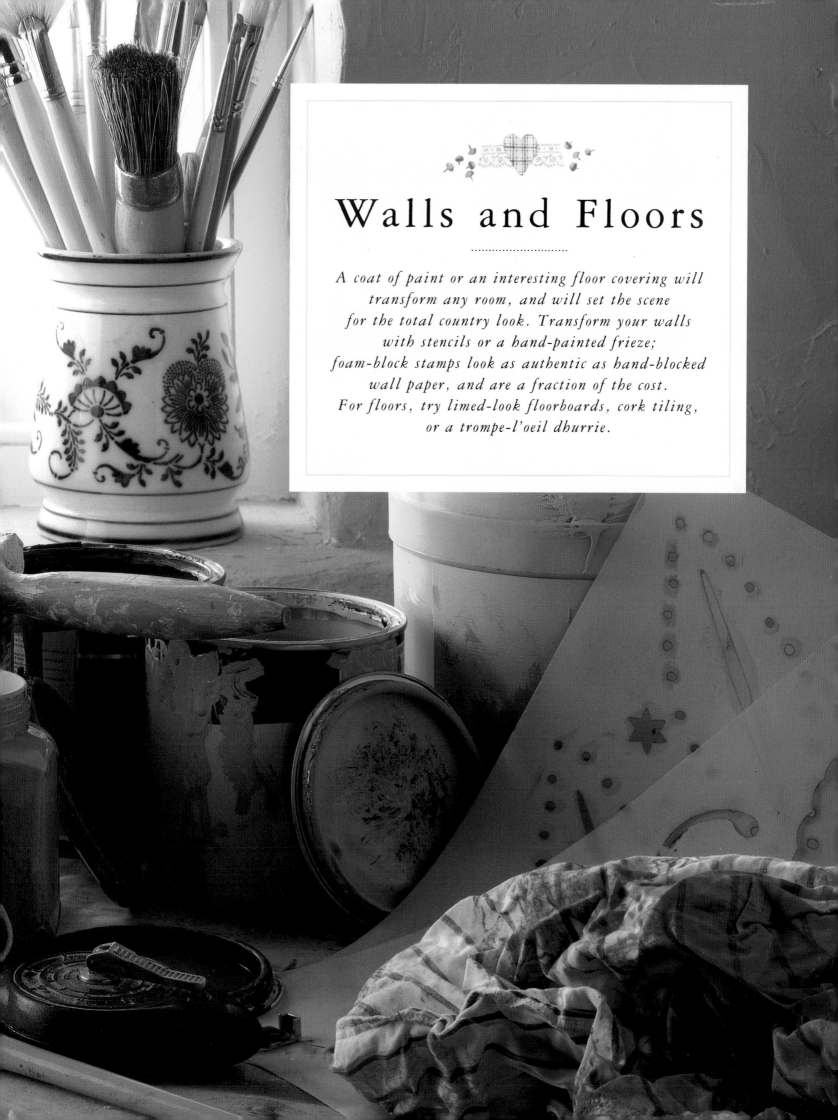

Walls and Floors

·····················

*A coat of paint or an interesting floor covering will
transform any room, and will set the scene
for the total country look. Transform your walls
with stencils or a hand-painted frieze;
foam-block stamps look as authentic as hand-blocked
wall paper, and are a fraction of the cost.
For floors, try limed-look floorboards, cork tiling,
or a trompe-l'oeil dhurrie.*

The Country Palette

Colour has a great influence on us: it can affect our moods quite dramatically. Choose your palette from nature's harmonies, avoiding artificially brilliant colours. It would be a mistake to think that natural colours are all shades of beige; just think of autumn and the huge variety of yellows, oranges and scarlets that mingle among the trees.

When painting the walls country-style it is best to avoid a perfect, even finish – go instead for a patchy, glowing, colour-washed effect. By doing this you can use strong colour, but in a transparent way that is not as heavy as solid colour. Don't avoid strong colours like brick red, deep green or dusky blue. The furniture, rugs, pictures, ornaments, cushions and curtains will all combine to absorb the strength of the wall colour and dilute its power. If your rooms are dark, use the strong colours below dado-rail height only, with a creamy, light colour on the upper walls and ceiling. Darker colours can be very cosy in a large room, but if you want a room to look bigger it would be best to stick to a lighter scheme, and use a stencil or free-hand border to add colour and interest.

If mixing your own paint is too daunting a prospect, you could go for one of the new 'historic' ranges made by specialist producers. These paints are a lot more expensive than ordinary brands, but the colour ranges are designed to harmonize with antiques, natural building materials and old textiles, and if your budget can stretch to them, they really are wonderful.

If your courage fails and you choose white walls, think about highlighting the woodwork. Paint a deep, rich colour on the skirtings and the window- and door-frames, allow it to dry and then

ABOVE: *Colours derived from nature are not necessarily sombre. Think of clear blue skies or a field of wildflowers.*

paint a light colour on top. Use a damp cloth to wipe off some of the topcoat, and sandpaper to lift colour that has dried. This will give you an effect of flashes of brilliance to add warmth to the room.

Choose natural colours that make you happy, and remember that country-style decorating is not about having everything matching. You don't need co-ordinating curtains, carpets and lampshades. On the contrary, the more eclectic the choice, the more stunning the effect can often be.

Giving your home the country look requires attention to the basics – the walls and floors. Get these right and the rest is easy. A bare room with powdery wall-paint, stencilling and a stripped, limed floor has a real country feeling, whereas no amount of folk artefacts and rustic furniture can transform to 'country' a tastefully wallpapered, corniced and thick-pile carpeted drawing room!

The ideal way to begin would be to clear the house, remove all the old wallpaper

and carpets and start from scratch, but this is a luxury that few can afford. It's more practical to think in terms of a room at a time, repainting the walls and adding one of the country-style floors that are featured in this chapter.

This chapter shows how the basic elements of a room can be changed to make it feel more individual. When you paint, stencil or print on your walls, they truly become your own, and this never happens with wallpaper, however good you are at hanging it! We sometimes suggest cheating a little: roughening up smooth surfaces, wiping off more paint than is put on, or stencilling unevenly, for a worn-away look. You can't wait a hundred years for this to occur naturally!

The ideas for the projects have been inspired by folk art and by real-life examples of country decorating of period homes. There has been a recent revival of interest in the subject and it is now possible to buy kits to age practically anything, with a plethora of equipment required for the job.

Whatever you choose for your walls and floor, it is important to see them in terms of a backdrop for your own tastes and possessions. Paintings, mirrors, lamps, plants, shelves, rugs and furniture will all add to the final effect. A painted border may appear to be too dominant in an empty room, but the effect will be much more subtle when the furnishings, accessories and personal details have been added.

Remember that country style is more about relaxation, comfort and harmony than precision and fashion; this is the type of decorating that is a pleasure to involve yourself in, so enjoy the process as well as the result.

CLOCKWISE FROM TOP LEFT: *The walls and floors have been coated with tinted varnish to simulate the patina of age.*
Deep, brick red is bold, yet warm in a sitting room. The soft colours of this crazy patchwork quilt
are punctuated with vibrant stitching.

Brushed-out Colour Glaze

This soft, patchy wall finish is pure country. It's traditionally achieved using either a very runny colour-wash, or an oil-based glaze tinted with oil colour, over eggshell paint. This project gives the same effect, but is easier to achieve.

The unusual element in the glaze is wallpaper paste, which is mixed in the usual way before the addition of PVA glue. The wallpaper paste adds a translucency to the colour and the PVA seals the surface when dry. To tint the glaze you can use powder, gouache or acrylic paint, mixed with a small amount of water first, so that it blends easily.

Use a large decorator's brush to apply the glaze, dabbing glaze on to the wall about five times within an arm's reach. Then use light, random strokes to sweep the glaze across the area, to use up the dabs and cover the area. Move along the wall, blending each area with the next.

This is a very cheap way of painting a room, so you can afford to mix up more glaze than you will use, and throw some away. This is preferable to running out before you finish, because it is so difficult to match the original colour. A litre / 1¾ pints of glaze will cover almost 40 square metres / yards.

MATERIALS

*PVA glue
wallpaper paste
acrylic, gouache or powder paint,
to colour the glaze
large decorator's brush*

1

Prepare your wall-surface: ideally it should be an off-white vinyl silk, but any plain, light colour will do, if it is clean. Wash old paint with sugar soap and leave it to dry. Mix up the glaze, using 1 part PVA glue, 5 parts water and ¼ part wallpaper paste. Tint it with three 20 cm / 8 in squirts from an acrylic or gouache tube, or about 15 ml / 1 tbsp of powder paint. Vary the intensity of colour to your own taste. Experiment on scrap lining paper painted with the same background colour as your walls. Get the feel of the glaze and brush, and adjust the colour at this stage if necessary.

2

Begin applying the glaze in an area of the room that will be hidden by furniture or pictures; as your technique improves you will be painting the more obvious areas. Start near the top of the wall, dabbing glaze on with the brush and then sweeping it over the surface with random strokes, as described previously.

3

The effect is streaky and the brushstrokes do show, but they can be softened before they are completely dry. After about 5 minutes brush the surface lightly with your brush but don't use any glaze. The brush will pick up any surplus glaze on the surface and leave a softer, less streaky effect. When working on edges and corners, apply the glaze and then brush it away from the corner or edge. You will still find that the colour may be more concentrated in some places, but it will all look very different when the room is furnished.

'Powdery' Paint Finish for Walls

You may need to 'rough-up' your walls a bit to achieve this look; this is easily done with a tub of filler, a spatula and some rough-grade sandpaper. Think of it as a reversal of the usual preparations!

This paint finish imitates the opaque, soft colour and powdery bloom of distemper, the wall finish most used before the invention of emulsion paint. The joy of decorating with this 'powdery finish' paint, is that it can be used directly on concrete, plaster or plasterboard – indeed almost any surface – without lining paper or special undercoats. The paint is diluted with water, to the consistency required, and is slapped on with a large brush. Mistakes and runs can be wiped off with a damp cloth, and the paint is a pleasure to use. It takes about two hours to dry, and the colour lightens considerably as it does so, until the final effect is revealed – a soft powdery surface of matt colour that will bring instant warmth to any room.

The 'distressed' plaster effect has a charmingly country feel. Perhaps we imagine that real country folk didn't have the time or inclination to decorate to a perfect finish; for whatever reasons, there is something very comfortable about walls with irregular surfaces and faded paint.

MATERIALS

Polyfilla or similar filler
spatula
rough-grade sandpaper
Brats 'Mediterranean Palette'
paint in shade 'Asia'
large decorator's brush

1

Prepare the walls by stripping off any wallpaper down to the bare plaster. Spread the filler irregularly with the spatula to simulate the uneven texture of old plaster. Use thin layers, applied randomly from different directions. Don't worry about overdoing the effect; you can always rub it back with sandpaper when it's dry, after about an hour.

2

Blend the dried filler into the original wall surface using the sandpaper, leaving rougher areas for a more obvious distressed effect. Mix the paint with water in the ratio 2 parts water to 1 part paint.

3

Begin painting at ceiling height. The paint is likely to splash a bit, so protect any surfaces with an old sheet or decorator's cloth. Use the paintbrush in a random way, rather than in straight lines, and expect a patchy effect – it will fade as the paint dries. The second coat needs to be stronger, so use less water in the mixture. Stir the paint well; it should have the consistency of single cream.

Apply the second coat in the same way, working the brush into any cracks or rough plaster areas. Two hours later the 'bloom' of the powdery finish will have appeared. The element of surprise makes decorating with this paint exciting, especially as the final texture is so mellow and effective at covering, but not concealing, the irregularities of the wall's surface. We used this surface as a base for the stencilled border on the following page.

Stencilled Border

Stencilling tends to spread around the house like a climbing plant, appearing round doorways and winding along picture rails, up staircases and across floors! It is a delightful and habit-forming activity and it's extremely difficult to be a minimalist when it comes to stencilling.

The design used for this border came from a Rhode Island house that was built and decorated in the eighteenth century. Stencilling was an extremely popular means of decorating interiors, and stencils were used to create pillars and friezes as well as all-over patterns, with as many as seven different designs on a single wall.

A border design like this one is perfectly suited for use above a dado-rail, but there is no reason why you should not use it at picture-rail, or skirting-board height, or even as a frame around a window. Or you may not have a dado-rail but still like the effect of a wall divided in this way. In this case it is a simple matter of marking the division with paint or varnish.

Use a plumb-line and a long ruler to divide the wall, marking the line in pencil. The wall below the line can be painted a darker shade, or, if you are using the 'Mediterranean Palette' colour, a coat of clear satin varnish will darken the colour and add a sheen. The stencilled border will visually integrate the two sections of wall and soften the edges between them. If you vary the depth of stencilled colour, it will look naturally faded by time.

MATERIALS

tracing paper
Mylar or stencil card
spray adhesive
scalpel or craft knife
masking tape
Brats Mediterranean Palette paint
in shade 'Asia' (optional)
varnish in shade 'Antique Pine'
household paintbrush
stencil paint
stencil brush

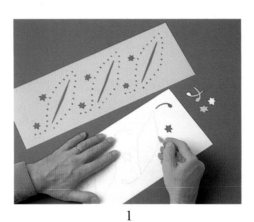

1

Trace and enlarge the pattern from the template section. Stick it on the Mylar using spray adhesive. Use a scalpel or craft knife to cut out the stencil carefully. Repair any mistakes with masking tape and always use a very sharp blade which will give you the most control when cutting. Peel off the remaining tracing paper.

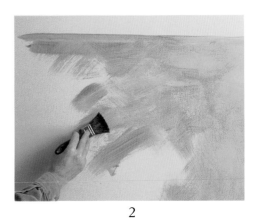

2

If desired, prepare the powdery paint finish on the previous page, then paint the whole wall in 'Asia'. Paint the lower half of the wall with a coat of Antique Pine tinted varnish. Use random brush strokes for a rough finish.

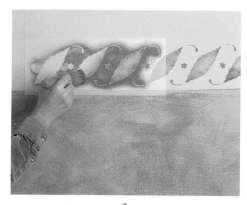

3

Apply a light spray of adhesive to the back of
the stencil and leave it to dry for 5 minutes.
Position the stencil at a corner and paint the
first colour. Use the paint very sparingly,
wiping the brush on absorbent kitchen paper
before using it on the wall. You can always
go over a light area to darken it later, but
excess paint on the brush will cause blobs,
and bleed through to the back of the stencil.
Lift the stencil and wipe any excess paint
from the pattern edges before positioning it
alongside the stencilling. Continue along
the top of the dado-rail until the first colour
is complete.

4

Stencil paint is fast-drying, so you can
immediately begin to add the next colour,
starting at the same point as you did with the
first. Work your way around the border,
remembering to wipe the stencil clean
as you go.

Free-hand Frieze with Half-gloss to Dado Height

This project combines the idea of dividing up the wall with textures and colours, and the free-hand painting of a vine frieze. The frieze will take some planning and preparation to achieve the casual free-hand effect, but the finished painting will look effortless and be unique.

A coat of gloss paint below the dado-rail will provide a practical, tough, wipe-clean surface where you most need it, and the gloss gives the colour a marvellous reflective shine. The lighter colour above the dado has a matt texture and the shade is reminiscent of cream straight from the dairy. If you don't have a dado-rail dividing your wall, this project is just as effective on a plain wall.

The secret of painting free-hand curves on a vertical surface, is to steady your hand on a mahlstick, which is quite simply a piece of dowel about 45 cm / 18 in long. Make a small pad of cotton wool at one end, cover it with a small square of cotton or muslin and secure it with a rubber band. Use the stick by pressing the pad against the wall with your spare hand, holding the stick free of the wall. Rest your brush hand lightly on it to prevent wobbles and jerks. Practise the curves with the mahlstick before starting the frieze, but remember that the charm of hand-painting is its variability, so relax and enjoy yourself.

MATERIALS

National Trust paint in shades 51 (Sudbury Yellow) emulsion, 14 (Berrington Blue) full gloss and 43 (Eating Room Red) oil eggshell paint-roller and tray gloss-roller 2.5 cm / 1 in decorator's brush masking tape, if necessary chalk line or ruler chalk stencil card with design

medium-weight card scalpel or craft knife 1 cm / ½ in square-ended artist's brush gouache paint in Indian red and raw sienna 45 cm / 18 in length of dowelling (of pencil thickness) small wad of cotton wool square of cotton fabric rubber band number 6 round-ended artist's brush

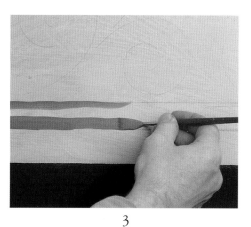

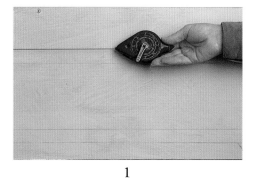

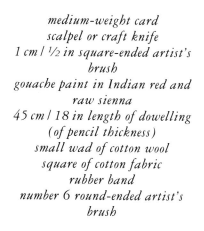

1

Apply yellow emulsion to the prepared wall with the paint-roller, from ceiling to dado. Paint blue gloss colour between the dado and skirting, using the gloss-roller. Using the red eggshell paint, and the 2.5 cm / 1 in brush, paint the skirting board and the dado-rail, if you have one. Use masking tape, if necessary, to give a clean line. Use a chalk line or ruler to draw light chalk guide-lines, marking out the depth of the frieze.

2

Using your chosen stencil, lightly mark out the position of the frieze by drawing through the stencil.

3

Paint the thick and thin lines, using the square-ended brush, flat and on its side, and the gouache paints. To add variety to the line, mix up two different shades of the same colour and use both randomly.

4

Make up your mahlstick as described on the previous page.

5

Paint in the curved stems, using the round-ended brush and gouache, supporting your hand on the mahlstick. Try to make your movements as fluid as possible.

6

Add the bunches of grapes, above and below the stems using the round-ended brush. Overlap the double lines in some places: remember that you are aiming for a hand-painted look, not a regular-repeat pattern.

Foam-block Painting

Printing with cut-out foam blocks must be the easiest possible way to achieve the effect of hand-blocked wallpaper, and it gives an irregularity of pattern that is impossible in machine-produced papers. Another special feature of this project is the paint that we have used – a combination of wallpaper paste, PVA glue and gouache colour. This is not only cheap, but it also has a wonderful translucent quality all of its own. The combination of sponge and paint works well, because pressing and lifting the sponge emphasizes the texture that results from using a slightly sticky paint.

The best foam for cutting is high in density but still soft, such as upholsterer's foam; it needs to be at least 2.5 cm / 1 in thick. You need to be able to hold the foam firmly without distorting the printing surface.

Paint some of your background colour on to sheets of scrap paper, and then use this to try out your sponge-printing; use different densities and combinations of colour, making a note of the proportions of colour to paste in each one. This means you will be able to mix up the same colour in a larger amount when you print on the wall (although the paint will go a very long way). The background used here is painted using the brushed-out colour glaze described on page 16.

MATERIALS

*tracing paper, if necessary
upholsterer's foam off-cuts
felt-tipped pen
scalpel or craft knife
plumb-line
paper square measuring
15 × 15 cm / 6 × 6 in, or
according to your chosen spacing
wallpaper paste
PVA glue
gouache paint or ready-mixed
watercolour paint in viridian,
deep green and off-white
saucer
clear matt varnish (optional)*

1

Photocopy or trace the design from the template section and cut out the shapes to leave a stencil. Trace the design on to the foam and outline it using a felt-tipped pen.

2

Cut out the shapes using a sharp scalpel or craft knife: first cut around the pattern, and then part the foam slightly and cut through the entire thickness.

3

Attach the plumb-line to the wall/ceiling join in one corner. Now turn the square sheet of paper on the diagonal and let the plumb-line fall through the centre, lining up the top and bottom corners with the line. Make pencil dots on the wall at each corner. Move the square down the line, marking the corner points each time. Then move the line along sideways. Continue until the whole wall is marked with a grid of dots.

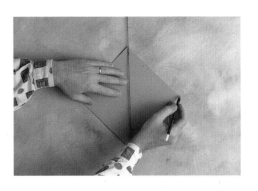

4

Mix wallpaper paste and water according to the manufacturer's instructions. Add PVA glue, in the proportion 3 parts paste to 1 part PVA. Add a squeeze of viridian and deep green gouache paint or ready-mixed watercolour, and blend the ingredients until well mixed. Test the mixture on scrap paper, adding more colour if necessary.

5

Put some paint into a saucer and dip the first sponge into it. Wipe off excess paint, and then print with the sponge using a light rolling motion. Lift and print again, using the pencil dots as a positioning guide.

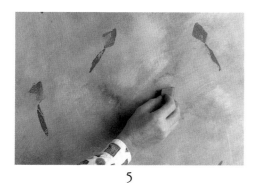

6

Use the second sponge to complete the sprig design with leaf shapes, varying the position slightly to add life.

7

Use the dot-shaped sponge and the off-white colour to complete the motif with berries, adding the colour to the PVA mixture as before. Go over the leaves or stalks on some sprigs and let others 'float' alongside. If your walls are to be exposed to steam or splashes, or even fingerprints, you may like to protect this finish with a coat of clear matt varnish.

'Limed' Floorboards

Liming sanded wooden floorboards gives a much softer impression than stains or tinted varnishes, reminiscent of scrubbed pine kitchen-tables, washed-out wooden spoons, or driftwood bleached by the sun and the sea. If you are lucky enough to possess a sandable floor, try this easy alternative to time-consuming conventional liming. The floor can be a traditional off-white, or tinted to any pastel shade.

Raking-out the grain with a wire brush makes the channels for the paint, as well as clearing out any residual polish or varnish. If you like the wood grain to show as much as possible, wipe the surface with a damp cloth before it dries; the colour will then be concentrated in the raked-out grain of the floorboards. When the floor is dry, a coat of acrylic floor varnish will seal the colour.

MATERIALS

coarse wire brush
white emulsion paint
acrylic paint in raw umber
large decorator's brush
clean damp cloth
clear matt varnish

1

Use a wire brush to rake-out the wood following the grain direction at all times. Brush and vacuum the floor very carefully.

2

Mix up the wash, using 3 parts of water to 1 part of emulsion. Tint the colour with raw umber acrylic, or, if you prefer, use a pastel colour: pink, blue, green or yellow will all look good in the right setting, and very little of the actual colour will show. Experiment on spare boards.

3

Apply the wash with the decorator's brush, beginning in a corner at the skirting board and following the direction of the grain to the other edge.

4

Use a damp cloth to wipe away any excess paint and reveal the grain. A wet cloth will just wash away the paint, so keep it just damp for this. When the floor is completely dry, apply several coats of varnish to protect and seal the surface, allowing plenty of drying time between each coat.

Hardboard Floor with Trompe-l'œil Dhurrie

It is a sad fact that not every home is blessed with handsome floorboards, to be sanded and waxed to a golden gleam. Most older houses have a mixture of new and old boards that aren't good enough to be made into a feature.

Hardboard can be a surprisingly attractive solution if you're faced with a low budget and a patchy selection of floorboards. The utilitarian appearance of hardboard means it is most often used as a levelling surface below vinyl; used in its own right, however, and decorated with stencils, it can look very stylish.

To counteract the potential drabness of a large area of hardboard this project shows how to paint a trompe-l'œil dhurrie in the centre of the room, so that the plain board becomes the border for the dhurrie. Hardboard provides a wonderfully smooth surface for painting and the dhurrie will provide a focal point that is guaranteed to be a talking point as well!

MATERIALS

newspaper
hardboard to fit the floor area
small hammer
panel pins
Stanley knife
ruler
tape measure
Crown Compatibles emulsion paint in shades 'Dusky Blue', 'Splash Blue' and 'Regency Cream'
2.5 cm / 1 in square-ended brush
acrylic paint in dark blue and black
decorator's brushes
masking tape
stencil card or Mylar
scalpel or craft knife
2 cm / ½ in stencil brush
clear matt varnish

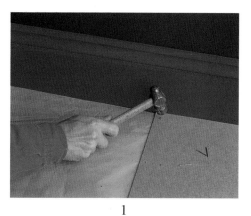

1

Lay sheets of newspaper on the floor to make an even surface. Fit the first sheet of hardboard into the corner nearest the door. Hammer in panel pins 7.5 cm / 3 in apart and 1.5 cm / ⅝ in in from the edge and fasten the hardboard to the existing floor.

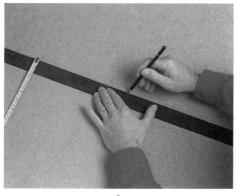

2

Lay the next sheet of hardboard alongside the first, butting it hard up against the first sheet, and right up to the skirting board. Continue laying the whole boards across the room until you reach the point at which the hardboard needs to be trimmed to fit. Measure the space, at least twice, if it is not too large or awkwardly shaped; if it is irregularly shaped, make a newsprint pattern to be sure of getting a good fit. Cut the hardboard using a Stanley knife and a ruler on the shiny side, then breaking along the cut.

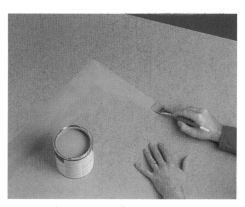

3

If you decide to place your dhurrie in the centre of the room, use a tape measure to find the centre line, and then measure out from it. The dhurrie can be as large or small as you like; this rug is made up of units 150 × 75 cm / 5 × 2½ feet, which you can multiply or divide to suit your room size. Mark the outline of the dhurrie on the floor. Outline the area with the square-ended brush and then fill in the Dusky Blue colour. Leave to dry for 2 hours.

4

Tint the blue to a darker shade by adding a squeeze of black acrylic, and then paint over the area with a dryish brush, to give the dhurrie a woven texture.

. . . continued

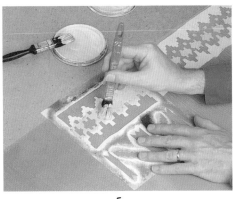

5

Trace and cut out the stencil design from the template section. Mask off the outer patterns with tape. Position the stencil 2 cm / ¾ in from the edge, and stencil the central design in Splash Blue emulsion. Remove the tape and clean the stencil.

6

Now mask off the central pattern and stencil the pattern on either side in Regency Cream emulsion.

7

Position the medallion stencil along the edge of the border and paint all the pattern, except for the outermost lines, in dark blue acrylic. You can mask off these lines with tape, as in the previous steps.

8

Mask off the central medallion and stencil the outer lines cream.

9

Soften the dark blue of the central medallions with light dabs of Splash Blue emulsion.

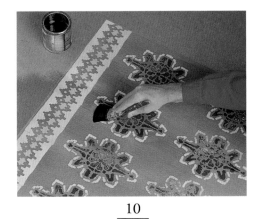

10

Apply at least two coats of clear varnish to the whole area.

Cork-tile Chequer-board Floor

Cork is a wonderful natural material that provides a warm, quiet and relatively cheap floor-covering. It has been largely confined to the kitchen and bathroom in the past, but should not be overlooked when choosing a floor for living areas.

It is important to lay cork tiles on an even surface, so tack a layer of hardboard across the floorboards first. Use only floor-grade cork tiles. The unsealed tiles used here absorbed the coloured varnish well; two coats of clear polyurethane varnish with a satin finish gave a protective seal. You may prefer a proprietary brand of cork tile sealant.

MATERIALS

cork floor tiles
wood-stains in shades 'Dark Jacobean Oak' and 'Antique Pine'
large decorator's brush
cork-tile adhesive, if necessary
clear satin varnish

1

Paint half of the tiles with the Dark Jacobean Oak wood-stain and the remaining tiles with the Antique Pine wood-stain and leave them to dry overnight. Measure the floor length to establish the number of Jacobean Oak tiles needed and cut half that number in half diagonally. Begin laying tiles in the corner that will be seen most; then, if you have to trim a tile at the other end, it will not be so obvious. If you are using self-adhesive tiles, simply peel off the backing.

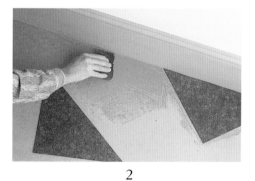

2

Lay the contrasting tiles next, tight up against the first row, wiping off any excess adhesive that has been forced up between the tiles, if you're using adhesive. Once you have laid the two rows, measure the nearest adjoining wall and cut half-tiles to fit the length of that skirting as well. Stick these down.

3

Now, work to fill the floor space diagonally. Trim the tiles at the opposite edge to fit snugly against the skirting board. Apply two coats of clear varnish to seal the floor. It is important to make sure that the first coat is bone-dry before you apply the next one, so be patient, and let it dry overnight.

Acorn and Oak-leaf Border

A painted border can offset the austerity of plain wooden floorboards, while the pattern links different areas without dominating the room. The scale of the oak-leaf pattern can be adjusted to suit the size of your room, but try to 'think big' and enlarge the design to at least four times larger than life size, otherwise the impact will be lost.

Acorns and oak leaves have been used to decorate homes for hundreds of years, and they have a special place in country decorating. William Morris, the famous designer of the Arts and Crafts movement, used many country trees and plants in his patterns, and designed a wonderful wallpaper called 'Acorns'. Let the old saying 'Tall oaks from little acorns grow' be your inspiration, and use this painted-floor border as the basis for a warm and welcoming country-style living room.

Paint the background a dark colour and use paint with a matt finish as this will 'hold' your outline drawings better than a smooth or glossy paint. Begin at the corners and work towards the middle, using the templates as a measuring guide to work out your spacing. Once you have planned the placing of your design, work on a 60 cm / 24 in area at a time, using your whole arm to make the curves, not just the wrist. This way your painting will flow in a more natural way.

MATERIALS

medium-weight card
spray adhesive
scalpel or craft knife
masking tape
ruler
set square
National Trust paint in shade
'Off Black'
decorator's brush
white chinagraph pencil or chalk
white plate
gouache paint in yellow, sienna,
umber, etc.
soft artist's brush
plank or long ruler
lining brush
clear matt varnish

1

Use a photocopier to enlarge the oak-leaf and acorn pattern from the template section to at least four times life size (larger if you have a big room). Stick the enlargement on to medium-weight card and cut around the shape with scalpel or craft knife, to leave a cardboard template. Use masking tape, with a ruler and set square to outline the dark background colour. Apply the colour using the decorator's brush and leave to dry.

2

Beginning at the corner, draw around the oak-leaf template with the chinagraph pencil or chalk. Add stems or acorns to make the pattern fit around the corner, and then continue along the border. Use the template as a measuring guide, to make sure that the design fits comfortably.

3

Using a white plate as a palette, squeeze out several different tones of yellow, sienna, umber, etc. Mix them as you paint; this adds variety.

4

Fill in the oak-leaf shapes, using subtle variations in colour for added interest.

5

Add the finishing touches and flourishes like the leaf veining, stems and acorns.

6

Use a straight edge, such as a plank, and a lining brush to paint the lines that enclose the border about 2.5 cm / 1 in from the edge. Apply 3–4 coats of clear varnish, allowing generous drying time (overnight if possible) between coats.

Painted Canvas Floorcloth

Canvas floorcloths were first used by the early American settlers, who had travelled across the sea from Europe. They recycled canvas sailcloth, painting it to imitate the oriental carpets that were popular with the rich merchants and aristocrats in their native lands. Many layers of linseed oil were applied to the painted canvas to make them waterproof and hard-wearing.

The floorcloths were superseded by linoleum, and, unfortunately, few good old examples remain; they had no intrinsic value and were discarded when worn. Recently, however, they have undergone something of a revival. With the tough modern varnishes now available, they provide an unusual and hard-wearing alternative to the ubiquitous oriental rug.

The design for this floorcloth is based on a nineteenth-century quilt pattern called 'Sun, Moon and Stars'. The original quilt was made in very bright primary colours, but more muted shades work well for the floorcloth.

MATERIALS

craft knife or pair of sharp scissors
heavy artist's canvas (to order from art supply shops)
pencil
ruler
strong fabric adhesive
drawing pin and 1 m / 1 yd length of string
cardboard
acrylic paints in red, blue and green
medium-size square-ended artist's brush
medium-sized pointed artist's brush
varnish in shade 'Antique Pine'
household paintbrush
medium-grade sandpaper

1

Cut the canvas to the size required, allowing an extra 4 cm / 1½ in all around. Draw a 4 cm / 1½ in wide border around the edge of the canvas and mitre the corners. Apply fabric adhesive to the border and fold it flat.

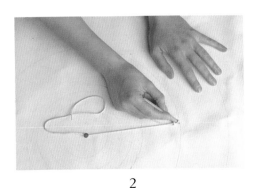

2

Referring to the diagram in the template section, find the centre-point of the canvas and secure the string to the drawing pin at this point. You will now be able to draw the five circles needed for the design, by holding a pencil at various distances along the length of the tautly pulled string. Keep the tension on the string to draw a perfect circle.

3

Cut three differently sized cardboard triangles to make the saw-toothed edges of the two circles and the outside border. Just move the triangle along the pencil guidelines using the card as a template to draw around.

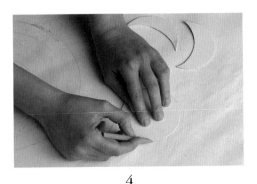

4

Cut a card circle to make a template for the full moons and draw them in position. Then trim the circle to make the crescent and then the sickle moons, drawing them in position. Do the same for the stars.

5

Now start filling in the red. Use the flat-ended brush for larger areas and the pointed brush for outlines and fine work.

6

Fill in the pale blue and green circles of colour.

7

Apply 3–4 coats of Antique Pine varnish with a clean household brush, rubbing down each dried coat with sandpaper before applying the next one. Overnight drying is best.

Furniture and Furnishings

....

Hand-painted furniture is all part of the country look, but unless you have the luck to inherit beautiful old pieces they often remain a distant dream. However, there are still bargains to be had from junk shops and flea markets, and they can be transformed fairly inexpensively. Renovate a table with a colorful border, paint a chair for a French country kitchen, or create your own shelves or kitchen dresser.

Country-style Motifs and Patterns

There are three main sources of motifs in country style – nature, local tradition and religion. Nature and the elements are the strongest influences of all and are celebrated in the decoration of rural homes throughout the world. Flowers and foliage vary according to climate; this is reflected in patterns and motifs, although some plants, like the vine for instance,'have been used decoratively since classical times and are found in the art of many cultures.

Many fruit, flower and foliage motifs have symbolic meanings too, and these were incorporated into homes for their protective value in warding off evil, or for the bringing of good fortune. The rose is used as a symbol of love, both divine and earthly, and the tulip stands for prosperity. The oak leaf and acorn are associated with great potential and the future, while ivy symbolizes tenacity. The sunflower radiates warmth and is guaranteed to bring thoughts of summer to winter days.

Animals, birds and fish feature as well. Wild creatures, farm animals, faithful pets and feathered friends all find their way into country crafts and patterns. The rooster has been used since early Christian times as a symbol of faith, but it is more likely to feature in country

ABOVE: *The tulip is a popular folk motif, and symbolizes prosperity.*

decorating in celebration of his great decorative shape, coupled with his early-morning tyranny.

Cats and dogs are often commemorated in embroideries or paintings, as are horses and other farmyard friends. Patchwork quilts feature many animal and fruit designs that have been stylized to great effect, and this, in turn, has created a style of stencilling whose origins are the quilt-maker's patterns rather than the original inspiration.

Religious influences are especially noticeable in Roman Catholic countries, where there is more emphasis on the visual celebration of faith. Shrines, altars, festive decorations and votive offerings are all a part of the decoration of rural homes in countries like Mexico, Spain, Italy and France.

Harvest motifs, like the wheat sheaf or the cornucopia are popular in most cultures. Fruits have been incorporated into woven and printed textiles, and vegetables are a favourite subject in 'theorem' paintings, a style of stencil paintings used in American folk art.

One of the most common country motifs is the heart: whether punched out of tin, carved out of planks or stencilled on to walls, the heart is everywhere. It symbolizes love and it is a uniquely simple and adaptable motif. The shape hardly changes at all, yet it can be used in many different ways without diminishing its effect. The heart has been used for many centuries across many cultures, and yet there still seems to be an infinite number of new ways to use it.

Geometric shapes have been borrowed from patchwork quilts, and suns, moons and stars will always be popular motifs. They are universal.

The beauty of country-style decorating is the nonchalance with which motifs, styles and patterns can be mixed. The only decorative effect to be avoided is mass-produced adulterated versions of country-style designs, because they will have lost their heart and soul in the manufacturing process!

LEFT: *Decorative surface detail is characteristic of country style, as in this free-hand painted box.*

RIGHT: *The heart, a perennial favourite, is appliquéd in a repeat pattern on this patchwork piece.*

CLOCKWISE FROM TOP LEFT: *Stencilled details give this chair a look of pure country. Geometric patterns are always popular choices for textiles. The free-hand, organic design on this box is inspired by nature. A tin heart is decorated with punched geometric patterns.*

Painted Table

It is still possible, thank goodness, to find bargain tables in junk shops, and this one cost less than a tenth of the price of a new one. It is the sort of table that you can imagine standing in a country cottage parlour, covered with a lace-edged cloth and laden with tea-time treats. There is no guarantee that you will find a similar table, but any old table could be decorated in the same way.

Before you decorate your bargain, you may have to strip off the old paint or varnish and treat it for wood-worm, as we did. Any serious holes can be filled with wood-filler and then sanded and stained to match. The trick is to emphasize the good features and play down the bad. Old table-tops look more interesting than new ones and are well worth sanding, bleaching and staining. The stain on the table legs contrasts well with the red and green paint used on the table-top. The lining can be attempted free-hand, but masking tape makes the job much easier. Mark the position lightly in pencil so that all the lines are the same distance from the edge.

MATERIALS

table
wood-stain in shade 'Dark Jacobean Oak'
household paintbrush
emulsion paint in red and green
1 cm / ½ in square-ended artist's brush
masking tape
shellac
beeswax polish
soft clean cloth

1

Prepare and treat the table as necessary. Use a rag to rub the wood-stain into the table legs, applying more as it is absorbed into the wood. The finish should be an even, almost black tone.

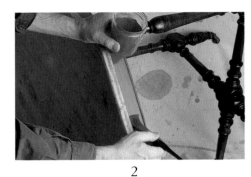

2

Paint the base of the table-top with red emulsion.

3

Measure 5 cm / 2 in in from the edge of the table and place a strip of masking tape this distance in from each of the edges. Leave a 2 cm / ¾ in gap and then place the next strips of tape to run parallel with the first set.

4

Fill in the strip between the tape with the green paint and leave to dry.

<u>5</u>

Apply two coats of shellac to the table.

<u>6</u>

Finish the table with a coat of beeswax
polish, buffing it to a warm sheen with a soft
clean cloth.

Painted Chest

Before the eighteenth century, throughout northern Europe and Scandinavia a country bride took her own decorated linen chest into her new home. The dowry chest would have been made by her father, lovingly carved and painted as a farewell gift to his daughter. Marriage customs accounted for many rural crafts, and the family took great pride in providing a handsome chest for a bride. This custom was continued among the first settlers in North America.

The chest used in this project is a mixture of Old- and New-World influences. The shape is English, but the painted decoration was inspired by an old American dowry chest. The pattern used on the chest is geometric, but the paint finish is very loosely applied, to give a good contrast between two styles. You can use the pattern to decorate any blanket chest, old or new, and then give it an antique finish with tinted varnish.

The most time-consuming aspect is the accurate drawing-up of the pattern shapes, but it is worth spending time to get the proportions right. The combing and spotting has to be done quickly, so the effect is one of controlled chaos!

MATERIALS

blanket chest
shellac, if necessary
Crown Compatibles paint in shades 'Dusky Blue' and 'Regency Cream'
household paintbrushes
tracing paper
pair of compasses
ruler
acrylic varnish in shade 'Antique Pine'
graining comb
clean damp cloth

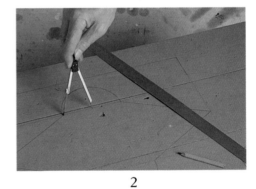

1

If you are starting with bare wood, apply a coat of shellac to seal the surface.

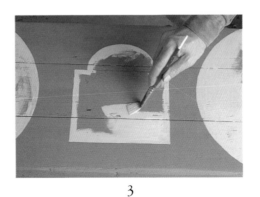

2

Paint the chest with Dusky Blue emulsion. Trace and enlarge the pattern from the template section and use it as a guide to position the panels. Draw the panels with a pair of compasses and ruler.

3

Fill in all the panels with cream emulsion.

4

Apply a thick coat of varnish to one panel only.

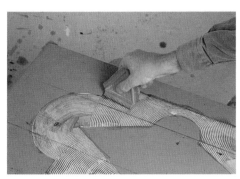

5

Quickly comb the varnish in a pattern, following the shape of the panel. Make one smooth combing movement into the wet varnish, and then wipe the comb to prevent any build-up of varnish. Complete one panel before repeating steps 4 and 5 for the others.

6

Apply a coat of varnish to the whole chest. Immediately take a just-damp cloth, screw it into a ball and use it to dab off spots of the varnish.

Painted Bench

*Every home should have a bench like this, to squeeze extra guests around the
dinner table and to keep by the back door for comfortable boot-changing.
This bench was made by a carpenter, from a photograph seen in a book of
old country furniture. The wood is reclaimed floorboards, which give just the
right rustic feel to the bench.*

The decoration is applied in a rough
folk-art style that adds a touch of
humour. You can use this style to
decorate any bench, and even a plain
modern design will lose its hard edges
and take on the character of a piece of
rustic hand-made furniture.

MATERIALS

bench
medium-grade sandpaper
shellac
household paintbrushes
emulsion paint in deep red,

dark blue-grey and light
blue-green
small piece of sponge
varnish in shade 'Antique Pine'
clear matt varnish

1

Sand the bare wood and seal it with a
coat of shellac.

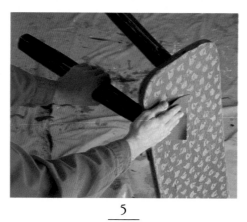

2

Paint the legs in dark blue-grey emulsion,
working directly on to the wood.

3

Paint the seat with the
deep red emulsion.

4

Use the sponge to dab an even pattern of
blue-green spots across the whole surface of
the seat.

5

When the paint is dry, rub the seat and edges
with sandpaper, to simulate the wear and tear
of a thousand harvest suppers.

6

Apply one coat of Antique Pine varnish to
the whole bench. Then apply two more coats
of matt varnish for a strong finish.

Shaker-inspired Peg Rail

The Shakers were a religious movement whose ideals inspired a style of furnishings and furniture of great simplicity and beauty of form. They did not believe in ornamentation or decoration for its own sake, but held that functional objects should be as beautiful and as well made as possible. The name 'Shaker' comes from the ecstatic movements that occurred in their worship.

Peg rails were very characteristic of Shaker homes, and were used for hanging all kinds of utensils and even chairs, keeping the floor clear. Our rail is a very inexpensive and simplified version of the Shaker idea, and what it lacks in fine craftsmanship it makes up for in practicality. We have used a pine plank, with a sawn-up broom-handle to make the pegs. These rails work well all around the house, but are especially useful in hallways, children's rooms and bathrooms. The coat of paint is not strictly Shaker in style, but will disguise the rail's humble origins.

MATERIALS

pine plank 2.5 cm / 1 in thick
ruler
saw
plane
drill with bit for broom-handle holes
1 or 2 broom-handles
medium-grade sandpaper
wood glue
wooden block and hammer
shellac
household paintbrushes
Crown Compatibles emulsion paint in shade 'Dusky Blue'
varnish in shade 'Antique Pine'
white spirit, if necessary
spirit-level
rawl plugs and long screws

1

Measure and cut the wood to the length required. Plane it to smooth and round the edges.

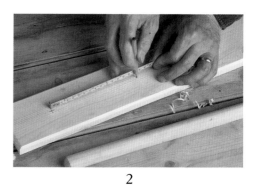

2

Mark the peg positions 20 cm / 8 in apart along the length. The spacing can be altered to suit your requirements.

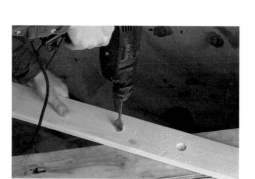

3

Drill holes 1.5 cm / ⅝ in deep in which to recess the pegs.

4

Cut up the broom-handles into 13 cm / 5 in lengths. Sand the edges to round them off.

5

Apply wood glue and fit the pegs into their holes using a small wooden block and hammer to fit them securely.

6

Apply one coat of shellac to seal the surface of the wood.

7

Paint the rail blue.

8

Use medium-grade sandpaper to rub back to bare wood along the edges.

9

Give the whole shelf a coat of Antique Pine varnish. Dip a rag in white spirit (for polyurethane varnish) or water (for acrylic varnish) and rub off some of the varnish. Use a spirit-level and ruler to mark the position of the rail on the wall. Drill holes through the rail at 40 cm / 18 in intervals. Drill into the wall, using suitable wall-fixings and screws.

Painted and Lined Country Chair

It is always worth buying interesting individual chairs when you spot them, as they are often very inexpensive if they need 'doing up'. Four mismatching chairs painted the same way will make a convincing and charming set, and the effect is pure country.

This is a typical French, country-style, rush-seated chair, with curvaceous lines just begging to be accentuated with lining. The essentials of sturdiness and comfort have not been ignored, the seat is generously woven and it is very comfortable. (It is always worth sitting on your chair before you buy because it may have been custom-made for a differently shaped person!)

Colour is a real revitalizer and we have chosen a yellow and blue colour scheme reminiscent of the painter Monet's kitchen, to bring out the French character of the chair. It is worth spending time preparing the wood, and this may mean stripping all the paint if there are several layers of gloss. If you do have the chair professionally stripped, the joints will need to be re-glued, because the caustic stripper dissolves glue as well as paint.

MATERIALS

country-style chair
medium-grade sandpaper
undercoat
household paintbrushes
shellac and wood primer,
if necessary
Crown Satinwood paint in yellow
wire wool
hard pencil
tube of artist's oil colour in
ultramarine blue
white spirit
long-haired square-ended
artist's brush
varnish in shade 'Antique Pine'

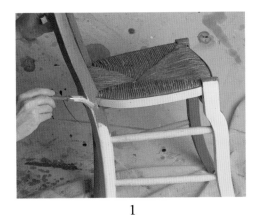

1

If the chair hasn't been stripped, rub it down well with medium-grade sandpaper. Apply the undercoat, or if the chair has been stripped, give it a coat of shellac followed by wood primer. Paint the chair yellow.

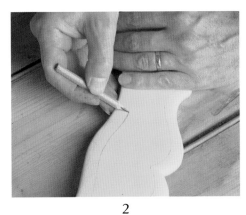

2

When this coat has dried, use wire wool to rub the paint back along the edges where natural wearing away would take place. With a pencil draw the lining, following the curves of the chair.

3

Mix the oil paint with white spirit in the proportions 3 parts paint to 1 part white spirit. You need paint that flows smoothly from the brush and allows you to retain control. If you find the paint too runny, add more colour. Practise the brushstroke with the artist's brush on scrap paper or board, supporting your brush-hand with your spare hand. Controlling your lines is a matter of confidence, which grows as you paint. Paint the lining on the legs, chairback and seat.

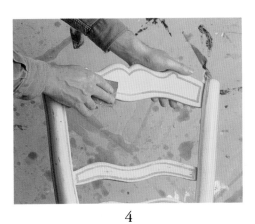

4

When dry, rub back with wire wool in places, as you did with the yellow.

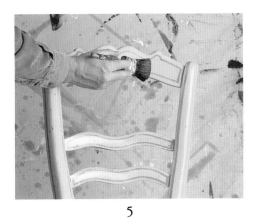

5

Finally apply a coat or two of varnish to soften the colour and protect the lining.

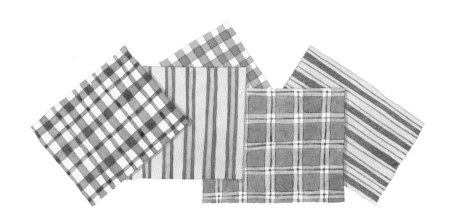

Pie-safe Cupboard

Cupboards like this one were mainly used in America as cooling cupboards for freshly baked goods. The doors were made out of decoratively punched and pierced tin sheets that allowed the delicious aromas to waft out, but prevented flies from getting in. They were called 'safes' because they were fitted with locks to keep temptation out of reach of little fingers lured by delicious smells!

We used an existing old pine cupboard to make the pie-safe, replacing the wooden front panels with newly pierced tin ones. Milled-steel sheet can be bought from sheet-metal suppliers, or try asking at a hardware store or looking in Yellow Pages. Care must be taken, as the edges of the sheet are very sharp, and need to be folded over to make a safe seam. You can crimp or flatten the edges using pliers.

The actual patterning is done with a hammer and nail, or, for more linear piercing, you can use a small chisel. This pattern is our own interpretation of a traditional design, but once you begin, your own style will emerge. You may find other ways of making patterns, perhaps using the end of a Phillips screwdriver, for instance – really anything goes. If the cupboard is to be used in the kitchen, add a protective backing sheet behind the tin, to cover the sharp edges. To get rid of the very new gleam of pierced metal, rub vinegar into the surface.

MATERIALS

old cupboard with one or two panelled doors
tracing paper
medium-grade sandpaper
shellac, if necessary
24- or 26-gauge milled-steel sheet(s) to fit (allow 1 cm / ½ in all around for the seams)
pliers and tinsnips, if necessary
masking tape

pair of compasses or transfer paper
chinagraph pencil
hammer
selection of different nails, screwdrivers and chisels
backing material such as hardboard, if necessary
panel pins
varnish in shade 'Antique Pine'
household paintbrush

1

Remove any beading and ease out the existing panels from the cupboard doors. Measure the space and use tracing paper to plan the design to fit. Rub down the cupboard with sandpaper. If it has been stripped, re-seal it with a coat of shellac. Trim the metal sheet, if necessary. Fold over the sharp edge of the metal sheet, to make a seam about 1 cm / ½ in deep around the edge. Crimp firmly with pliers. Put masking tape over sharp edges, to prevent accidental cuts.

2

Transfer your design on to the tin surface, using a pair of compasses. If you find this tricky, trace the whole design and use transfer paper to put it on to the metal. Add any extra designs with the chinagraph pencil.

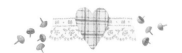

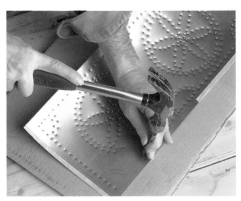

3

Practise piercing on a scrap of tin, such as a biscuit-tin lid, so that you know how hard you need to hit the nail to pierce a hole, and also how just to dent the surface without piercing it. Place thick cardboard or an old towel or blanket beneath the tin to absorb the noise and protect the surface underneath. Once you are confident with the hammer and nail, or whatever tool you want to use, hammer out the pattern.

4

Fit the pierced panels, and the backing if you are using it, into the door and replace the beading to secure it. Use short panel pins at a distance of 4 cm / 1½ in apart, all around the panel to fix in place.

5

Sandpaper the edges to simulate a time-worn effect. Give the wood a protective coat of antiquing varnish.

Shelf with Hanging Hooks

This large shelf with a backboard and hooks would suit a kitchen, entrance hall or large bathroom. It is really simple to make, requiring only the most basic of carpentry skills and tools. The shelf can be painted or varnished, depending on the wood, and it's a really handsome and useful piece of furniture.

The very best wood to use is reclaimed pine, usually floorboards. Demolition or builder's reclamation yards usually have stocks of old wood, but be prepared to pay more for old than new pine. If you're leaving the shelf unpainted it's definitely worth the extra money for old wood. If you intend to paint the shelf, new wood can be used for the backing board, to cut down on the price.

The best feature of the shelf is the very generously sized brackets, which were copied from an old farm storeroom. They have been cut from a section of old pine door, using a jig-saw. The brackets will support the shelf and balance the weight, but the shelf should be screwed into a sound brick wall, using suitable rawl plugs and long steel screws.

This type of shelf is very popular in rural eastern European communities. The hooks can either be new brass or wrought-iron coathooks; or you may be lucky enough to find an old set. Either way they are bound to be concealed, as hooks usually attract more than they were ever intended to hold!

MATERIALS

tracing paper
piece of pine 34 cm × 18 cm × 3 cm / 14½ in × 7 in × 1¼ in thick, for the brackets
jig-saw
drill with No. 5 and 6 bits
pine plank 100 cm × 15 cm × 2 cm / 3 ft 4 in × 6 in × ¾ in thick, for the backboard
pine plank 130 cm × 22 cm × 2 cm / 4 ft 4 in × 8½ in × ¾ in thick, for the shelf
wood glue
wood-screws
shellac
household paintbrush
2.5 cm / 1 in brush
Crown Compatibles emulsion paint in shades 'Dusky Blue', 'Aqua Spring', and 'Precious Jade'
clean damp cloth
wire wool
medium-grade sandpaper
6 coathooks
rawl plugs, if necessary
3 long screws

1

Trace the bracket pattern from the template section and enlarge it until the longest side measures 33.5 cm / 13½ in. Trace this on to the wood, fitting it into one corner, and then flip the pattern over and trace it again into the opposite-end corner. The two can be cut out at the same time, using a jig-saw. Use the number 5 drill bit to make two holes through the backboard into the brackets; and also through the shelf down into the brackets. Spread wood glue on all the joining edges, and then screw them together with wood-screws.

2

Apply one coat of shellac to the whole unit.

3

Use the 2.5 cm / 1 in brush to apply a coat of Dusky Blue emulsion.

4

When dry, apply a coat of Aqua Spring.

5

Immediately afterwards, use a damp cloth to wipe the paint off in some areas.

6

Paint the edges of the shelf and brackets with Precious Jade.

7

Rub away some of the dried paint using wire wool. This will reveal the wood grain along the edges.

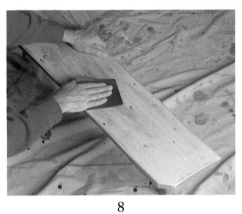

8

Finally rub down with medium-grade sandpaper to smooth the finish and reveal the grain. Screw in the hooks. Attach to the wall by drilling through the backboard to make holes for long wood-screws. Use suitable wall fixings, if necessary.

Painted Dresser

If there is one item of furniture that typifies country style in most people's minds, it must surely be the dresser. A sturdy base cupboard topped with china-laden shelves is an irresistible sight.

This dresser was made by a local carpenter using reclaimed pine, but a dresser can easily be made up using a sturdy chest of drawers combined with a set of bookshelves. The trick is to make sure that the two are balanced visually, with the height and depth of the shelves suiting the width of the base. You can join the two unobtrusively by using strong steel brackets at the back, and painting will complete the illusion that the two were made for each other.

The washed-out paint finish is achieved by using no undercoat and rubbing the dried paint back to the wood with sandpaper and wire wool. Alternatively you can rub some areas of the wood with candle wax before you begin painting; the candle wax will resist the paint, leaving the wood bare.

MATERIALS

dresser, or combination of shelves and base cupboard
shellac
household paintbrushes
Crown Compatibles emulsion paint in shades 'Dusky Blue',
'Quarry-tile Red' (optional) and 'Regency Cream'
household candle (optional)
medium-grade sandpaper and wire wool
varnish in shade 'Antique Pine'

1

Apply a coat of shellac to seal the bare wood.

2

Paint the dresser Dusky Blue, following the direction of the grain. Allow to dry.

3

If desired, rub candle wax along the edges of the dresser before painting with a second colour.

4

The wax will prevent the second colour from adhering completely, and will create a distressed effect. Add the second colour, if using.

5

Paint the backing boards Regency Cream, again following the direction of the grain.

6

When the paint has dried, use medium-grade sandpaper and wire wool to rub back to bare wood along the edges, to simulate wear and tear.

7

Finally apply a coat of Antique Pine varnish to the whole dresser to protect the surface.

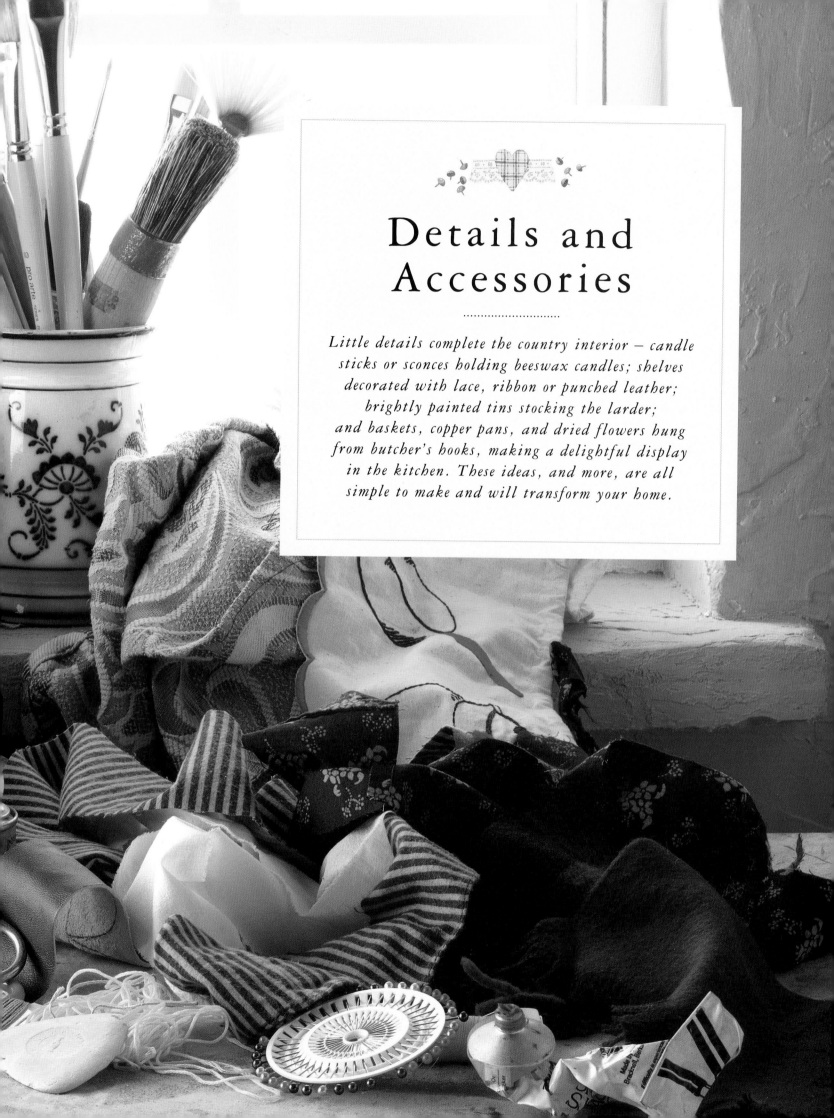

Details and Accessories

Little details complete the country interior – candle sticks or sconces holding beeswax candles; shelves decorated with lace, ribbon or punched leather; brightly painted tins stocking the larder; and baskets, copper pans, and dried flowers hung from butcher's hooks, making a delightful display in the kitchen. These ideas, and more, are all simple to make and will transform your home.

Finishing Touches

Once you have transformed your home with country-style paint finishes, furniture and flooring, it is time to add the finishing touches. The accumulation of 'finds' that add personality to a home does take time, and should be a gradual process; it often depends on your being in the right place at the right time. An unlimited supply of money would buy you folk-art treasures and an interior-designed country look, but you would certainly miss out on the pleasure of making your own accessories.

There are projects in this section to suit most talents and skills, whether your talent lies with a needle and thread, carpenter's tools or paintbrushes.

A simple broom-handle can be used to display a collection of baskets hanging from the ceiling and découpage transforms any ordinary tray into one to be displayed on the wall as 'art'.

Shelving can be dressed up with lace, ribbons, paper or even punched leather, to make something functional into a decorative feature. It is well worth seeking out a local carpenter if you lack

ABOVE: *This punched-tin sconce creates a wonderful backdrop for candles.*

the space or inclination to make your own shelving, because reclaimed timber like pine floorboarding is really worth using for its character and colour.

Candlelight is essential for adding a cosy atmosphere, and whether you choose to make the baluster candlesticks or the rustic wall sconce, you will be enriching the room with something unusual and hand-made. Use the ideas suggested as a starting point, adding your own colour schemes and patterns to give each thing you make a personal touch.

The embroidered pelmet looks very special, and the shapes do not require any particular needlecraft skill to follow. A simple chain stitch could be used to outline all the shapes, and satin stitch for the scallops. The more advanced embroiderer could elaborate upon the designs, filling the background as well as the kitchen implements with a variety of colours and fancy stitchwork.

Similarly, the patchwork throw does not need any more than basic sewing-machine skills to fit it together. The design will vary, depending on your selection of warm winter scarves and backing fabric, and the more experienced seamstress will be tempted to make the pattern more complicated by adding differently shaped patches. Whether you choose to make the basic throw or a more complicated variation, you are bound to be delighted with the result. It looks great draped over a chair and is marvellously warm and insulating on a cold country evening.

There are many country crafts that can be studied and mastered, like basket-making, weaving or the carving of decoy ducks. If you have time to explore and learn about how things are traditionally made, it is very enriching. Our projects are more about taking short cuts and making an impact, which is a good creative starting point. Once you realize the pleasure that is to be gained from both making and displaying your own creations, you are bound to continue to experiment and to enjoy country crafts.

LEFT AND RIGHT: *Beauty and practicality are the keynotes of any country kitchen. Utensils are displayed within easy reach, and dried goods may be kept in colourfully painted tins.*

CLOCKWISE FROM TOP LEFT: *A painted salt box, Shaker-style doll and varnished trug all add a feeling of country. Candles complete the scene. Sewing odds and ends can be kept tidy in a wooden box. These whirligigs form an eye-catching still-life with a collection of plates in complementary colours. A colour-washed tin lantern sets off a display of beeswax candles.*

Wall Sconce

These fashionable room accessories were once essential to every household; however, one wonders what our ancestors would make of us forsaking the convenience of electricity for the 'romance' of candlelight. The truth is that technology and mass-production seem to take the humanity out of our homes, making us long for the irregularity of candlelight, hand-stitching and country-crafted furniture.

MATERIALS

*old piece of wood
saw
hammer
brass and black upholstery tacks
wood glue
nails*

1

Saw through the wood, making two sections to be joined at right angles. Begin the pattern by hammering the upholstery tacks in a central line; the pattern can then radiate from it.

2

Form arrows, diamonds and crosses, using the contrast between the brass and black tacks to enhance your design.

3

Apply a coating of wood glue to the sawn edge of the base. Hammer fine nails through the back into the base.

Découpage Tray

A good tray will be strong enough to carry the tea things and handsome enough to hang up as a decoration when not in use. This one has been découpaged with a selection of old engraving tools, but you could follow the method using any design you choose.

Découpage takes you back to childhood; cutting out and gluing is a favourite activity of children between the ages of five and ten. The grown-up version is slightly more sophisticated, but the fun remains.

The secret of good découpage lies in accurate cutting and in putting on enough coats of varnish. Serious enthusiasts use 30 layers, rubbing back with fine sandpaper between the coats. The idea is to bring the background up to the level of the applied decoration, and then to add further depth with more coats, possibly to include crackle glaze and antique varnish. The final result should be convincing to both eye and touch.

MATERIALS

tray
Paint Magic woodwash in shade 'Maize'
household paintbrush
fine-grade sandpaper
photocopied motifs to cut out
sharp-pointed scissors or scalpel
wallpaper paste and brush
soft cloth
new paintbrush for varnishing
clear satin varnish
crackle glaze (optional)
artist's oil paint in raw umber

1

Prepare the tray by painting it with Maize as a base colour. When dry, rub the surface with fine-grade sandpaper.

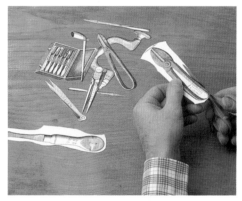

2

Cut out your paper shapes carefully, moving the paper towards the scissors, or around on the cutting surface, so that you are always using the scissors or scalpel in the most comfortable and fluid way.

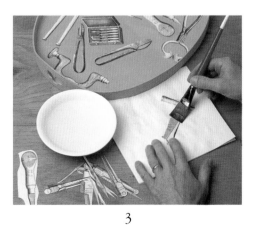

3

Turn the cut-outs over and paste the backs with wallpaper paste, right up to the edges, covering the whole area.

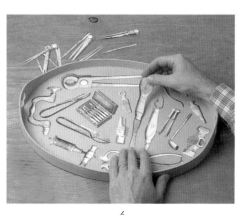

4

Stick them down in position on the tray.

. . . *continued*

5

Use a soft cloth to smooth out any bubbles.
Leave to dry overnight.

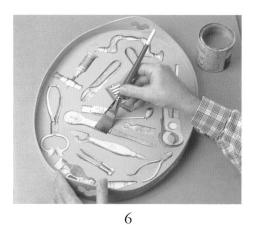

6

Begin varnishing, using a clean new brush
and applying a sparing coat to the whole
surface of the tray. When dry, rub lightly
with fine-grade sandpaper and repeat as many
times as possible.

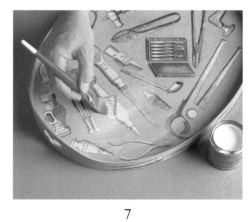

7

A further dimension has been added to this
découpage, by the application of a crackle
glaze. There are several brands on the
market. It is best to follow the specific
instructions for the product you use.
Here the base varnish is being painted
on to the tray

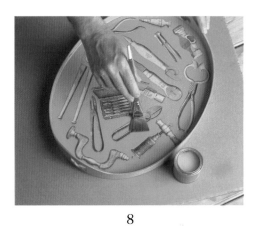

8

When this coat is dry (after 20 minutes),
apply an even coat of crackle glaze and leave
it to dry for 20 minutes.

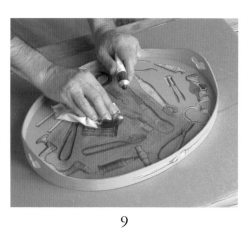

9

Rub a small amount of artist's oil paint into
the cracks, using a cotton cloth. Raw umber
was used here, which gives a naturally aged
effect but any colour can be used.

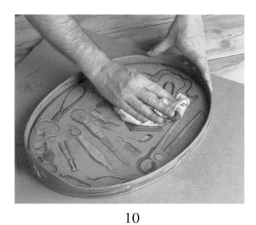

10

When the cracks have been coloured,
gently rub the excess paint from the surface,
using a soft cloth.

11

Give the tray at least two more coats of clear
satin varnish; many more if time and
patience allow.

Wooden Candlesticks

This pair of matching wooden candlesticks have been made from old balusters that were removed from a stair rail. This is an easy way to make something from turned wood without having to operate a lathe yourself. Balusters can be bought singly from wood merchants or DIY stores.

The only special equipment needed is a vice and a flat-head drill bit, to make a hole in the top of the baluster large enough to hold a candle.

The candlesticks have been painted in bright earthy colours, giving a matching pair fit to grace any country table.

MATERIALS

saw
2 wooden balusters (reclaimed or new)
2 square wood off-cuts
medium- and fine-grade sandpaper
wood glue
vice

electric drill fitted with a flat-head drill bit
acrylic paint in bright yellow, red and raw umber or burnt sienna
household and artist's brushes
clear matt acrylic varnish
soft clean cloth

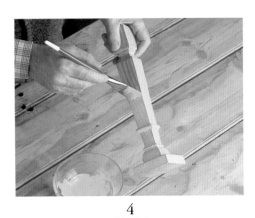

1

Cut out the most interesting section of the baluster and a square base; this one measures 7.5 × 7.5 cm / 3 × 3 in. Roughen the bottom of the baluster with sandpaper.

2

Very slightly, chamfer the base with fine-grade sandpaper. Glue the two sections together with wood glue.

3

Hold the candlestick securely in the vice and drill a hole for the candle 2 cm / ¾ in in diameter and 2 cm / ¾ in deep.

4

Paint with two or three coats of bright yellow acrylic paint.

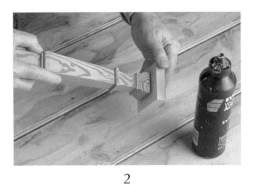

5

Apply a coat of orange acrylic paint (add a touch of red to the yellow acrylic).

6

Tint the varnish to a muddy brown, by adding a squeeze of raw umber or burnt sienna. Brush this over the orange.

_____
7

Use a crumpled cloth to lift some varnish and reveal the colour below.

Woollen Patchwork Throw

*Believe it or not, this stunning chair throw cost next to nothing to make, and was
finished in an afternoon! It is made from pure woollen scarves and remnant
wool fabric. The scarves come from charity shops, and can be bought for pennies.
You will be spoilt for choice, so choose a colour scheme derived from your remnant.
The throw is lined with a length of old brocade curtain, but a flannel sheet
would also be suitable, especially if you dyed it a dark colour.*

The only skill you need for this project is
the ability to sew a straight line on a
sewing machine: and tartan scarves
provide good guidelines to follow. Clear
a good space on the floor and lay the
fabric and scarves out, moving them
around until you are happy with the
colour combinations. Cut out the first
central square. The diamond shape will
need to be hemmed and tacked before
you sew it to the centre of the first
square; after this, each strip of scarf
will just need to be pinned and sewn
in position.

The throw could easily be adapted to
make a bedcover, and, because of the
fine-quality wool used for scarves, it will
be exceptionally warm. The challenge
with this throw is to resist draping
yourself in it, instead of the chair!

MATERIALS

scissors
about 1 m / 1 yd wool fabric
selection of plaid and plain
woollen scarves
pins, thread and sewing machine
old curtain or flannel sheet,
for lining

1

Cut out a 46 × 46 cm / 18 × 18 in square of your 'background' fabric. Choose the pattern for your central diamond and cut a square, using the width of the scarf as the measurement for the sides. Turn the edges under 1 cm / ½ in and tack. Pin and sew the diamond in position.

2

Choose two scarves and cut them into four rectangles. Position them along the sides of the square, with the matching patterns facing each other. Sew them in place and trim off any excess.

3

Cut out four matching plain squares and pin and sew them into the corners. Check on the right side, to make sure that the corners meet accurately. Cut four strips of the background fabric to fit the sides.

4

Cut out four corner pieces of the scarf used for the central diamond, 14 cm × 14 cm / 5½ in × 5½ in. Sew a square to one end of each strip of background fabric.

5

Pin and then sew these long strips in position around the edge of the patchwork.

6

Cut a plain scarf into four strips lengthways and sew these around the outside edge, overlapping at the corners to complete the square.

7

Cut the lining to fit and sew the two pieces together, with their right sides facing inwards.

8

Turn inside out and sew up the seam by hand. Press, using a damp cloth and dry iron.

Plaited 'Rag-rug' Tie-backs

Tie-backs are an attractive way of getting the maximum amount of daylight into the house. It is surprising how much difference a few inches more exposure of window panes can make to the light in a room, so unless your windows are huge, it is well worth tying your curtains back into the wall. This idea has a real hands-on feel and can be made to co-ordinate or contrast with existing curtains.

This method of plaiting scraps of fabric has been stolen from rag-rug makers, and if you have always wanted to make one, this may be just the introduction that you need! If you have any fabric left over from your curtains, you could incorporate this into the plaits. If not, one plain colour that appears in your curtaining will have a harmonizing effect on the whole scheme.

MATERIALS

*scraps of fabric cut into 7.5-cm /
3-in wide strips
safety pin
needle and thread
scissors
strip of fabric for backing (one for
each tie-back)
2 D-rings for each tie-back*

1

Roll up the fabric strips, leaving a workable length unfurled.

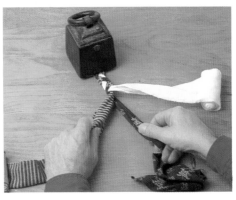

2

Join three strips together, rolling one fabric around the other two and pinning them together with the safety pin. Attach the ends to a chair or any suitable stationary object or anchor them under a heavy weight. Begin plaiting, rolling the strips into tubes as you go, so that the rough edges are turned in and concealed. Make tight plaits. The tie-back needs to be at least 50 cm / 20 in long and four plaits deep.

3

Work until you have the required length and number of plaits. Lay the plaits flat and sew the edges together using a large needle and strong thread pulled up tight. Keep the plaits flat when you turn at either end.

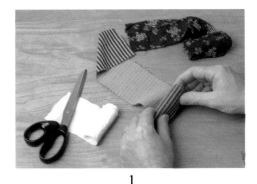

4

Cut a backing strip, allowing enough fabric to turn under 1.5 cm / ⅝ in all round. Attach the D-rings at either end as you slip-stitch the lining into place.

Quilted Tie-backs

This is a quilting project for the absolute beginner. All that is required is the ability to sew an even running stitch along a drawn line. The pattern is a standard quilting stencil (available from craft shops), which you draw through using a chalky coloured pencil. A layer of wadding is placed between two strips of fabric, which can then be tacked or pinned together.

The effect produced by the quilting is textural and the pattern shows up very well. The quilting is best done on plain fabrics, like the calico we used, but the tie-backs could be used with patterned curtains. Gingham or larger checked patterns look especially good teamed with quilted calico.

MATERIALS

1 m / 1 yd unbleached calico
scissors
50 cm / 20 in quilter's wadding
quilt stencil pattern
chalky coloured pencil
pins, needle and thread
2 D-rings for each tie-back

1

Cut the calico into strips 50 cm × 14 cm / 20 in × 5¾ in. Cut the wadding into strips 48 cm × 10 cm / 19 in × 4 in. Use the stencil to draw on to one piece of calico. Put a layer of wadding in between two layers of calico and pin.

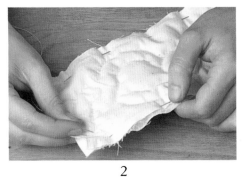

2

Sew a running stitch along the pattern lines. You may find it easiest to pull the needle through each time, rather than sewing in and out of all three layers at once.

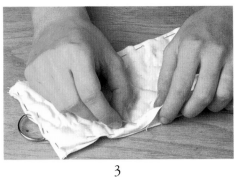

3

When the pattern is complete, fold in the edges and stitch them all around, either by hand or machine. Attach a D-ring at each end.

Leather-edged Shelf Trimming

Not all shelves are worthy of display, especially the new and inexpensive ones that are readily available in DIY stores. There is no denying that they are practical and functional, and a simple shelf trimming will transform them very quickly into a charming and individual room feature.

MATERIALS

leather off-cuts (sold by weight in craft shops)
round template with a 7.5 cm / 3 in diameter
pencil, ruler and chalk
pinking shears
multi-sized hole punch
double-sided tape or glue

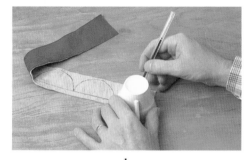

1

Cut strips of leather to fit the length of your shelf, using several sections to make up the length if necessary. The edging needs to be 6 cm / 2½ in deep. Draw a line 1 cm / ½ in from the edge (on the reverse side) and use the template to draw semi-circles along the length of the line.

2

Cut around these with pinking shears. Punch out holes around the edges, varying the sizes.

3

Draw stars on the semi-circles with chalk. Punch out holes around the star outlines in the same way. Run a strip of double-sided tape along the shelf, and use this to attach the leather trim; alternatively all-purpose glue can be used.

Lace and Gingham Shelf Trimming

The lacy look may not suit every room, but it can add a very French touch to a dresser or kitchen shelf. The contrast between stout enamel pans and fine cotton lace can be quite charming; in French country homes, crochet lace is pinned up for display on any shelf available.

There are so many different lace designs available, that the decision will have to be a personal one. You may go for an antique hand-crocheted piece or a simpler machine-made design. The pointed edging chosen here suits a china display very well.

There is something both cheerful and practical about gingham. It is perfectly suited to edging food-cupboard shelves, where the pattern is strong enough to stand out against all the different packaging designs. The combination with lace is fresh and pretty.

MATERIALS

strips of lace the length of the cupboard shelves, plus extra for turnings
cold tea
small bowl

scissors
double-sided tape
gingham ribbon the length of the sides of the shelves
all-purpose glue

1

To tone down the brightness of this new lace, it was dipped into a bowl of cold tea. The stronger the brew, the darker the colour, so adjust it by adding water to lighten the dye, if necessary. Press the lace when dry and cut it to the correct length.

2

Apply the double-sided tape to the vertical sides of the shelves and peel off the backing tape. Cut the gingham ribbon to fit and seal the ends with a little glue, which will dry clear and prevent the ends from fraying.

3

Stick the gingham ribbon to the verticals, carefully smoothing it out and keeping it straight. Start at one end, and keep the ribbon taut.

4

Apply double-sided tape to the edges of the shelves, overlapping the gingham.

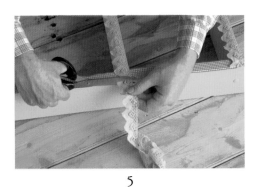

5

Seal one end of the lace with a small amount of glue. Stretch it along the tape, cut it to fit and seal the edge. Repeat for the other shelves.

French Bread Bin

*The kitchen and meal-times play a central role in country life, entailing warm
winter suppers when the nights have drawn in, or long, languorous lunches
in the height of summer. Crusty bread is an integral part of any meal, and
this stylish bread bin will bring a touch of French country style to your kitchen.
The same design could be used in a hallway or by the back door
to hold umbrellas or walking sticks.*

The pattern provided in the template
section could be given to a carpenter, or,
if woodworking is a hobby, made at
home. The stand has been made from
reclaimed pine floorboards, which are
quite heavy and give it stability, as does
the moulding used to broaden the base.

The decoration is called ferning and was
very popular in Victorian times. Dried or
imitation ferns (florists sell fake plastic
or silk ones) are sprayed with aerosol
mounting adhesive and arranged on the
surface, which is then spray-painted. It
dries very quickly and the ferns can then
be lifted off. The effect is stunning and
very easy to achieve.

MATERIALS

wood for the stand (see pattern)
tracing paper or transfer paper
jig-saw or coping saw
wood glue and 2.5 cm / 1 in
panel pins
hammer

For the decoration
shellac
household paintbrush
newspaper
masking tape
spray adhesive
selection of artificial ferns
spray-paint in black, dark green
or dark blue
fine-grade sandpaper
clear matt varnish

1

Apply two coats of shellac to seal and colour
the bare wood.

TO MAKE THE STAND

Cut the timber to the dimensions shown
on the pattern in the template section.
Mitre the edges. Trace the
pattern for the back detail and cut it out
using a jig-saw or coping saw.
Apply wood glue to all joining edges,
join them and then use panel pins
to secure them.

2

Working on one side at a time, mask off the
surrounding area with newspaper and masking
tape. Apply mounting spray to one side
of the ferns and arrange them on the surface.

3

Spray on the colour, using light, even sprays,
and building up the colour gradually.
Lift the ferns when the paint is dry.

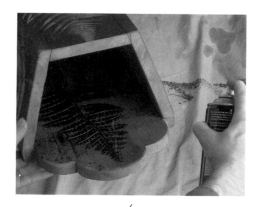

_4_

Work on all the sides and the inside back
panel in the same way.

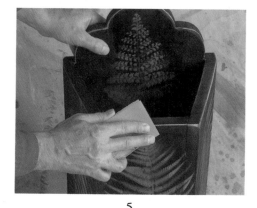

_5_

Sand the edges to simulate a time-worn look.

_6_

Finally, apply two coats of varnish
to protect the fernwork.

Rabbit Dummy Board

A free-standing oversized rabbit will certainly provide both a focal and a talking point! Dummy boards originated as shop or inn signs; in the days when few people could read, a painted sign would indicate the trade being practised on the premises. The signs would either hang above the doorway or stand on a wooden block. You can give this rabbit a support to make it stand up, or hang it on the wall.

This project employs a mixture of old and new, as it is an original nineteenth-century engraving enlarged on a photocopier. The fine lines of the original thicken up with enlargement, but not enough to lose the effect of an engraving.

This project is great fun and fairly simple, and the only real skill required is that of cutting the shape out with a jig-saw. Personal experience has shown us that there are people who delight in this; so if you don't have a jig-saw — find someone who does!

MATERIALS

*wallpaper paste and brush
A2 (59.5 × 42 cm /
23¾ × 16¾ in) sheet of marine
plywood (or similar)
jig-saw
fine-grade sandpaper
shellac
household paintbrushes
varnish in shade 'Antique Pine'
clear matt varnish
scrap of wood for stand
PVA glue*

1

Photocopy the rabbit pattern from the template section, enlarging it to the edges of an A4 sheet. Cut the enlargement in half to give two A5 sheets.

2

Enlarge both of these up to A3 size. Depending on the machine, this process can be done in one step, or might take several enlargements.

3

Apply a coat of wallpaper paste to the plywood. This seals the surface and provides a key for the pasted paper.

4

Trim the 'joining' edges of the photocopies right up to the print, so that they can butt up against each other with no overlap. Apply a thin layer of wallpaper paste right up to the edges and stick the two halves together on the board. Smooth out any bubbles with a soft cloth and leave it to dry overnight.

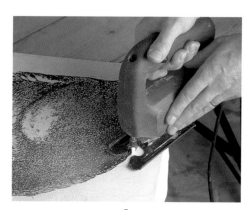

5

Use a jig-saw to cut out the shape, leaving a flat base. Using a jig-saw is not difficult, but you will need to practise to get the feel of it. Take your time.

6

Sand the edges of the rabbit smooth.

7

Seal the surface with a coat of shellac, which will give it a yellowish glow. Apply a coat of Antique Pine varnish, followed by several coats of clear varnish.

8

Trace the pattern from the template section. Use it to cut out the stand. Rub down the edges with fine sandpaper and glue in place

Painted Tin or Tôleware

Tin-painting reached its zenith in the early days of American settlement, when itinerant merchants would appear in a blaze of colour at farm gates, selling their decorated tin housewares. Even then, they were hard to resist and most homes boasted a display of painted tinware. The word 'tôleware' derives from the French tôle peinté *meaning 'painted tin', but the style of painting owes more to the Norwegian* rosemaling *than the elaborate French style.*

Our project does not require you to learn the specialized brushstrokes used in traditional tin-painting, although the colours and antiquing will ensure that it blends in well with any other tôleware pieces. These numbered tins were used by tea merchants as containers for different tea blends.

MATERIALS

metal primer
household paintbrushes
large metal tin (either tin or
aluminium) with a lid
emulsion paint in black,
brick-red and maize-yellow
selection of artist's brushes
tracing paper (optional)
soft pencil
masking tape
hard pencil
shellac
clear varnish tinted with
raw umber acrylic paint
clear satin varnish

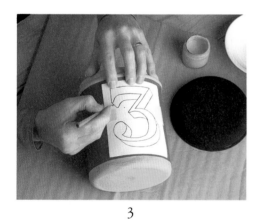

_1_

Prime the tin. Paint the lid with black
emulsion and the tin brick-red, with bands
of maize-yellow.

_2_

Trace or photocopy the pattern from the
template section and then cross-hatch over
the back with a soft pencil.

_3_

Use low-tack masking tape to hold the
pattern in position and then draw over it
with a hard pencil, transferring an outline
to the tin.

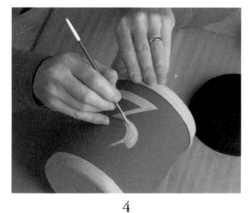

_4_

Fill in the main body of the '3'
in maize-yellow.

_5_

Fill in the shadow in black.

_6_

Varnish the tin with shellac to give it
a warm glow.

_7_

Apply a coat of tinted varnish and then
give it a coat of clear satin varnish
to protect the surface.

Curtain-pole Hanging Display

*The Victorian clothes airer made use of the warmth above the range in the days before
tumble driers. These days they are seldom used for their original purpose; instead
they are adorned with hooks that hold copper pans, baskets and other delights.*

However, not all ceilings are suitable for
a heavy airer, and some are not high
enough for a hanging display of this sort.
For the country look without the
creaking timbers and bumped heads, try
this attractive, painted curtain pole.

The wooden curtain poles used here can
be bought from any DIY store.

MATERIALS

*curtain pole, plus turned finials
(not brackets)
2 large 'eye' bolts for ceiling beam
medium-grade sandpaper
emulsion paint in green, red and
cream*

*household paintbrushes
clear varnish tinted with raw
umber acrylic paint
2 equal lengths of chain
cup hooks and butcher's hooks
for displays*

1

Using the pole as a measuring guide,
position and screw into the ceiling or beam
the two 'eye' bolts. These must be very
sturdy and firmly fixed. Sand down the pole
and finials, and then paint the finials green.

2

Paint the pole red. When the pole is dry,
paint the cream stripes 6 cm / 2½ in
from the ends.

3

Sand the paint in places to give an aged look.
Fit the finials on the ends of the pole. Apply
a coat of tinted varnish. Attach the lengths
of chain to the 'eye' bolts. Screw in two cup
hooks to the pole in the correct position to
line up with the bolts. Attach the butcher's
hooks for hanging your decorations,
hang up the pole and add your display.

Embroidered Pelmet

*In France, pelmets such as this one are often pinned up above windows
that do not need curtains, but that would otherwise be too plain.*

The embroidery is simply made from a
few basic stitches and is quite suitable
for a beginner to attempt. Gingham
curtains provide a simple contrast
without detracting from the embroidered
pattern, but you could make calico
curtains and embroider them with the
same designs – if you have time and have
fallen under the embroidery spell!

M A T E R I A L S

*tracing paper
dressmaker's transfer paper or
carbon pencil
1 m / 1 yd calico, cut into
2 strips 20 cm / 8 in deep
needle and embroidery threaa
in 4 colours
scissors
curtain wire*

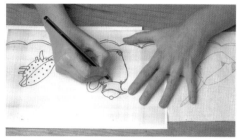

1

Enlarge the patterns from the template
section to approximately 10 cm / 4 in.
Use transfer paper or carbon pencil to
transfer the patterns on to the calico.

2

Depending on your knowledge and level of
skill, embroider each of the designs.
A simple chain-stitch can be used, but
cross-stitch, stem-stitch, back-stitch and
French knots will add variety.

3

Use satin-stitch to make the scalloped edge.
Carefully trim the edge. Sew a seam along
the top edge and thread a length of curtain
wire through it. Gather to fit the window.

Amish Sewing Box

The style adopted by the Amish communities of rural America sits very well with an overall 'country' look. 'Plainness and practicality' were the qualities to strive for and pride was to be avoided at all costs. This discipline produced simple but beautiful objects such as the sewing box that inspired this project. It is based on a box attributed to Henry Lapp (1862–1904), a versatile Amish carpenter who owned a shop supplying furniture, household objects and paint to his own community in the late 1800s.

This is a simple design, an oblong, with a lid, hinged to allow access to the largest compartment used for storing spools of thread, and a small drawer at the bottom for smaller sewing paraphernalia. The colouring and decoration is typical of the style of Henry Lapp – red paint, yellow graining, pale blue interiors and white ceramic handles. The box was commissioned from a local craftsman who used a photograph as a guide, but simpler wooden boxes could be adapted for the project.

MATERIALS

matt emulsion paint in duck-egg blue, brick red and beige
2.5 cm / 1 in artist's brush
2 thick-bristled varnishing brushes
small household paintbrush
clear water-based varnish
artist's acrylic paint in raw sienna and burnt umber
cloth
small white ceramic or plastic knob
screwdriver

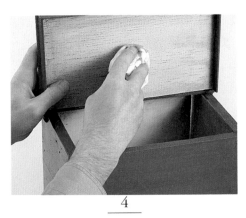

1

Paint the inside of the box with two coats of duck-egg blue, and apply a base coat of brick red to the outside, and beige to the drawer front.

2

Tint the varnish with a small squeeze of the raw sienna and burnt umber and paint the outside of the box. Apply it with a thick-bristled brush, using pressure to leave visible brushstrokes, sideways across the box and lengthways across the lid.

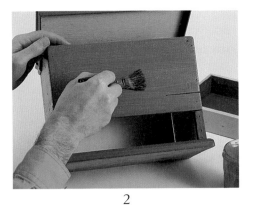

3

Apply the same varnish over the beige base coat on the drawer and while it is still wet, use a dry thick-bristled brush to lift some of the glaze to imitate woodgrain. Do not try for a realistic effect graining effect, but one like lines of static interference on a television screen.

4

Apply a coat of tinted varnish to the inside and while it is still wet wipe off patches of it with a damp cloth to imitate wear and tear. Follow this with a coat of clear varnish over the whole box. Finally, screw on the knob. 'Age' a new one by scratching the surface and rubbing it with a dab of burnt umber.

Painted Picture Frame

In the nineteenth century, country-style frames were often made of common woods painted and grained to imitate something much grander, such as walnut or bird's eye maple. However, some of the most appealing examples of woodgraining bear little resemblance to the real thing. The paint is vigorously applied, usually in a dark colour on a light background, using a piece of sponge, crumpled paper or a cloth. The paw print was a popular pattern in which the surface was covered with spots resembling animal tracks.

The frame for this project was painted in a naive, energetic style. It is an old frame from a junk shop and quite rustic, both in construction and texture. A silhouette was framed here, itself a typical folk technique. If you do not have anything suitable to go in the frame, try a mirror. Take the frame along to a glass merchant and have the mirror cut to fit, as old frames can be very quirkily shaped.

MATERIALS

matt emulsion paint in red ochre and pumpkin yellow
4 cm / 1½in decorator's brush
stencilling brush
small household paintbrush
artist's acrylic or stencil paint in black
absorbent paper towel
fine-grade steel wool
clear water-based varnish
artist's acrylic paint in raw sienna and burnt sienna

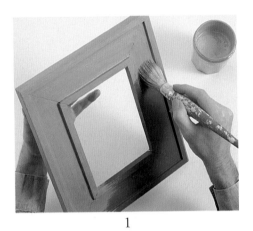

1

Paint the frame with a base coat of red ochre, allow to dry and then apply a coat of pumpkin yellow.

2

To paint the spots use black paint undiluted on a dry stencilling brush. Too much paint will 'blob' so rub the brush on paper towel between dipping and painting. Hold the brush in a vertical position and push down slightly while twisting it on the frame. The effect needs to be more wild than restrained.

3

When the paint is completely dry, rub the edges lightly with steel wool to simulate wear and tear.

4

Tint the clear varnish with a small amount of both raw and burnt sienna and apply to the frame. Add a coat of clear varnish.

Painted Glass

Painted glassware was a popular country art in Europe, with bright figures used to adorn bottles of spirit and drinking tumblers from France to Hungary. When emigration to America began in the early seventeenth century, glassmakers from Poland, Holland, England and Germany crossed the sea to make their fortunes, and some of them succeeded. Henry Wilhelm Stiegel (1729–1785) was the most influential glass manufacturer of his time. His name is still used to describe the type of enamel-painted glass that is featured in this project.

Painting on glass is not difficult provided that you thin the enamel paint sufficiently and relax enough to let the brushstrokes flow. Do not slavishly follow your tracing – use it as a positional guide for the main motif, but let the shape of your glass suggest the detailing. Enamel paints are available from most hobby shops. Try to find old glasses in junk or antique shops – a glass with a slight imperfection will cost next to nothing, but is perfect for folk painting.

MATERIALS

tape measure
tracing paper and pencil ·
low-tack masking tape
soft cloth
small pots of enamel paint in red,
green, yellow, blue, black and white
2 fine, short-haired artist's brushes
elastic band

1

Measure around your glass, top and bottom, and cut a piece of tracing paper to fit inside it. Draw the pattern on to the tracing paper and put it into the glass, using masking tape to secure it if necessary

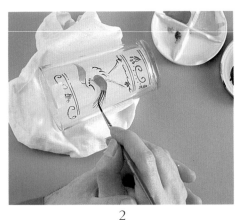

2

Rest the glass on a cloth and support your painting hand with your other hand. The paint should be thinned enough to make it flow nicely and be slightly transparent; if it is too thin it may run. Try to avoid overpainting, or the design will lose its freshness.

3

When the pattern has dried, place an elastic band around the glass to act as a guide, and paint stripes of colour around it. Support the glass as described in the previous step.

4

Add the small dots and motifs to suit your glass. Allow one side of the glass to dry first before painting the other, unless you can support the glass on its rim by using your other hand splayed inside the glass.

_5_

Finally, introduce some individuality by
adding embellishments of your own,
perhaps just a few squiggles, some dots or
even your initials.

Hanging Salt Box

Salt was even more important to cooks 300 years ago than it is today. It was the main preservative for meat and fish, which were salted down and stored ready for lean winter months. The hanging salt box is common to many European cultures, and the design is fairly standard. Decoration of the boxes varies; in Norway, for example, it usually featured a woodburnt repeat pattern using symbols and runes that date back thousands of years. In other parts of Europe, and later America, it was customary to paint the box with the year it was made, bordering the numerals with motifs such as hearts or tulips.

Scandinavian-style kitchenware is now widely available and you should not find it difficult to buy a plain pine hanging salt box like the one featured in this project. But if you are a keen woodworker you could easily make a box; the design is relatively simple.

The geometric motif used here was very popular with painters of American country furniture and objects. The design was drawn with a pair of compasses and the segments painted different colours. This box is painted with a green background, but natural wood, or another traditional colour would suit equally well.

MATERIALS

matt emulsion paint in emerald green
2 2.5 cm / 1 in artist's brushes
long-haired artist's brush
pair of compasses
artist's acrylics or stencil paints in brick red, off white and black
clear water-based varnish
artist's acrylic paint in raw and burnt umber

1

Apply the base coat of green emulsion, and allow to dry. Using the compasses draw a circle on the lid. Without adjusting the radius, move the compass point to the edge of the circle and draw an arc to intersect both sides of the circle. Move the point to one of these intersections and draw another arc; continue around the circle until you complete the pattern.

2

Repeat the pattern on the front and sides of the box and draw half of it on the backing plate. Fill in the background of the motif using brick red paint. Support your brush hand with your spare hand.

3

Use the compass to draw a circle 6mm / ¼in larger than the first, and fill this in with off white paint. Paint three sections of the motif and edges of the box with black paint.

4

Tint the water-based varnish with a small amount of raw and burnt umber and apply two coats to the outside of the box. When dry, apply a coat of clear varnish.

Stencilled Border

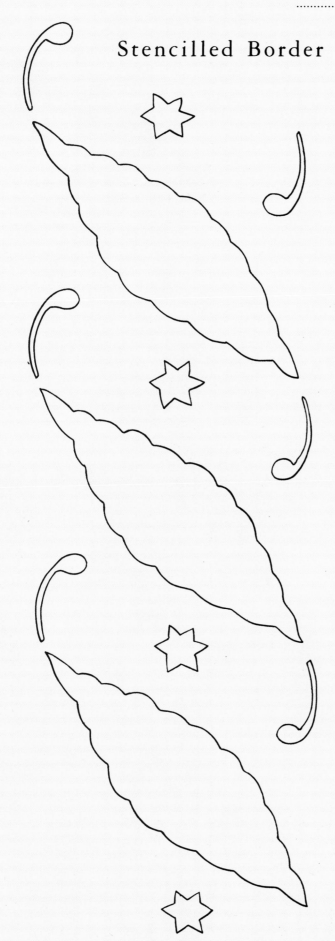

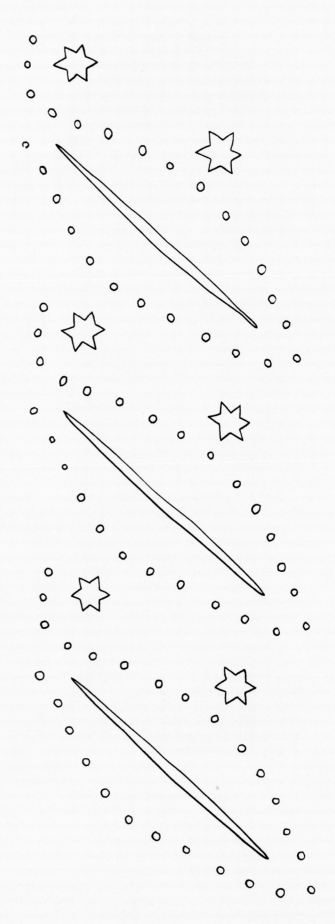

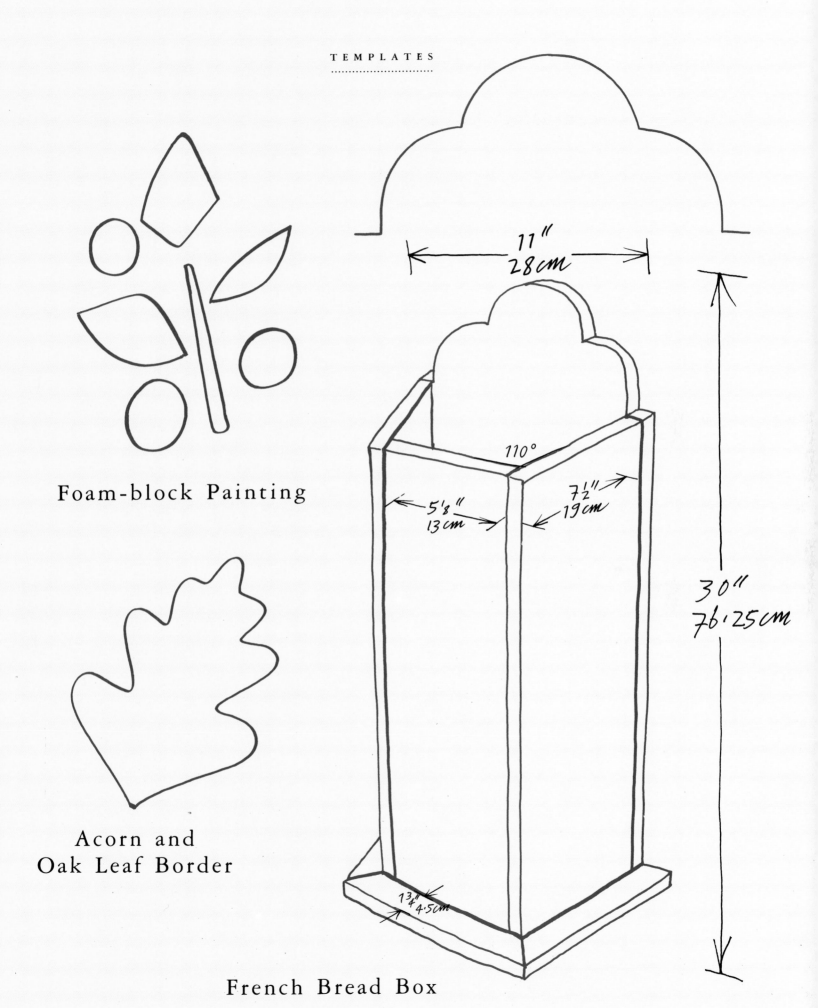

Foam-block Painting

Acorn and
Oak Leaf Border

11"
28cm

110°

7½"
19cm

5⅛"
13cm

30"
76·25cm

1¾"
4·5cm

French Bread Box

Trompe-l'oeil Dhurrie

Canvas Floor Cloth

Painted Chest

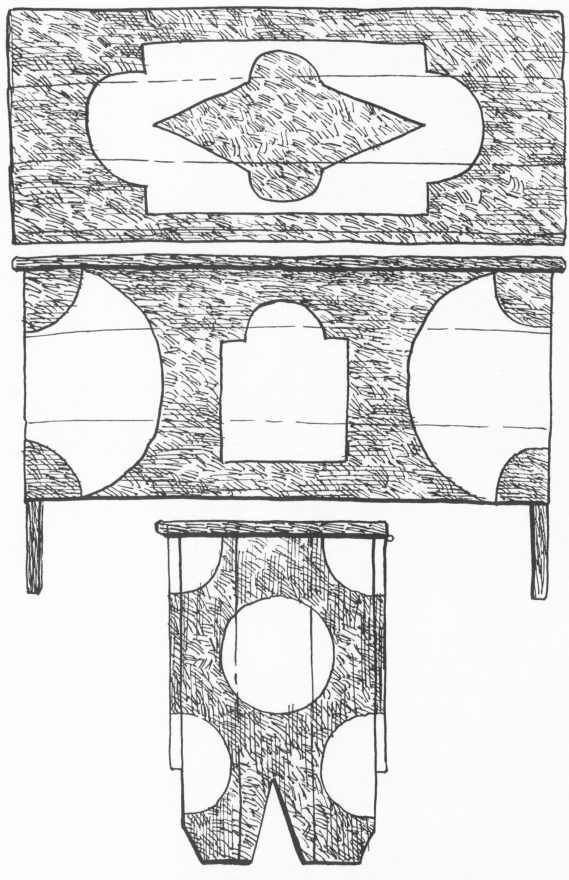

Shelf Bracket and Dummy Board Stand

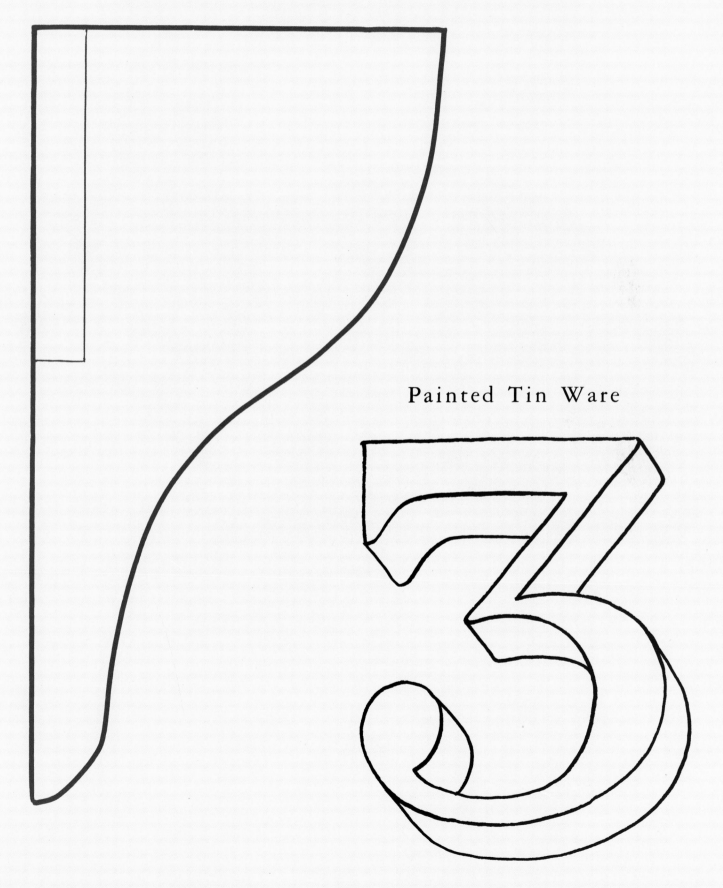

Painted Tin Ware

Rabbit Dummy Board

Embroidered Pelmet

COUNTRY
Quilts and Needlework

Patchwork
and Appliqué

*Create a nostalgic country mood with soft textiles, full
of associations with nature and folklore. Antique
patchwork quilts were mostly made by country people,
and they often tell the story of the changing seasons,
of animals, birds and flowers, and of weddings and
births. Choose cotton floral prints, gingham, checks
and stripes, mixing them together like an
old-fashioned cottage garden.*

The Country Quilt

ABOVE: *The Bear's Paw is a traditional motif in North American quilts.*

The needlework techniques of quilting, patchwork and appliqué have been with us for centuries. Quilting is the oldest of the three crafts, with its origins in the Far East, where ancient civilizations used quilted fabric for padded winter clothing. The technique was brought to the West by the Crusaders, and in the Middle Ages women adapted the idea to create warm bedcovers.

When the first pilgrims set sail for the New World, the idea travelled with them, and quilting became essentially a thrift craft, with the settlers recycling their outworn clothes, cutting the worn fabric into ever-smaller pieces and patching it together – and so the patchwork quilt was born. As the settlers prospered, the pioneering plainness of the quilts and patchworks became more elaborate and colourful. A whole variety of motifs and designs evolved, many of which are still popular today. Appliqué followed as a popular way of decorating quilts, and the craft of making patchwork quilts was born.

Most of the tools and equipment needed to work the projects in this section will be found in any well-equipped workbasket. In addition to good dressmaker's scissors, and the usual complement of matching threads, thimbles and pins and needles, a rotary cutter is invaluable when pieces with precise angles are needed. The cutter, which should always be used in conjunction with a cutting mat, makes it possible to cut several pieces at once, and this not only saves time but means that the pieces are exactly the same shape. Large embroidery hoops and frames are also useful for holding fabric taut, and some types of frame can be used with sewing machines. Seams should be pressed open or to the side to reduce bulk, and it is often convenient to have a small travelling iron for this purpose rather than having to set up the ironing board and domestic iron each time.

Although patchworks used to be pieced by hand, with the scraps of fabric carefully folded over pieces of paper, today's craft shops and department stores stock iron-on fusible bonding web and interfacing, isometric graph paper, special dressmaker's carbon paper, adjustable markers and gauges, vanishing markers, plastic and acetate templates – the list of gadgets and sewing aids is almost endless. None of these items is essential, but they all make the stitcher's task easy and help to give professional-looking results every time.

Patchwork is traditionally made from scraps and oddments left over from other sewing projects, but today most fabric, especially for large quilting projects, is bought specially. Cotton is the most often used fabric, and 100 per cent cotton is an immensely practical fabric, being easy to stitch and hard wearing, as well as being available in hundreds of different colours and patterns. Cotton sateen, which has a subtle sheen, is a great favourite with quilters. Silk, textured materials, synthetics and lightweight wool can also be used. Sort oddments into fabric types and weights, and use fabrics of similar weight in individual projects. New fabrics should always be prewashed before use to test for both colour-fastness and shrinkage.

The selection of appropriate fabrics is the key to a successful evocation of country style. To create a riot of colour and pattern, combine gingham with stripes, checks or tiny floral prints, which will appear as interesting tones in a large scheme. Plain colour can be used, and it is interesting to use historical examples and the shades of nature to inspire choices. Turkey red, a bright, deep colour, was an extremely popular shade for patchwork, for instance, and it is especially striking when it is teamed with white. Colours do not always have to coordinate, because country style is often an eclectic mix of patterns and colours. Fabrics and textures will have faded and become discoloured over time, and the aim should be to recreate this warm, comfortable and, above all, practical look.

LEFT: *Example of French quilting style.*

CLOCKWISE FROM TOP LEFT: *An American appliquéd quilt dating from c.1940 and a pieced quilt, made in Pennsylvania in the late nineteenth century. The Double Irish Chain is a popular pattern in both Britain and North America. Today, quilts are usually made from toning shades of pure cotton, but in the late nineteenth century crazy quilts were popular.*

Bear's Paw Quilt

There was a time when almost every woman in America was engaged in making a quilt, such was the scale of the fashion for quilting in the late nineteenth century. The craft was more or less abandoned during and after the Second World War, but it resurfaced in the 1960s, and there is now a huge revival of interest in it.

The quilt pattern used in this project is a traditional one called Bear's Paw. The pattern is made of squares, rectangles and triangles which require accurate cutting and stitching if the block is to lie flat. Use 100 per cent cotton fabric, prewashed and ironed flat. The Bear's Paw works best with a simple two-tone colour contrast, which shows off the pattern well.

The choice of machine or hand sewing is a personal one; hand sewing will take longer to do and will not be as strong as machine sewing, but it is infinitely more controllable. This example has been made with the help of a sewing machine.

MATERIALS

template plastic
pencil and ruler
red fabric, 3.5 m × 115 cm /
4 yd × 45 in
white fabric, 4.6 m × 115 cm /
5 yd × 45 in
needles, pins and scissors
thread to match and invisible
polyester thread
sewing machine
4.6 m / 5 yd white backing fabric
wadding (batting) to fit
4 cm / 1½ in masking tape
tape measure

Backing fabric
2.5 × 2 m / 100 × 8 in

Binding strips
2.5 m × 3.5 cm / 100 × 1½ in
2 m × 3.5 cm / 80 × 1½ in

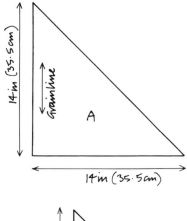

Template for triangles

Template	Quantity	Material
A	38	white
B	12	white

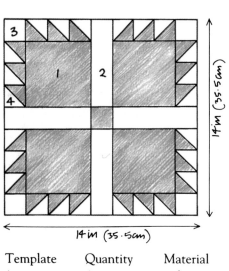

Template	Quantity	Material
1	4	red
2	4	white
3	4	white
3	1	red
4	24	white
4	24	red

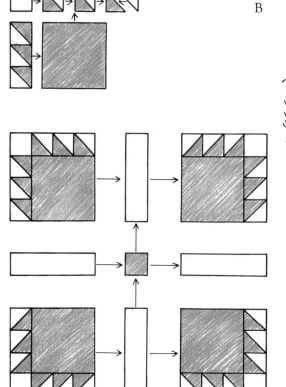

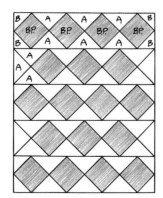

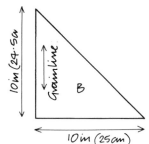

1

Enlarge the Bear's Paw block to 13.5 cm / 14 in square and number each template as shown. Trace out the 4 shapes on to template plastic and add a 6 mm / ¼ in seam allowance on all sides. Mark in the straight grain line. Cut out the templates. You will need enough shapes to make 18 blocks.

2

Lay out a block – start by joining the small triangles. Place the triangles right sides together, and pin and machine them one after the other, leaving a small 'chain' of thread between. This will speed up production and save on thread. Check the seams, then press them open and join the block as shown in the diagram.

3

Work methodically, pressing between each step. When all the blocks are patched, check the measurement, and make corrections if necessary.

4

When all the blocks are patched, join the large triangles (A and B). Following the quilt plan, join the rows in the order shown. Press the work well. If you are quilting by hand, mark out guidelines with a straight-edge and a sharp pencil.

5

On a large flat surface, lay the backing fabric right side down. Carefully centre the wadding, and over this place the quilt top right side up. Check that all the sides match, then, starting from the centre, pin then tack the layers together, smoothing any wrinkles towards the edge as you go. Work one side first, then the other starting from the centre again and tacking fairly closely so that the layers do not slip.

6

Quilt either by hand or machine. Starting from the centre, stick several lengths of masking tape as a guide, 4 cm / 1½ in apart. A walking or feed foot will help keep the stitches even on the machine. Use a polyester thread. You can re-use the masking tape several times. Quilt a 4 cm / 1½ in grid over the entire quilt.

<blockquote>
. . . *continued*
</blockquote>

7
___

When all the quilting is finished, trim the
edges and put on the binding, right sides
together and opposite sides first, then slip
stitch to finish. Do not forget to put a label
on the back with your name and date —
your quilt may be a future heirloom.

The Alphabet Cot Quilt

The design for this quilt is taken from one made in Pennsylvania in about 1900. Most examples of early cot quilts are simply scaled-down versions of patterns used on full-size quilts, but the original that inspired this project was unmistakably designed for a child. The letter forms follow the quirks of the original, some of them being reversed, and the building in the bottom right-hand corner represents a schoolhouse.

The colours of this quilt are strong compared with the pastel shades that are usually used for babies nowadays, but the quilt will brighten any nursery, and later make an attractive wall hanging for an older child's bedroom. It is best worked in fine cotton, which will not fray too much and will hold a firm crease well, which is important when sewing the pieces together. If you find the letters difficult to appliqué, try cutting actual-sized letters (without a seam allowance) from iron-on interfacing.

The choice of machine or hand sewing is a personal one; hand sewing will take longer to do and will not be strong as machine sewing, but it is infinitely more controllable.

The measurements include a 6 mm/ ¼ in seam allowance.

MATERIALS

pencil
thin cardboard and paper
iron-on interfacing
iron
red fabric, 2.3 m × 115 cm /
2½yd × 45 in
blue fabric, 90 × cm / 1 yd × 45 in
sewing machine
needles, pins, safety pins and scissors
thread to match and invisible nylon
thread
wadding (batting) to fit
tape measure

Blue fabric
28 15 cm/6 in squares
2 72 × 6.5 cm/28½ × 2½ in
2 1.3 m × 6.5 cm/51 × 2½ in

Red fabric
28 15 cm/6 in squares
1 1.35 m × 77 cm/53 × 30½in
2 60 × 6.5 cm/24 × 2½in
2 1.18 m × 6.5 cm/46½ × 2½in

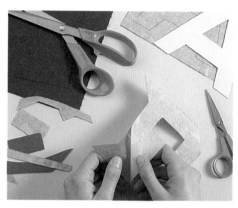

1

Enlarge the alphabet in the templates and draw it up on cardboard. Each letter should fit in the squares, allowing space around it. The alphabet should be in reverse at this stage. Trace it and the house on to iron-on interfacing and cut them out. Use a steam iron to press each letter in the centre of a blue square. Press the work.

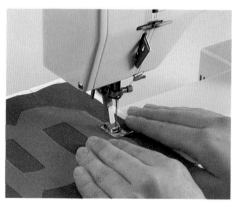

2

Fit an appliqué foot to your sewing machine if you have one and set the machine to satin stitch. Stitch the alphabet and house on to the squares, placing a piece of thin paper under each one as you work to stop puckers forming. Remove the paper after stitching.

. . . continued

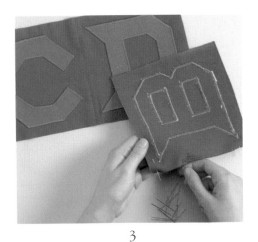

3

Lay out the quilt in the correct order and join the squares in pairs, pinning and tacking them first. Pass all the squares through the machine, running a short 'chain' of thread between each pair. This both speeds up production and saves thread.

4

Check and press the seams open, then lay out the squares and join them again to form rows. Join these rows together until the quilt is finished; press the work well.

5

Pin and tack the 2 shorter red strips to the top and bottom edges of the quilt, making sure the strip and quilt are right sides together. Sew and press, then join the remaining 2 red strips to the sides. Repeat, joining the blue borders to the red ones, then press the work well.

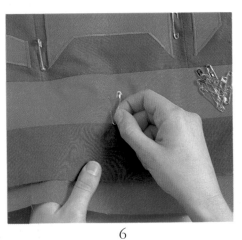

6

Lay the backing fabric on a flat surface, right side down and cover with wadding. The backing fabric is 5 cm/2 in larger than the quilt; place it, centred over the wadding (batting), right side up. Tack using safety-pins, one in each letter and around the borders.

7

Machine quilt using a walking or a feed foot if you have one. For the quilt shown here, invisible nylon thread was used on the top with red thread in the bobbin and it was quilted 'in the ditch' – stitched around each block along the valley that worms between the seams. Roll the quilt so that it will fit under the machine; you can use bicycle clips to hold it. When finished, pull the threads through to the back, knot the loose ends by sewing them into the back of the quilt.

8

Fold the red backing fabric around to form the binding. Pin it and then slip stitch.

Quilted Appliqué Cushion Cover

The album style of quiltmaking flourished in the state of Maryland in the mid-nineteenth century, and most particularly in the city of Baltimore, which gave its name to the style. These first appliqué album quilts were highly individual, depicting homes, families and pets as well as floral motifs.

If you have never tried appliqué work before, it would be unwise to launch yourself straight into making a bedcover. Instead, begin by making just one square of an album quilt, which can be framed as a picture, or made into a cushion cover.

This square was inspired by an intricate 25-block quilt known as the Baltimore Album, signed by Hannah Foote and dated 1850. Each block is different, depicting floral urns and baskets, wreaths, farm scenes, the eagle and flag and an anchor (the motif chosen for this project), which may represent a relative away or lost at sea.

MATERIALS

*template plastic or paper
3 pieces unbleached calico, 30 cm /
12 in square, 35.5 cm / 14 in square
and 48 × 35.5 cm / 19 × 14 in
scraps of material (finely woven pure
cotton is best)
cotton thread to match scraps
cream cotton thread
wadding (batting) 33 cm / 13 in
square
red print fabric for 4 strips, each
30 × 5 cm / 12 × 2 in
pins, needles, scissors
1.5 cm / ½in ribbon (optional)
iron
cushion pad*

1

Enlarge the pattern elements and cut out the templates, and then the pieces from your scraps of material. Look at the picture of the finished cushion and decide how many leaves to cut out.

2

Working on to the smallest calico square, begin with the ring. Snip the edges at 6 mm / ¼ in intervals and position it centrally on the square. Tack down the centre of the ring and begin sewing. Use a small slip stitch, and turn under the seam as you sew. Use this method for the other curved patterned pieces.

. . . continued

3

When cutting the bow, slit the fabric and snip around for the inside bow shapes, or the seam will rob your bow of body.

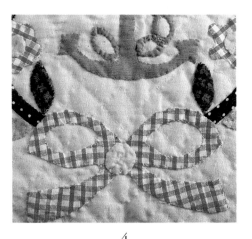

4

This picture shows the position of the bow. Then add the leaves and flowers, alternating between left and right to get an evenly matched wreath. You may find it easier to appliqué the flowers and leaves if you apply iron-on interfacing, without the seam allowance, to the backs of the pieces before you snip the edges.

5

This picture shows the position of the anchor. It should be slip stitched into place. The chain is a challenge, but it can be worked in embroidery silk using chain stitch if you prefer. Embroidery was used for detailing on these squares.

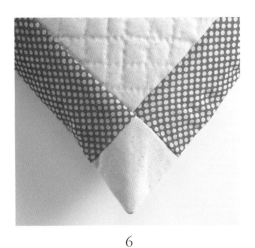

6

Attach the red border strips, adding a square connecting piece of plain calico at each corner. Then pin the wadding (batting) between your work and the backing square, which is the second calico square. Fold the appliquéd square over the edge of the wadding (batting), pin and sew around the edge using a running stitch.

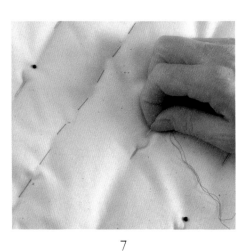

7

Tack the three layers diagonally and crosswise using a contrasting colour.

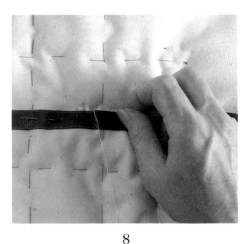

8

Sew through all three layers using a small running stitch. Keep the lines running up to the motifs and then beyond them in straight rows, first in one direction and then the other, until the background is quilted in a diamond pattern. Beginners will find it useful to pin a length of ribbon in a straight line, and stitch along either side of it. See the Pieced Cushion Cover for the back of the cushion.

Pieced Cushion Cover

The pattern for this cushion comes from a single block on a very large sampler quilt made in Lancaster County, Pennsylvania, in about 1870. The original quilt is a masterpiece of 85 different patchwork squares, 28 triangular edging patchworks and a green and red zigzagged frame within a patterned border. The squares are made to a mixture of traditional and original patterns, and the quilt is signed 'Salinda W Rupp'.

This project is worked in the original quilt colours; you can use another combination, but it is important to keep to the design by using darker and lighter colour tones. Accuracy is vital when cutting and sewing geometric patchwork and pure cotton fabrics are most suitable; they fold well and do not fray much. The finished cushion is 40 cm / 16 in square, but can be enlarged to any size.

MATERIALS

graph paper and pencil
template plastic
red fabric, 25 × 115 cm / 10 × 45 in
green fabric, 45 × 115 cm /
18 × 45 in
yellow fabric, 45 × 115 cm /
18 × 45 in
scraps of bright green and red
spotted fabric
scissors
sewing machine and iron
needles, pins and thread to match
cushion pad

1

Enlarge the design to the size you want. Number the templates as shown, then trace them out on to template plastic, leaving enough room for a 6 mm / ¼in seam allowance to be added on all sides. Follow the chart for the number of each template shape required, and cut out the shapes. Lay out the whole block to check that you have all the pieces you need.

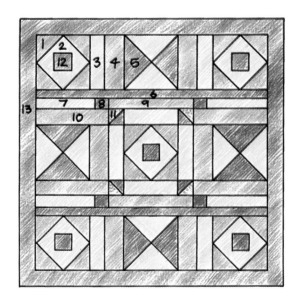

Red
20 of no. 1; 6 of no. 4;
2 of no. 9; 4 of no. 10

Green
8 of no. 5; 4 of no. 11; 2 of no. 6;
5 of no. 12; 4 of no. 13

Bright green
4 of no. 8

Yellow
5 of no. 2; 6 of no. 3; 8 of no. 5;
4 of no. 7

Red spotted
4 of no. 11

. . . continued

2

Start to join the pieces, working in rows. Take a yellow square, then pin and sew two red triangles on opposite sides of it, with the right sides together. Press the work, with the seam allowance under the darker fabric. Join the two remaining red triangles on opposite sides. Press the fabric.

3

Pin together and sew one yellow triangle and one green triangle. Press and repeat with the remaining triangles. Join them diagonally to make a square, then press the work.

4

Sew the yellow and red stripes together, then join all the pieces for the top strip, and press the work. Press in a 6 mm / ¼ in seam allowance on the 5 green squares and hand appliqué them using yellow thread and tiny stitches.

5

Continue patching each row, then join them, pressing between each step until the cushion is finished.

6

Cut out 2.5 cm / 1 in borders from the green fabric to fit two opposite sides of the piece. Pin, then sew and press the fabric. Cut two more borders to fit the remaining sides and repeat, then press the work.

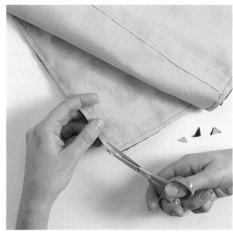

7

To make the back of the cushion cover, cut a piece of fabric the same width but about 13 cm / 5 in longer. Cut this fabric in half and turn in a hem at one end of each piece. Lay the 2 pieces on the cushion cover, right sides together, with the hemmed edges overlapping. Pin all the way around the edge, then sew it. Trim off the corners diagonally, within the seam allowance. Turn the cushion cover through, press it and insert a cushion pad.

Country Throw

This delightful cotton throw is made from checked patches alternating with plain ones. This appliqué project lends itself to a country image, with bold designs colouring plain squares.

MATERIALS

*calico, 60 × 90 cm /
24 × 36 in
checked cotton fabric,
60 × 90 cm / 24 × 36 in
dressmaker's scissors
tracing paper and pencil
iron-on fusible bonding web,
20 × 90 cm / 8 in × 36 in
iron
assortment of fabric scraps
dressmaker's pencil
crewel needle and
assortment of embroidery
threads
small glass beads
sewing machine and
matching thread
cotton drill, 1 m × 115 cm /
40 × 45 in
dressmaker's or safety pins
needle and tacking thread
shirt buttons*

Calico

13 pieces 17 × 19 cm /
6½ × 7½ in

Checked cotton

12 pieces 17 × 19 cm /
6½ × 7½ in

Enlarge the motifs from the template section and trace on to the bonding web. Cut 4 hearts, 3 birds, 2 hands, 1 pear, 1 strawberry, 1 grape and 1 flower.

1

Roughly cut round the shapes on the bonding web and iron them on to the scraps. Cut out, peel off the backing paper and fuse to the calico squares.

2

Mark design details with a dressmaker's pencil and embroider round each shape. Use a variety of stitches and coloured threads. Sew on beads for the birds' eyes and holly berries.

3

Alternate checked with appliquéd squares in 5 rows, each row with 5 blocks. Use the flag method to join the blocks, then join the rows.

4

Centre the patched piece on the cotton drill. Pin and tack through all the layers and round the outside edge. Stitch a small glass bead to each corner.

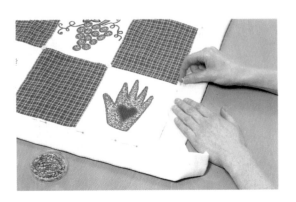

5

Press a 1 cm / ½ in hem round the outside edge, then fold in half to make a border. Pin, slip stitch in place and mitre the corners. Decorate the border with the shirt buttons.

Amish Bag

*The Amish people were already quilting when they first settled in America,
and this envelope bag is patched and quilted in Amish style.*

MATERIALS

*dressmaker's scissors
dark blue fabric,
50 × 90 cm / 20 × 36 in
light blue fabric,
50 × 90 cm / 20 × 36 in
dark green fabric,
50 × 90 cm / 20 × 36 in
wadding (batting),
50 × 90 cm / 20 × 36 in
dressmaker's pins
sewing machine and
matching thread
needle and tacking thread
red and green thread
bias binding, 2 m / 2 yd
press stud*

Dark blue fabric

1 18 cm / 7 in square

4 pieces, 24 × 6 cm /
9½ × 2½ in

Light blue fabric

2 13 cm / 5 in squares, cut in
half on the diagonals

4 6 cm / 2½ in squares

Dark green fabric

2 strips, 16 × 32 cm /
6¼ × 13 in

2 strips, 16 × 60 cm /
6¼ × 24 in

1

Pin and stitch the triangles to the large centre
square with a 1 cm / ½ in seam allowance.

2

Pin and stitch the 4 strips and the small squares to
the patched piece.

3

Attach the border to the patched piece. Cut the
wadding (batting) and the backing fabric to fit.
Layer the wadding, the patched piece and the
backing, then pin and tack through all the layers.

4

Machine a meandering filling stitch over the whole
piece using the red and green thread. Bind the
edges with bias binding. Fold 3 corners into the
centre like an envelope, pin and slip-stitch the
binding. Sew a press stud to both sides at the centre
to close the flap.

Patchwork Frame

Patchwork squares are sewn into strips to make the cover for this pretty picture frame.

Cut a window in one piece of card, with a 5 cm/2 in frame. The second piece is for the backing board. Trace the frame on to the wadding (batting), cut out and stick together with double-sided tape. Draw round the backing board on to the calico, and cut out with a seam allowance. Fold over the seam allowance and glue to the back. Cut a calico facing for the inner and outer frame. Cut the gingham scraps into 3.5 cm/1½ in squares.

MATERIALS

2 pieces of thick A4-size card
craft knife
fabric marker
scraps of wadding (batting)
dressmaker's scissors
double-sided tape
calico, 20 × 90 cm/ 8 × 36 in
fabric glue
scraps of gingham
dressmaker's pins
sewing machine and matching thread
iron
needle and matching thread

1

Pin the squares in pairs and stitch with a 6 mm/¼ in seam allowance, using the flag method. Make 4 strips of 10 patches, and 4 strips of 3 patches. Sew pairs of strips together. Press and then join the short strips to the long ones to make a frame.

2

Right sides together, stitch the facings round the inner and outer frame. Clip the corners, trim and press. Lay the fabric frame on the card, fold over the facings and secure them with double-sided tape. Put the front and back of the frame together and slip stitch round 3 sides.

Appliqué Wool Scarf

MATERIALS

tracing paper and pencil
thin card
craft knife
dressmaker's pencil
scraps of suede, corduroy
and wool
dressmaker's scissors
rotary cutter
needle and tacking thread
wool fabric, 30 × 150 cm /
12 × 60 in
sewing machine and
matching thread
crewel needle and contrasting
embroidery threads

1

Enlarge and transfer the 4 motifs to the card and cut them out. Draw round the templates on to the fabric scraps with a dressmaker's pencil and cut out the shapes. Tack the motifs to the scarf edge. Machine zigzag round the motifs.

2

Turn a hem on the long sides of the scarf and use your machine to top stitch both hems in place. Work large buttonhole stitch along the other two sides using a contrasting colour. Embroider a few stitches on to the motifs.

Motifs 25%

Sunflower Shelf Edging

MATERIALS

thin card and pencil
craft knife
calico, 16 × 90 cm /
6½ × 36 in
dressmaker's pencil
iron-on fusible bonding
web
dressmaker's scissors
iron
yellow, green and brown
gingham fabric scraps
needle and cream thread
spray starch
pinking shears

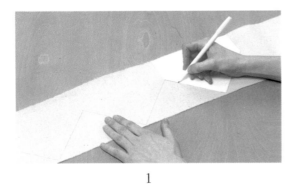

1

Enlarge and trace the template on to card and cut out with a craft knife. Place it at one end of the calico strip and trace along the length of fabric.

2

Trace 5 flowers, 5 centres and 10 leaves on to the fusible bonding web. Iron on to the fabric scraps and cut round the outlines.

3

Peel off the backing paper and place 2 leaves above the first point on the calico. Place the sunflower on top, overlapping the leaves, and iron in place. Work along the strip in this way using the points as guides.

4

Turn under the top edge and press a 1 cm / ½ in hem. Slip stitch in place. Spray the piece with starch and then pink the marked line.

50%

Bolster Cushion

Enlarge the end piece and copy on to paper. Cut a rectangle 47 × 70 cm / 18½ × 27½ in and 2 end pieces in the main fabric. Draw 8 patch templates on to the fusible bonding web. Iron to the fabric scraps and cut out. Press under a hem on both short sides of the main fabric piece and machine stitch. Make 2 buttonholes along one of these hemmed edges and iron the rectangular patches to one of the long edges. To make the patchwork base, cut the scraps into 7 × 4.5 cm / 3 × 2 in rectangles and sew into short strips.

MATERIALS

dressmaker's paper and pencil
dressmaker's scissors
iron-on fusible bonding web
iron
cotton fabric, 50 × 90 cm / 20 × 36 in
assorted fabric scraps
sewing machine and matching thread
2 buttons
bolster pad, 45 × 18 cm / 18 × 7 in

Patch template 50%

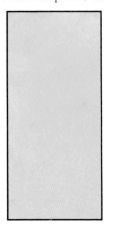

End piece 25%

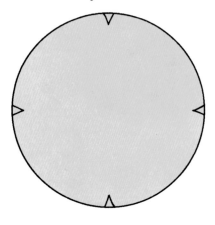

___1___

Set the machine to zigzag and outline each rectangular patch in satin stitch.

___2___

Pin and stitch the strips together to make a patch to fit the end piece. Lay the patch on one end piece, stitch round the edge and trim to fit. Pin the main piece into a tube. Insert the end pieces, sew, clip the curves and press. Turn right side out, and sew on the buttons. Insert pad.

Country Wreath Cushion

Enlarge the templates and trace 8 flowers, 18 flower centres and 24 leaves on to the fusible bonding web. Cut out roughly and iron on to the fabric scraps then cut round the outline. Fold the ticking into quarters to find the middle, centre a dinner plate on top and draw round it with the dressmaker's pencil.

MATERIALS

tracing paper and pencil
iron-on fusible bonding
web
iron
assortment of fabric scraps
dressmaker's scissors
striped ticking,
45 × 95 cm / 18 × 38 in
dinner plate
dressmaker's pencil
assortment of embroidery
threads
crewel needle
sewing machine and
matching thread
cushion pad,
45 cm / 18 in square

1

Position the flowers on the ticking, spacing them evenly round the circle, and trace round them with the dressmaker's pencil. Peel off the backing paper.

2

Slip the leaves under the flowers – mix the colours, vary the angles and iron in place. Fix a centre on each flower and arrange the extra circles round the wreath to fill the gaps.

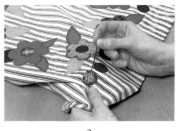

3

Using 3 strands of various colours of embroidery thread, work round the edges of the shapes with bold blanket stitches to emphasize the outlines.

4

Press under a 1 cm/½ in hem on both short ends and stitch. Mark 25 cm/10 in from one edge, fold over the appliquéd front and pin in place. Repeat on the other side. Sew both edges, clip the corners and turn right side out before inserting the cushion pad.

Flower and flower centre
50%

Leaves 50%

Calico Rag Doll

Make a rag doll from some calico scraps and dress her up in patchwork clothes. The same template could be used to make another doll from a piece of patched fabric.

Enlarge and trace the doll template from the template section and cut two shapes from the calico pieces, adding a 1 cm / ½ in seam allowance.

MATERIALS

*tracing paper and pencil
dressmaker's scissors
calico, 25 × 50 cm /
10 × 20 in
dressmaker's pins
sewing machine and
matching threads
polyester toy stuffing
needle
crewel needle and black,
white, blue and red
embroidery threads
non-toxic pink crayon
ball of yellow cotton
crochet thread
18 cm / 7 in square thin
card
narrow ribbons
assortment of fabric scraps
iron
scrap of broderie anglaise*

1

With right sides facing, pin and stitch the calico pieces together with a 1 cm / ½ in seam allowance. Leave a 4 cm / 1½ in gap under one arm. Clip the curves, trim any excess fabric and turn right side out. Fill the doll with polyester toy stuffing and slip stitch the gap closed.

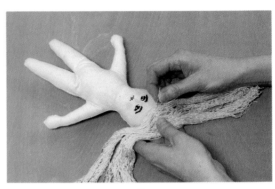

2

Embroider the features and colour the cheeks pink. Make the hair by winding crochet cotton round the card. Join with back stitch for the hair line, slip off the card and cut the other end. Sew to the head and twist into 2 plaits. Secure with ribbons.

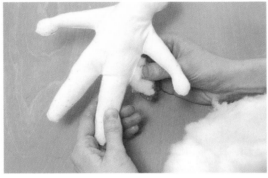

3

To make the body of the dress, cut 78 patches 3 cm / 1¼ in square from fabric scraps. Using the flag method, join in blocks of 6. Make a 13-row patchwork block. To make the sleeves, cut another 32 squares, and join 4 blocks in 4 rows, then make another the same. Press flat, and work running stitches either side of every seam. Join each block into a tube and hem the lower edge. Cut an angled opening either side of the dress and cut the sleeves to match. Sew in the sleeves.

4

Put the dress on the doll. Gather the neck opening and trim with a collar of broderie anglaise. For the underskirt, make a broderie anglaise tube 11 × 22 cm / 4½ × 8½ in, run gathering thread to one end and sew to the doll's waist.

Rag Book

Rag books have always been safe and practical toys for small babies.

MATERIALS

*tracing paper and pencil
iron
iron-on fusible bonding
web
assorted fabric scraps
dressmaker's scissors
calico, 60 × 90 cm /
24 × 36 in
floral cotton fabric,
20 × 90 cm / 8 × 36 in
sewing machine and
matching thread
dressmaker's pins*

Calico

10 20 cm / 8 in squares

1 rectangle, 14 × 17 cm /
5½ × 6½ in

Floral fabric

2 20 cm / 8 in squares

1

Select some simple images, letters and numbers. Trace on to the bonding web. Iron to the reverse of the fabric scraps and cut out. Remove the backing paper and iron the shapes to the calico.

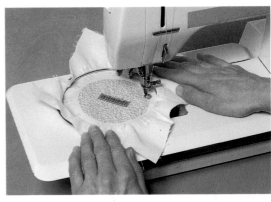

2

Set the machine to zigzag and secure with satin stitch. Make the picture for the front cover on the small calico rectangle, centre and stitch to one of the floral squares.

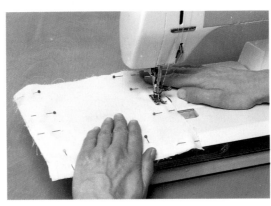

3

Pin and stitch the squares, right sides facing, to form pages. Back pages 1 and 10 with the floral squares. Turn right side out and collate.

4

Cut a wide bias strip from the floral fabric to bind the pages. Pin and stitch the strip to the centre seam as the 'spine' of the book.

Appliqué T-shirt

MATERIALS

tracing paper and pencil
iron-on fusible bonding
web
iron
assorted fabric scraps
dressmaker's scissors
needle and tacking thread
dressmaker's pins
plain T-shirt
matching thread

1

Trace the templates on to the bonding web and iron to the fabric scraps. Cut out with a small seam allowance. Clip and tack under the seam allowance round all of the shapes.

2

Arrange the flowerpot motif on the T-shirt, pin and slip stitch in place.

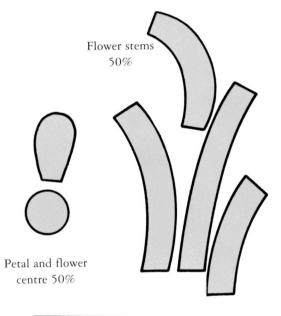

Flower stems 50%

Petal and flower centre 50%

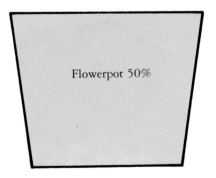

Flowerpot rim 50%

Flowerpot 50%

Autumn Leaf Shoe Bag

Enlarge the templates and trace on to the fusible bonding web. Roughly cut out the shapes and then iron to the fabric scraps.

MATERIALS

tracing paper and pencil
iron-on fusible bonding web,
20 × 50 cm / 8 × 20 in
dressmaker's scissors
iron
assorted fabric scraps
cotton waffle fabric,
50 × 56 cm / 20 × 22 in
sewing machine
red and cream thread
1 m / 1 yd narrow tape
safety pin

1

Carefully cut round the outline of each leaf and flower. Peel off the backing paper, arrange the shapes on the waffle fabric and iron on.

2

Set the machine to zigzag, and outline each shape in red satin stitch. Work a straight red line for the stems.

Leaf templates 50%

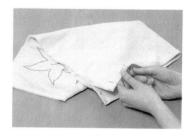

3

Right sides facing, make up the bag, finishing the side seam 7 cm / 2¾ in from the top edge. Fold the top edge down 3 cm / 1¼ in and stitch. Thread the tape through the channel using a safety pin. Tie the two ends together and trim the excess tape.

Hanging Heart Sachet

Enlarge the templates and make paper patterns. Cut out one of each shape from the fabric scraps.

MATERIALS

dressmaker's paper and pencil
scraps of cotton fabric
dressmaker's scissors
dressmaker's pins
needle and matching thread
iron
dried lavender or pot pourri
50 coloured glass beads
50 coloured headed pins
scrap of ribbon

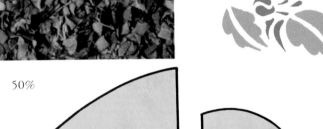

50%

1

Right sides facing, pin and stitch the pieces to make a heart shape, taking a small seam allowance. Trim the raw edges. Use the patched piece as a template to cut out another heart in plain fabric.

2

Right sides facing, pin and stitch round the heart, leaving a 5 cm / 2 in gap on one side. Clip the curves, press and turn right side out. Fill with lavender or pot pourri and slip stitch the gap closed.

3

Thread the beads on to the coloured pins and space evenly round the edge. Sew a ribbon loop to the top.

Heart Appliqué Pillowslip

Customize plain bed linen to give it country appeal, by stitching appliqué hearts to a pillowslip. Emphasize the hearts and raise the design with a halo of multi-coloured running stitches.

MATERIALS

pencil and paper
25 cm / 10 in square iron-on interfacing
dressmaker's scissors
iron
assorted scraps of brightly coloured cotton
needle and tacking thread
pillowslip
dressmaker's pins
matching thread
assortment of embroidery threads
crewel needle

1

Draw 17 hearts, varying the sizes, on the interfacing and cut out. Iron the interfacing to the fabric scraps and cut out the shapes with a 6 mm / ¼ in seam allowance.

2

Clip the seam allowance round the curves, fold over and tack in place.

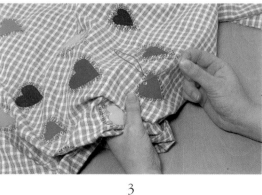

3

Arrange the hearts randomly on the pillowslip. Pin, tack and then slip stitch in place. Using an assortment of coloured threads in one strand, work lines of tiny stitches around each heart in halos. Press to complete.

Child's Strip Patchwork Rucksack

Enlarge and trace the templates for a base and a flap on to paper. Make a paper template for the straps measuring 50 × 4 cm / 20 × 1½ in. Cut a rectangle 36 × 85 cm / 14 × 34 in and a base, a flap and two straps in both the wadding (batting) and gingham. Cut a gingham casing for the rope tie 1 m × 10 cm / 1 yd × 4 in, and a gingham bias strip 1.5 m × 4 cm / 1½ yd × 1½ in. Cut the scraps into strips 6 × 36 cm / 2½ × 14 in. Taking a 6 mm / ¼ in seam allowance, sew the strips into a patched piece. From this cut a rectangle, a base, a flap and 2 straps. Lay the patchwork on top of the matching wadding and gingham pieces, tack through all layers and then quilt along the seam lines. Join the 2 short ends to make a tube. Centre the wadding along the gingham straps and fold the fabric round it. Turn under the raw edge, and stitch along the centre. Layer the patchwork, wadding and gingham base and flap pieces and quilt diagonally.

MATERIALS

dressmaker's paper and pencil
dressmaker's scissors
60 cm × 1 m / 24 in × 1 yd wadding (batting)
1 m × 90 cm / 1 yd × 36 in gingham fabric
assorted floral and gingham cotton scraps
sewing machine and matching thread
needle and tacking thread
dressmaker's pins
1 m / 1 yd rope
wooden toggle

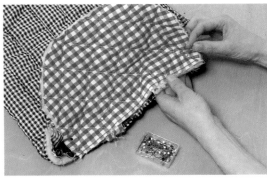

1

Wrong sides facing, pin the base to the tube. Insert the straps at either end, centred 5 cm / 2 in apart and pin to the bag. Bind the raw edges with the gingham bias strip.

2

Bind the top edge with the casing strip so that the ends meet at the centre front of the bag. Fold the binding over to right side, turn under a hem and top stitch below the previous seam.

3

Bind the shaped edge of the flap with the gingham bias strip. Right sides facing, pin the flap to back of bag below the casing. Stitch 2 rows, 1 cm / ½ in apart, close to the edge. Thread the rope through the casing and knot. Make a narrow rouleau and sew to the flap. Sew on the toggle.

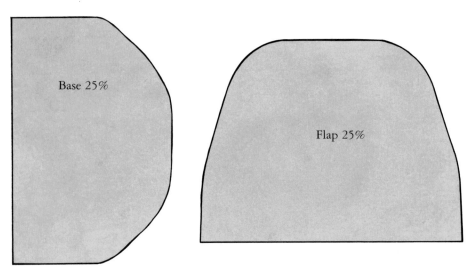

Base 25%

Flap 25%

Toy Bag

Drawstring bags like this one make excellent storage space for all those tiny toys which most children seem to collect in large quantities. This bag has two rag dollies appliquéd on its pockets.

Trace as many shapes as you need to make two dolls on to the fusible bonding web. Iron on to the fabric scraps and cut them out.

MATERIALS

tracing paper and pencil
iron-on fusible bonding web
iron
red, green and cream
fabric scraps
dressmaker's scissors
striped cotton fabric,
70 × 115 cm / 27½ × 45 in
20 × 90 cm / 8 × 36 in
checked cotton fabric
sewing machine and
matching thread
small amount of brown
yarn
lace scraps
blue and red embroidery
threads
crewel needle
dressmaker's pins
3 m / 3 yd cord

Striped fabric
1 rectangle, 70 × 100 cm /
27½ × 40 in

Checked fabric
2 pockets, 20 × 25 cm /
8 × 10 in

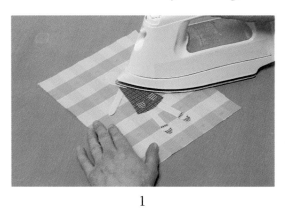

1

Assemble the fabric shapes and iron on to the pockets to make 2 dolls. Secure the pieces with machine zigzag. Sew lengths of yarn for hair and a scrap of lace on the dress hem. Sew blue French knots for eyes and sew a red smile.

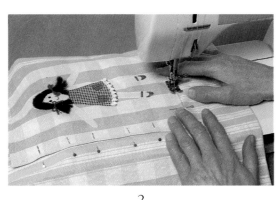

2

Hem the long side of the striped fabric, fold in half and press. Hem the pocket tops, and press under the seam allowance on the other 3 sides. Pin the pockets to the front of the bag and top stitch them in place.

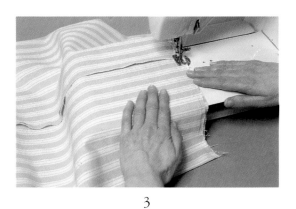

3

Pin and stitch the bag along 2 sides. Fold over 10 cm / 4 in along the top edge and press.

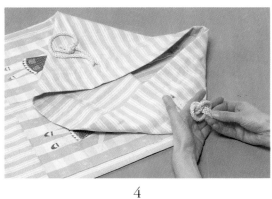

4

Make 2 buttonholes each side of the seam, 15 cm / 6 in from the top edge. Stitch a line either side of the buttonholes. Cut the cord in half, thread through the buttonholes and knot.

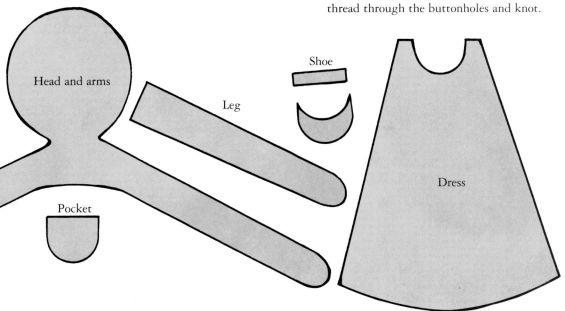

Head and arms

Leg

Shoe

Pocket

Dress

Child's Strip Patchwork Waistcoat

This waistcoat is made from patched strips. You can use long, narrow pieces of fabric left over from previous projects. Fold the fabric like a concertina and cut into strips.

Fabric amounts are given for a waistcoat to fit chest 64 cm / 26 in. To make the patched piece, join 5 6 × 90 cm / 2½ × 36 in strips, taking a 6 mm / ¼ in seam allowance. Halve the patched piece and cut out 2 waistcoat fronts. Cut 2 backs, 2 fronts and 2 interfacings in plain cotton.

MATERIALS

commercial waistcoat pattern
assorted floral scraps in toning shades
dressmaker's scissors
sewing machine and matching thread
iron
plain fabric, 85 × 90 cm / 34 × 36 in
dressmaker's pins
needle
4 buttons

1

Right sides facing, machine the interfacings to the fronts and press the seams. Stitch the fronts to the back. Make up the lining and pin to the waistcoat, matching shoulder seams.

2

Stitch round the outer edges, leaving the side seams open. Trim and clip the edges. Turn the waistcoat right side out and press. Pin the back to the fronts at the side seams and stitch, leaving a small gap.

3

Clip and press open the seam allowances. Make 4 evenly spaced buttonholes on the right front and sew 4 buttons to the left.

Child's Strip Patchwork Skirt

This gathered skirt is made from pieced strips to match the child's waistcoat. The skirt is finished with a double hem band made from a floral and striped patchwork strip.

Fabric amounts are given for a skirt to fit waist 58 cm / 23 in, with a back length of 50 cm / 20 in. To make the patched piece, cut 32 strips 6 × 40 cm / 2½ × 16 in from the floral and striped fabrics. Join together, taking a 6 mm / ¼ in seam allowance. Cut a striped and floral strip 6 × 160 cm / 2½ × 63 in and join, long sides together, for the hem band. Right sides facing, join one edge of the hem band to the base of the skirt and the other to the lining fabric. Press and turn right sides out. For a waistband, cut a piece 12 × 80 cm / 4¾ × 31½ in.

MATERIALS

dressmaker's scissors
assorted scraps of floral and striped fabric
sewing machine and matching thread
40 × 160 cm / 16 × 63 in plain fabric for lining
iron
needle
dressmaker's pins
elastic

1

Sew 2 rows of running stitch 6 mm / ¼ in and 1.5 cm / ½ in from the top of the skirt. Pull up the threads to gather the skirt to the size of the waistband.

2

Pin the waistband to the gathered edge and stitch. Fold over to the right side and pin. Top stitch along the waistband, just below the previous seam line, leaving a gap. Thread the elastic through the waistband and secure.

Log Cabin Throw

The Log Cabin is a traditional patchwork design. Although you can use any number of colours, a limited combination will help to unify the whole design.

The finished piece measures 1.8 × 2.3 m / 71 × 90½ in and is made from 12 blue pieced centres, 6 red pieced centres and 17 plain blue squares. It is edged with 3 borders. Cut out 12 blue and 6 red needlecord 10 cm / 4 in squares. Cut the floral scraps, and some blue and red needlecord into strips 4 cm / 1½ in wide. Cut 17 plain blue 32 cm / 13 in squares. For the borders cut 4 red floral strips and 4 blue needlecord strips 8 cm / 3 in wide. The pieced centres are worked from the middle out.

To finish, sew the borders to the patched piece. Lay on top of the backing piece and, starting in the middle, tack through all the layers. Stitch round each pieced square to outline the quilt. Trim the backing to overlap the patchwork all round by 13 cm / 5 in. Fold the backing over to the front of the throw to make an outer border. Turn under the raw edges and top stitch. Mitre the corners if wished.

MATERIALS

dressmaker's scissors
blue needlecord, 20 × 90 cm / 8 × 36 in
red needlecord, 1 m × 90 cm / 1 yd × 36 in
assortment of floral fabric scraps in red and blue
plain blue fabric, 2 × 2.5 m / 2½ × 3 yd

dressmaker's pins
sewing machine and matching thread iron
red floral backing fabric, 2 × 2.5 m / 2½ × 3 yd

1

Sew a blue needlecord square to a red floral strip and trim even with the square. Sew a red floral strip across the top edge of the pieced centre and trim even with the pieced centre. Sew a red floral strip to the left edge and trim.

2

To complete the centre, sew a fourth red floral strip to the lower edge, trim and press.

3

Continue to add strips round the centre. First add the blue floral strips, then the red floral strips and finally the blue needlecord strips. Press and trim to 32 cm / 13 in square. Make up 12 blue centred squares and 6 red centred squares, alternating red and blue floral strips.

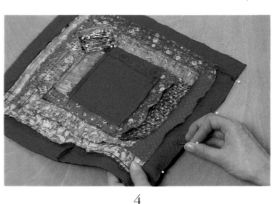

4

Sew a blue pieced centre to a plain blue square using the flag technique. Repeat, until 4 blue pieced centres are separated by 3 plain blue squares. Make 2 more rows the same, then 2 rows with 3 red pieced centres separated by 4 plain blue squares. Join the rows so the colours alternate.

Patchwork Tea and Egg Cosies

Templates 25%

Fabric amounts are for one tea cosy and 2 egg cosies. Enlarge the templates and cut out 2 large and 4 small pieces in wadding (batting). Cut the scraps into 12 cm / 5 in strips and stitch with a 6 mm / ¼ in seam allowance into one piece. Cut 4 small and 2 large pieces in patchwork and lining fabric. Pin one patched piece to the wadding and machine quilt along the seam lines. Trim the edges and repeat with the other side. Sew a ribbon loop to the centre top of one side.

MATERIALS

dressmaker's paper and pencil
dressmaker's scissors
51 × 90 cm / 20 × 36 in wadding (batting)
assorted scraps of tartan cotton fabric
sewing machine and matching thread
30 × 90 cm / 12 × 36 in cotton lining fabric
dressmaker's pins
12 cm / 4½ in of 1 cm / ½ in tartan ribbon

1

Right sides facing, pin the 2 sides together and stitch round the top and sides. Stitch the linings together, leaving a gap at the top.

2

Put the cosy inside the lining, right sides together. Pin and stitch along the lower edge, turn right side out and slip stitch the opening.

3

Push the lining inside the cosy, leaving a band on the right side. Top stitch along the seam line.

Napkin and Napkin Ring

These table accessories are appliquéd with fabric scraps and decorated with wooden buttons.

For the napkin, iron the bonding web to the assorted scraps and cut into 6 cm / 2½ in squares. Cut 4 plain blue 6 cm / 2½ in squares and, right sides facing, stitch to each corner of the napkin along 2 sides. Cut 4 calico strips as long as the napkin and 6 cm / 2½ in wide. Iron the assorted squares to the calico strips.

MATERIALS

iron
iron-on fusible bonding web
assorted blue and blue and white fabric scraps
dressmaker's scissors
sewing machine and matching thread
linen or cotton napkin
strips of calico scraps
navy embroidery thread
crewel needle
needle and matching thread
5 wooden buttons

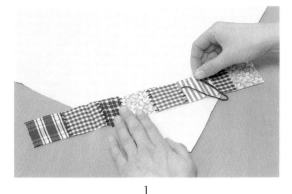

1

Work large navy stab stitches along the seam lines between each square to create a random pattern of evenly sized stitches. Right sides facing, machine the 4 strips along the edges of the napkin. Turn right side out and press.

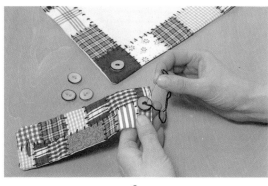

2

Work navy stab stitch along all four edges and sew a button in each corner. Make the napkin ring in the same way from 2 patched strips. Make a buttonhole on one short edge and attach a button to the other to match.

Dresden Plate Herb Cushion

This cushion is made from a ring of patched pieces that copy the design of a Dresden plate.

MATERIALS

*calico, 1 m × 90 cm /
1 yd × 36 in
dressmaker's scissors
pencil and paper
card
craft knife
assorted scraps of patterned
fabric in blue, mauve
and white
embroidery scissors
needle and tacking thread
31 cm / 12¼ in square
wadding (batting)
pale and dark purple
embroidery threads
crewel needle
2 m / 2 yd of 6 mm / ¼ in
lilac ribbon
sewing machine and
matching thread
muslin, 1 m × 90 cm /
1 yd × 36 in
dried herbs or lavender*

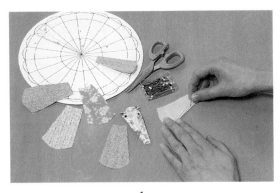

1

Cut one 33 cm / 13 in square in calico. Enlarge and trace the design from the template below on to the paper, then make templates of all the shapes in card. Cut out of fabric scraps, adding a 6 mm / ¼ in seam allowance. Tack the fabric scraps to the card templates, fold over the edges and whip stitch together. Remove the tacking threads and templates.

2

Centre the finished patchwork on the calico square, right side uppermost, with the wadding (batting) sandwiched between. Tack through all 3 layers. Outline all the shapes in running stitch, using both shades of embroidery thread.

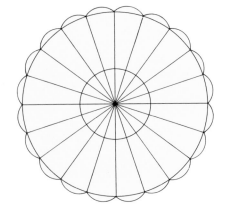

3

Pin the ribbon round the cushion square and top stitch along both edges, mitring the corners. Cut a calico strip 13 cm × 3 m / 5 in × 3 yd, joining the fabric as necessary, and hem one long edge. Stitch 2 rows along the other edge and pull up the threads to gather into a frill.

4

Right sides facing, pin the frill to the cushion and stitch. Cut 2 pieces of calico 33 × 18 cm / 13 × 7 in for the backing and make a envelope cushion cover. Cut 2 square pieces of muslin slightly smaller than the cushion and stitch together, leaving one side open. Fill with herbs or lavender and slip stitch the opening. Insert the pad inside the cushion cover.

Diamond-in-a-Square Quilt

Using the Log Cabin technique, offset a centre square with four triangles to make a traditional Diamond-in-a-Square pattern. The finished piece is edged with a magnificent red sawtooth border.

The finished wall hanging measures 2 × 2.5 m / 6½ × 8 ft and is made from 12 blue patchwork centres, 6 red patchwork centres and 17 plain squares. From the printed fabric, cut out 93 red and 94 blue 15 cm / 6 in squares. Cut red and blue printed strips 8 cm / 3 in wide, you need 4 for each block (see step 1). Make a plain blue border 8 m × 8 cm / 8¾ yd × 3 in. For the sawtooth border, make a plain red strip 9 m × 20 cm / 10 yd × 8 in and press in half lengthways. Press under a 6 mm / ¼ in hem along the top edge and mark at 7 cm / 2¾ in intervals, 4.5 cm / 1¾ in below the fold line and 3 cm / 1¼ in from the top. Stitch from point to point. Cut triangles out of the folded edge, close to the stitching, and clip into the corners. Turn right side out and press.

MATERIALS

assorted red and blue printed cotton fabric
dressmaker's scissors
red cotton fabric,
3 m × 90 cm / 3 yd × 36 in
blue cotton fabric,
4.5 m × 115 cm / 5 yd × 45 in
dressmaker's pins
sewing machine and matching thread
iron
9 m / 9 yd of 2 cm / ¾ in blue ribbon
needle and tacking thread

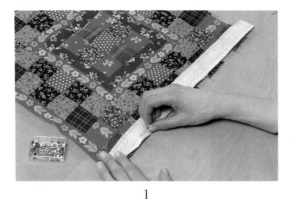

1

Using the flag method. join 3 squares to make a row and then 3 rows to make a 9-patch block. Sew a blue strip to both short and long sides, and trim. Sew 4 red strips to the block in the same way. Join 5 squares to make a row, make another the same and stitch either side of the patchwork centre. Make 2 rows of 7 squares to complete the square. Pin and stitch a border of the red strip to the square. Make 2 more identical squares.

2

For the sawtooth border, press 2 of the pieced patchwork squares diagonally in half. Cut along the fold to make 4 triangles, pin and stitch to the square. Make 2 rows of 14 squares and join to both ends.

3

Pin the ribbon along the raw edge of the sawtooth border. Top stitch along both edges of the ribbon. Right side facing, stitch the blue border round the patchwork. Cut a backing from the plain blue fabric to fit and lay the patchwork on top. Starting in the middle, tack through all layers. Outline the quilt with machine stitches. Stitch the border to the backing, fold to the front and top stitch.

Cherry Basket Patchwork Cushion

The cherry basket used to decorate this striking cushion is a traditional patchwork design.

Enlarge the triangle from the template section and cut out 18 card templates. Cut out 12 triangles in red fabric and six in white fabric, adding a 6 mm / ¼ in seam allowance. Cut out 2 38 cm / 15 in squares in cotton poplin. Tack the wadding (batting) to the reverse of one square.

MATERIALS

*paper and pencil
card
craft knife
scraps of red and white
cotton fabric
dressmaker's scissors
cotton poplin, 38 × 90 cm /
15 × 36 in
38 cm / 15 in square
wadding (batting)
needle and tacking thread
dressmaker's pins
needle and matching
thread
25 cm / 10 in square
iron-on interfacing
iron
backing fabric
sewing machine and
matching thread
square cushion pad*

1

Pin and sew the triangles in pairs. Join 8 triangles into a square, then join 4 more to the 2 top corners to make a large triangular shape. Follow the photographs for reference.

2

Pin the basket to the prepared poplin square, fold under the seam allowance and slip stitch in place. Slip stitch the 2 remaining triangles to make the base.

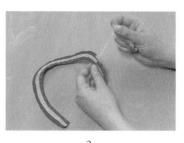

3

Draw a semicircle on the interfacing with a 25 cm / 10 in base line and use this to cut out a handle 1 cm / ½ in wide. Iron on to a scrap of red fabric. Cut out, adding a 6 mm / ¼ in seam allowance, fold under the seam allowance and slip stitch to the top of the basket. Work stab stitch round each triangle and around the basket handle. Make a cushion cover. Insert the cushion pad.

Hexagon Pincushion

Make this boldly patterned pincushion from navy and white fabrics.

Enlarge and trace the hexagon on to paper and cut out 14 card templates. Cut out 2 plain navy patches, and 4 patches in 3 other navy fabrics, adding a 6 mm / ¼ in seam allowance. Pin and tack the patches to the card templates.

MATERIALS

assorted plain and print scraps of navy fabric
tracing paper and pencil
card
craft knife
dressmaker's pins
needle and tacking thread
matching thread
wadding (batting)

1

Join the hexagons into 2 flower shapes, with 6 patterned patches round a central navy patch. Oversew the piece neatly. Make a second flower shape the same way.

2

Wrong sides facing, pin and tack the 2 pieces together. Slip stitch round the outside edge, leaving a small gap. Turn right side out. Fill with wadding (batting) and then slip stitch the gap.

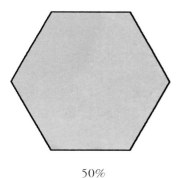

50%

Crazy Patchwork Bootees

These pull-on quilted booties have tops made from tiny pieces of crazy patchwork. Lined with gingham and secured at the top with elastic, they are a warm and comfortable gift for a baby.

Enlarge the pattern pieces from this page and from the template section. Cut out 2 tops, 2 soles and 2 front and side pieces in denim. Cut out 2 soles and 4 linings in gingham, and 2 soles in wadding (batting).

MATERIALS

paper and pencil
paper scissors
blue cotton denim,
20 × 90 cm / 8 × 36 in
gingham fabric,
20 × 90 cm / 8 × 36 in
dressmaker's scissors
scrap of wadding (batting)
assorted blue fabric scraps
dressmaker's pins
needle and tacking thread
sewing machine and
matching thread
elastic
50 cm / 20 in bias binding

1

Cut small scraps of blue fabric and tack to the bootee tops, turning under the edges. Secure with machine zigzag stitch.

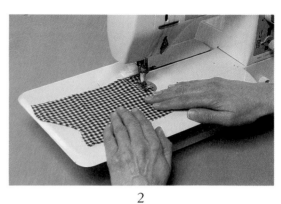

2

Machine stitch the lining pieces together along the 2 short edges.

3

Right sides facing, insert the patchwork top into the denim front and side pieces. Pin the elastic along the top edge and stitch. Join the back seam. Right sides facing, attach the lining to the top edge, clip and turn through.

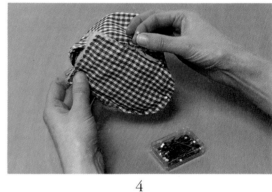

4

Sandwich the wadding (batting) soles between the denim and gingham soles. Tack through all the layers. Turn the bootees inside out, and pin and stitch the soles in place. Cover the seams with bias binding to neaten.

Front and sides 50%

fold

Lining 50%

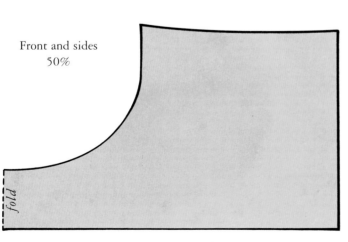
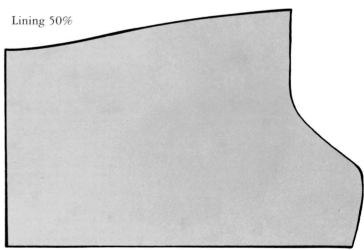

Small Quilt

This richly coloured quilt will fit a doll's bed, but it is also large enough for a Moses basket or a baby's crib. This project uses a clever method to secure the appliqué parts until they are needed.

Cut borders 13 cm / 5 in wide in contrasting fabric, 2 50 cm / 20 in long and 2 90 cm / 36 in long. Stitch to the main piece of fabric. Make card templates of the enlarged motifs and cut each one out several times from the scraps.

MATERIALS

contrasting fabric,
50 × 90 cm / 20 × 36 in
dressmaker's scissors
sewing machine and
matching thread
main fabric, 50 × 65 cm /
20 × 26 in
paper and pencil
card
paper scissors
assorted fabric scraps
iron-on interfacing
tissue paper
iron
needle and tacking thread
assorted green cotton fabric,
10 × 90 cm / 4 × 36 in
matching thread
wadding (batting),
50 × 65 cm / 20 × 26 in
backing fabric,
50 × 65 cm / 20 × 26 in

1

Lay the fabric pieces for each bird on to the interfacing, cover with tissue paper and iron – this keeps the pieces together. Prepare all the birds in this way and cut them out.

2

Arrange the birds on the quilt in rows. Tack the pieces on top of each other and secure with a small machine zigzag stitch.

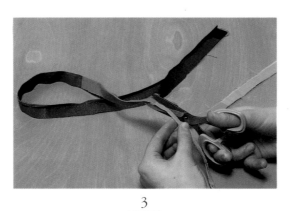

3

Cut a 2 cm / ¾ in wide bias strip in green cotton. Press in half, and stitch along the fold. Fold to cover the stitches and press. Trim back to the seam. Weave the strip round the birds, pin in place, then slip stitch along both edges.

4 ·

Appliqué the leaves to the branches then fill in the spaces with stars. Sandwich the wadding between the cover and backing, right sides out, and tack through all three layers. Make up the quilt.

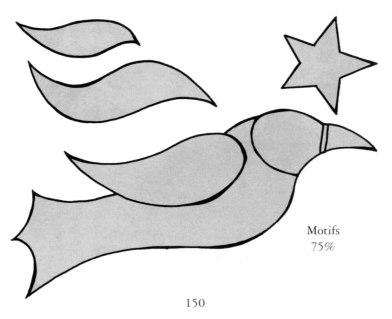

Motifs
75%

150

Baby's Appliqué Pillow

This little pillow is appliquéd with naive bird and star motifs.

Trace the motifs from the template section and transfer on to the interfacing. Iron to the fabric scraps and cut out. Cut out a 25 cm / 10 in square and a 36 cm / 14 in square in calico. Set the machine to zigzag and stitch the shapes on to the small calico square. Embellish with embroidery and sew on the button (optional). Cut 4 gingham strips 6 × 25 cm / 2½ × 10 in. Cut 4, strips, in the striped fabric 6 × 36 cm / 2½ × 14 in.

MATERIALS

pencil and paper
iron-on interfacing
assorted fabric scraps
iron
dressmaker's scissors
calico, 36 × 90 cm /
14 × 36 in
sewing machine and
matching thread
blue and brown
embroidery threads
crewel needle
small button (optional)
scraps of blue gingham
scraps of blue striped fabric
25 cm / 10 in square
cushion pad
needle and matching
thread

1

Right sides facing, make the gingham border, mitering the corners.

2

Pin and stitch the borders round the appliquéd square. Make up the striped border the same way and stitch round the first border. Clip the corners and press. Right sides facing, stitch the two calico squares together, leaving a small gap. Clip the corners and press. Turn right side out. Insert the pad and slip stitch the gap.

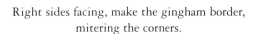

Patchwork Cube

This soft baby's toy is a perfect project for a beginner to work.

Cut each strip into 13 7 cm / 2¾ in squares. Following the illustrations, arrange the squares into 6 blocks, cutting some to make triangles. You can use a different patchwork design for each side of the cube. If you wish, finish by making a small rouleau loop and stitching it to one corner.

MATERIALS

7 × 90 cm / 2¾ × 36 in fabric strips, in 5 colours dressmaker's scissors dressmaker's pins sewing machine and matching thread wadding (batting) needle and matching thread

1

Using the flag method, pin and stitch the squares together to make 6 square blocks. Right sides facing, pin and stitch 4 blocks to the central one. Join the top block to one side block.

2

Stitch the sides in pairs, leaving a small gap on the last one to turn through. Fill with wadding (batting) and slip stitch the gap.

Oak Leaf Seat Cushion

*This appliquéd patchwork cushion is worked in sturdy contrasting colours. The leaves are out-
lined with rows of quilting, to raise them from the background fabric.*

Make a 15 cm / 5½ in square
card template, and cut out 5
red squares and 4 white
squares. Draw an oak leaf
freehand on to card and
cut it out.

MATERIALS

*ruler and pencil
card
craft knife
red cotton fabric,
30 × 90 cm / 12 × 36 in
white cotton fabric,
46 × 90 cm / 18 × 36 in
dressmaker's scissors
vanishing marker
dressmaker's pins
needle and thread
red embroidery thread
crewel needle
sewing machine and
matching thread
wadding (batting)*

1

Trace the leaf on to scraps of red fabric. Add a
6 mm / ¼ in seam allowance and cut out the shapes.
Clip the fabric back to the pencil line,
and pin under the edges.

2

Tack each leaf to a white square, as shown.
Appliqué the leaves in place with a single strand
of red embroidery thread.

3

Run rows of red stitches, like haloes, round each
leaf. Using the flag method, join the squares into a
block of 9. Make 2 rouleau ties from a 4 cm /
1½ in wide strip of white fabric. Cut 2 backing
pieces 42 × 28 cm / 16½ × 11 in, and make an
envelope cushion cover Stitch the ties to the back
corners of the cover. Stuff the cushion with
wadding (batting).

Hanging Hearts

Enlarge the heart and cut out of card. Cut out 12 5 cm / 2 in squares from assorted fabric scraps.

To finish, clip the curves and press the heart. Turn right side out and fill with pot pourri. Insert a ribbon loop and slip stitch the opening closed. Decorate with shirt buttons.

MATERIALS

paper and pencil
card
craft knife
assorted fabric scraps
dressmaker's scissors
dressmaker's pins
sewing machine and
matching thread
15 cm / 6 in square
backing fabric
iron
potpourri
scrap of ribbon
shirt buttons

<u>1</u>

Using the flag method, join the squares, with 6 mm / ¼ in seams. Make a block 4 rows across and 3 rows deep.

<u>2</u>

Pin the heart template to the patchwork and cut out. Cut another heart to match from the backing fabric.

<u>3</u>

Right sides facing, stitch the 2 hearts together, leaving a small opening in one of the sides.

33⅓%

Hanging Fan

This little pot pourri sachet is made from a small piece of patchwork sewn into the shape of a fan.

Make a card template of the fan shape. Trace on to the white felt and cut out the whole shape in backing fabric, adding a 1 cm / ½ in seam allowance. Cut the card into segments and use to cut out the individual pieces in scraps of fabric, adding a 6 mm / ¼ in seam allowance.

MATERIALS

paper and pencil
card
craft knife
5 cm / 2 in square white felt
dressmaker's scissors
7 cm / 2¾ in square backing fabric
assorted fabric scraps
dressmaker's pins
needle and matching thread
coloured thread
sewing machine and matching thread
iron
pot pourri
scrap of ribbon

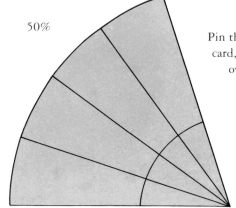

50%

1

Pin the fabric fan shapes to the card, fold the seam allowance over the card and tack.

2

To assemble the fan shape, oversew the segments with whip stitch. Centre the felt fan on the reverse of the patched piece and tack in place. Outline the fan segments on the right side with lines of coloured running stitches.

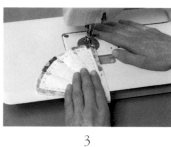

3

Right sides facing, stitch the patchwork piece to the backing, leaving a gap. Clip the curves and press the fan. Turn right side out and fill with pot pourri. Slip stitch the opening closed and add a ribbon loop to the centre of the top edge.

Child's Suffolk Puff Waistcoat

These pretty gathered rosettes are also known as bonbons and yo-yos. The Suffolk puffs are pieced together in a circle, like patchwork.

To fit 51 cm / 20 in chest. Enlarge the waistcoat outlines from the template section, adding a 1 cm / ½ in seam allowance. Cut out 2 backs and 4 fronts in dark print fabric. Cut an 8 cm / 3 in card circle. Trace 14 circles on to the assorted scraps of fabric.

MATERIALS

paper and pencil
dark print cotton fabric,
50 × 90 cm / 20 × 36 in
pair of compasses
card
craft knife
scraps of pastel print, plain pastel and bright print cotton fabrics
needle and matching thread
sewing machine and matching thread
pinking shears
needle and tacking thread
iron
dressmaker's pins
3 buttons
matching embroidery thread
crewel needle

1

Turn under a small hem on each fabric circle and make a row of running stitches round the edges.

2

Pull up the thread tightly to gather the fabric. Secure the end of the thread. Make all the puffs in the same way.

3

Oversew the individual Suffolk puffs in groups of 7 to make a circle.

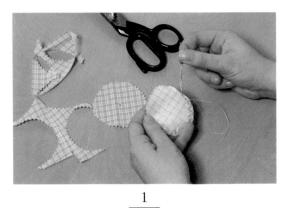

4

Stitch 2 waistcoat fronts to one back at the shoulders. Repeat with the other pieces to make the lining. Press the seams. Right sides facing, pin the lining to the waistcoat, matching the shoulder seams. Stitch the outer edges, leaving the side seams open, trim and clip. Turn to the right side and press. Pin and stitch the fronts to the backs at the side seams, leaving a gap to turn through. Make 3 buttonholes and sew on the buttons.

5

Pin and tack the Suffolk puffs to the waistcoat fronts. Using embroidery thread, work buttonhole stitch round the puffs so that they are attached to the top layer.

Cross Stitch

From its humble origins as thongs holding together pieces of animal skins, cross stitch has advanced from a primitive functional tool to a sophisticated decorative craft. The beautiful threads and exquisite fabrics of these traditional country-style items combine delicate yet elaborate designs. The inspiration for the projects comes from traditional needlework and from nature, and they bring the spirit and feel of the country into the home in items large and small.

Cross Stitch Motifs and Patterns

Since the Middle Ages embroidery and needlework has played an important part in the decoration of churches and the homes of the nobility, and from the twelfth to the fourteenth centuries. English ecclesiastical embroidery was renowned throughout Europe. Much early embroidery was done by guilds of craftworkers or in convents and monasteries, but it was not until the early sixteenth century that counted thread embroidery became popular.

With rising prosperity, there was a great demand for embellished clothes and furnishing as outward symbols of newly acquired wealth, and although much was still done professionally, the practical purposes to which so much of the work was put meant that it became an increasingly domestic occupation, with chair seats, bed quilts, curtains and even carpets being worked to imitate tapestries. These pieces were worked on canvas or linen in half cross stitch or tent stitch.

Early samplers were portable records of patterns and stitches. They were originally worked on long strips of linen, which were kept in sewing boxes to remind stitchers of colours and patterns and of different decorative stitches. Later, samplers began to include alphabets and numbers, and these may have been stitched as teaching aids for children. Interestingly, sampler patterns were often derived from oriental carpets, with the result that the patterns copied by one culture were incorporated into another country's folk art, and in this way girls in the New World stitched the same carnation borders that had been woven into the rugs of the Ottoman Empire. Over the years the number of stitches used in samplers gradually dwindled, until by the end of the eighteenth century cross stitch was the predominant stitch. Birds, trees, butterflies and animals became increasingly popular, and were used in combination with alphabets and numbers to record events such as births, christening and marriages.

The taste for lavishly embroidered and decorated household furnishings has now passed, and today cross stitch is more often used to add pretty embellishments to articles ranging from bed linen to lavender bags. Motifs are often stylized flowers, leaves, birds and animals, stitched in stranded cotton on evenweave fabric. However, as the projects in this section show, there is no limit to the ways in which cross stitch can be used to add a distinctive country look to everyday household items.

LEFT: *Worked in silks on wool tammy, this sampler from 1806 contains alphabets, border patterns, a religious verse and motifs, including flowers and butterflies associated with English country gardens (Whitney Antiques).*

Although stranded cotton is probably the most popular and versatile thread for cross stitch embroidery, there is an amazing range of different threads available. Coton perlé produces attractive raised stitches, while tapestry wool makes large, chunky crosses on 7- or 8-count canvas. Some of the projects in this section use other familiar threads, such as coton à broder or soft cotton, and some are worked in new threads such as silky Marlitt or the more rustic flower thread, which is ideal for stitching on linen. Look out for unusual flower threads that have been dyed in shaded natural colours and for metallic threads that have been especially made for cross stitching.

The most suitable fabric for cross stitch is evenweave, which has the same number of threads running in each direction. The numbers of threads in each 2.5 cm/1 in of fabric determines the gauge or 'count' of the fabric. The larger the number of threads, the finer the fabric. Aida and Hardanger are woven and measured in blocks of threads. However, cross stitches worked on 28-count linen are the same size as those on 14-count Aida because the stitches are worked over two threads of linen.

Pure linen was traditionally used for cross stitching, but there are now several different mixed-fibre evenweave fabrics in a wide range of colours. Cotton gingham can also be used and can look very attractive. Fabrics specially woven with distinct areas for cross stitching are suitable for making into napkins, tablecloths and cot covers. There are also some unusual evenweave fabrics with linen or Lurex threads interwoven into the fabric for special effects.

162

CLOCKWISE FROM TOP LEFT: *The wool-work sampler from 1850 has an innovative three-dimensional look (Whitney Antiques).*
The barnyard scene by Mary Rees, worked c.1827, reveals both careful colour selection and stitch direction. The set of table
linen was embroidered in England in the late 1940s, while the detail is taken from an eighteenth-century Persian embroidery.

Shaker Box

These oval beechwood boxes were used by the Shakers to hold all sorts of things.

MATERIALS

maroon 18-count Aida,
20 × 25 cm / 8 × 10 in
tacking thread
needle
embroidery hoop
Anchor Nordin nos. 150,
275 and 316
tapestry needle
beechwood box
paper
pencil
scissors
thin wadding (batting),
15 × 20 cm / 6 × 8 in
double-sided tape
60 cm / 24 in of 15 mm /
⅝ in cream ribbon
60 cm / 24 in of 12 mm /
½ in navy ribbon

1

Tack along the centre line of the Aida in both directions and work the cross stitch using the thread as it comes, then complete the back stitch.

Anchor Nordin		Backstitch	
⁊⁊	275	——	316
←←	150	☆	Middle point

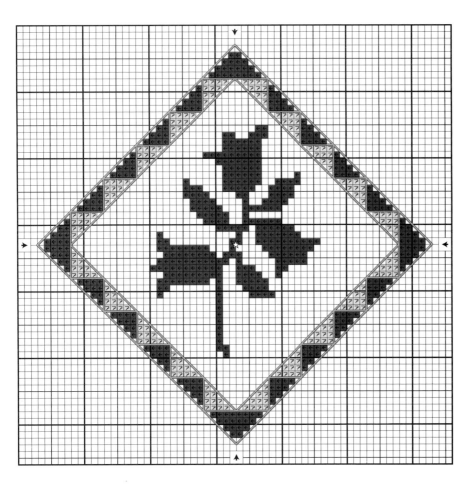

2

To make up, draw round the lid to make a template. Use this to cut out an oval of wadding (batting). Stick it onto the lid. Cut out the cover adding a 1 cm / ½ in allowance. Put some double-sided tape round the lid. Centre the design and stretch the fabric down the sides, making sure it is completely smooth and taut.

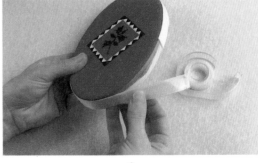

3

Put another layer of tape round the rim and stick on the cream ribbon. Trim and butt the ends together.

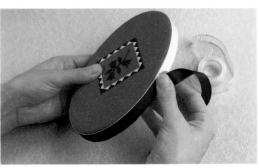

4

Repeat this process with the blue ribbon, leaving a touch of cream showing. This time turn under the raw end and stick it down.

Nine Star Picture

A simple design inspired by early American patchwork heart and star pictures.

MATERIALS

*46 cm / 18 in square of
antique white 28-count
Cashel linen, Zweigart
E3281
vanishing marker pen
tracing paper
pencil
paper scissors
tacking thread
needle
stranded cotton Anchor
nos. 39, 150, 169, 246
and 305
tapestry needle
30 cm / 12 in square of
mount board
strong thread
frame*

1

Mark a 25 cm/10 in square in
the middle of the linen and
stitch the border design,
sewing 20 hearts across and
24 down. Fold the fabric in
half both ways to find the
centre and mark with the
vanishing marker pen. Work
the heart cross stitch pattern
within the lines, beginning
with a heart on the centre
mark. To make up, trace and
cut out the star template. Place
it in the centre of the border
and draw round it carefully
with the pen.

2

Following the grain of the fabric make a second mark
on the left 8 cm/3 in from the centre. Draw round the
star template and fill with another cross stitch pattern.
Continue in this way, spacing the centres 8 cm/3 in
apart, until all 9 stars are complete. Finish the design by
stitching a grid of blue running stitch midway between
the stars to make 9 equal 8 cm/3 in boxes.

3

Stretch the linen over the mount board and put in a
simple frame.

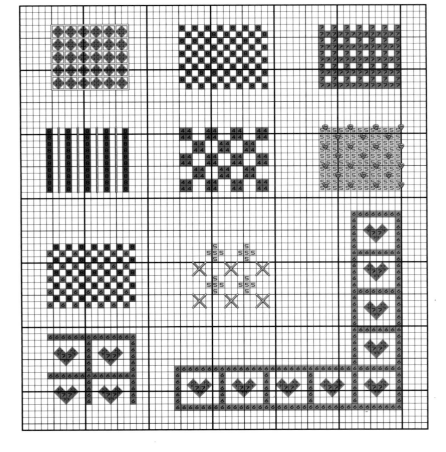

	Anchor		Backstitch
4 4	246	—	39
5 5	305	—	305
6 6	169	—	246
7 7	39		French knots
8 8	150	♥	150

Utensil Box

This simple box could be used to store candles, paintbrushes or pens and pencils.

1

Tack guidelines across the centre of the linen in both directions and work the cross stitch using two strands of cotton over two threads. Press the embroidery on the reverse side when it is complete.

2

To make up, paint the box with two coats of dark blue paint. Allow the paint to dry between coats.

3

Trim the card to fit the front of the box. Stretch the linen over it, mitring the corners neatly, and stick the panel onto the front of the box.

MATERIALS

28-count natural evenweave linen, 15 × 20 cm / 6 × 8 in
tacking (basting) thread
needle
embroidery hoop
stranded cotton Anchor nos. 150, 1034, 1036
tapestry needle
scissors
plain utensil box
emulsion paint in dark blue
paintbrush
thin card, 8 × 15 cm / 3 × 6 in
craft knife
all-purpose glue

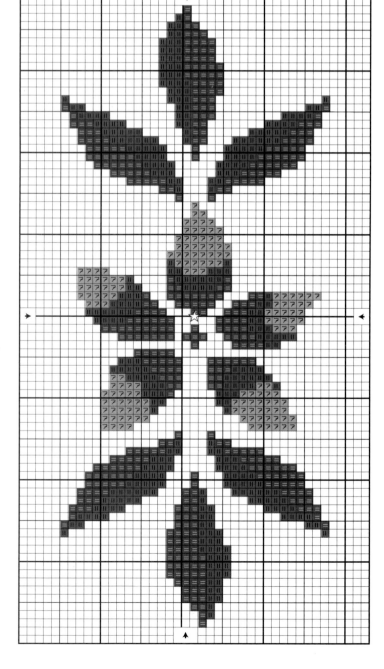

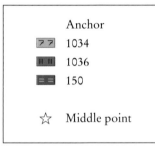

Anchor
⫘ 1034
▥ 1036
⊟ 150

☆ Middle point

Heart Vine Wreath

Make the wreath with fresh Virginia creeper or clematis stems and let it dry out under a weight to hold the heart shape. If you do not feel confident about making a wreath, look out for ready-made wreaths in dried flower and florist's shops. They are available in a range of materials and sizes. Embroider the six hearts onto the linen using one strand of Nordin over two threads of linen, leaving about 2.5 cm / 1 in round each design.

MATERIALS

antique white 28-count Cashel linen, Zweigart E3281, 20 × 30 cm / 8 × 12 in
small embroidery hoop
red Anchor Nordin no. 47
embroidery needle
lightweight iron-on interfacing, 15 × 23 cm / 6 × 9 in
scissors
pencil
pins
scraps of different red gingham fabrics
sewing thread
polyester stuffing
Virginia creeper or clematis stems
string

1

To make up, iron on 8 cm / 3 in squares of interfacing to the reverse side and cut out. Draw a heart on each piece, pin to a square of gingham and stitch. Trim the seams, turn through and stuff then slip stitch the gap.

2

Cut 8 60 cm / 24 in lengths of vine. Split the bundle in 2 and make into a heart shape securing the ends with vine. Wind some more vine round and round the rest of the wreath to hold it together.

3

Sew a 13 cm / 5 in length of embroidery thread through the back of each heart and use it to tie the hearts round the wreath. Add a loop for hanging or fit over a nail.

	Anchor Nordin
⊞⊞	47
Backstitch	
——	47

Tray Cloth

This design could be adapted slightly to fit a tray of any size.

MATERIALS

ruler
paper
pencil
scissors
4 different fat quarters
of gingham
medium weight iron-on
interfacing
sewing machine
sewing thread
fusible bonding web
stranded cotton
Anchor Nordin no. 144
embroidery needle
cotton lining
9 buttons

1

Measure your tray and using a scaled up template draw out a paper pattern to fit inside. Adding 1.5 cm / ¾ in seam allowances all round, cut out a triangle and a strip from each of the 4 kinds of gingham. Iron interfacing to the reverse side of each piece. With right sides facing, sew each pair of triangles together along the short sides and sew 2 strips together for each end. Stitch the large triangles together to make a square and sew the strips on opposite sides.

2

To make up, cut 4 hearts from the bonding web and iron onto the reverse side of different ginghams. Cut out leaving a 6 mm / ¼ in seam allowance. Remove the paper, snip the seams, fold over and press.

3

Position the hearts on the tray cloth and iron again. Sew large cross stitches round each heart and along the seams of the triangles and side panels.

4

With right sides together, sew the lining to the mat leaving a gap. Trim the seams and turn through. Slip stitch the gap and press. Sew a button in the centre and space the other buttons down each of the sides to complete.

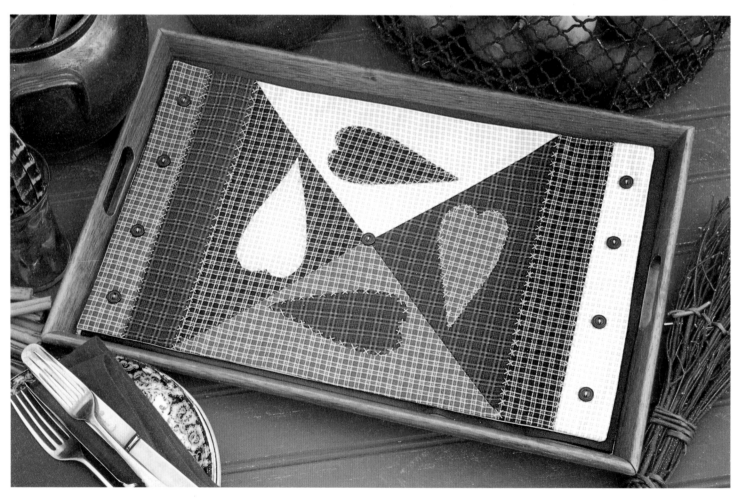

Curtain Pelmet

These delightful geese in their colourful carts would be ideal for a child's bedroom.

1

Measure the width of the window and cut a piece of gingham twice as wide and about 50 cm / 20 in deep. Tack the squares of waste canvas about 15 cm / 6 in apart along the bottom of the fabric, allowing for the hem and side turnings. Try to position the centre lines of the canvas on the same check each time. Work the cross stitch using 3 strands of cotton.

2

To make up, once the embroidery is complete, carefully remove the canvas threads one at a time and press the fabric on the reverse side.

3

Finish the raw edges at the side of the pelmet and turn under 5 cm / 2 in. Turn up the hem of the pelmet and stitch. Add curtain tape along the top edge or simply wrap the fabric round a curtain pole and adjust the gathers.

MATERIALS

tape measure
red, green and cream gingham
10-count waste canvas,
10 cm / 4 in square for each motif

tacking thread
needle
stranded cotton Anchor nos. 386,
879 and 1006
embroidery needle
sewing thread
curtain tape (optional)

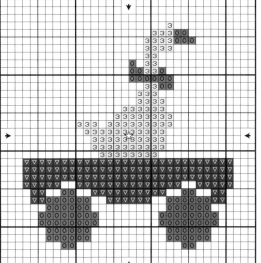

Anchor	
3 3	386
0 0	1006
▽ ▽	879
☆	Middle point

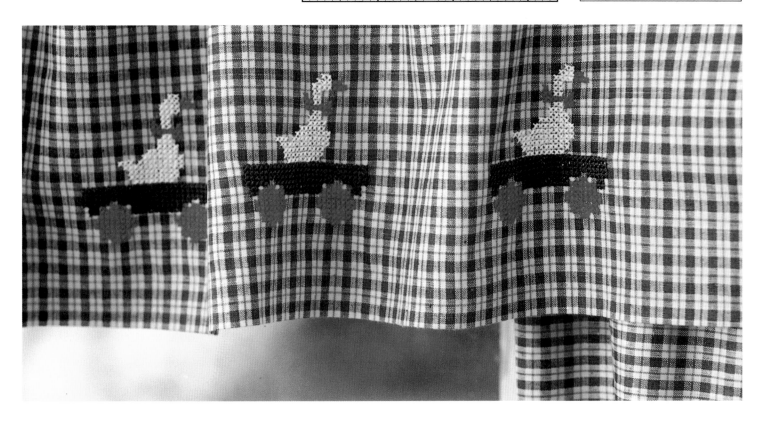

Game Board

This game board is quite easy to make with only basic woodworking skills.
It is antiqued using crackle varnish and oil paint.

MATERIALS

*gold 32-count evenweave
linen, 30 × 36 cm /
12 × 14 in
scissors
tacking thread
needle
embroidery hoop
stranded cotton Anchor in
white and nos. 44, 170,
211 and 403
tapestry needle
28 × 51 cm / 11 × 20 in of
6 mm / ¼ in medium density
fibreboard (MDF)
acrylic or emulsion paint
in off-white
paintbrush
ruler
pencil
blackboard paint
1.6 m / 1 ¾ yd of 2.5 cm /
1 in wood edging
56 cm / 22 in of 2 cm /
¾ in wood edging
fretsaw
wood glue
masking tape
2-step Craquelure varnish
oil paint in raw umber
soft cloth
antique brown wax
mount board, 23 × 28 cm /
9 × 11 in
safety ruler
craft knife
double-sided tape*

1

Cut the linen in half lengthways. Tack guidelines down the centre in both directions and work the cross stitch using 2 strands of cotton over 2 threads. Stitch the second piece to match and press on the reverse side.

2

To make up, paint a 28 cm / 11 in square in off-white in the middle of the MDF and allow to dry. Beginning in the middle of one side, mark every 33 mm / 1¼ in. Repeat on the other edges and draw out the squares. (There should be an 8 mm / ½ in border all round.) Paint the left-hand square black, then paint every second square black in alternate rows. When these are dry, paint the remaining black squares.

3

Cut 2 51 cm / 20 in pieces and 2 28 cm / 11 in pieces from the 2.5 cm / 1 in wood edging. Glue these to the side of the board and hold in place with masking tape. Cut the narrower strip to fit inside and stick it down across the board. Paint the completed board with an even coat of the first varnish and allow to dry according to the manufacturer's instructions. Brush on the second varnish, which takes a little longer to dry. Cracks will appear but may not be obvious as the varnish is transparent.

4

Next day rub some raw umber oil paint into the cracks with a soft cloth and leave to dry. Rub the entire board with antique brown wax. Measure the end sections and cut the mount board slightly smaller. Stretch the embroidery over the board and stick securely inside the end sections, using double-sided tape to complete.

Anchor		French knots
170	♥	403
211		
403	☆	Middle point
1		
44		

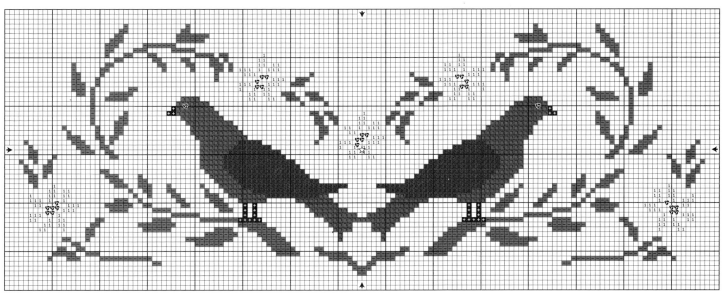

Napkin

This napkin has been finished with a pretty two-colour border to match the heart design.

MATERIALS

*40 cm / 16 in square grey /
blue 28-count Jobelan
sewing machine
sewing thread
scissors
Anchor Nordin nos. 127,
150, 326 and 341
embroidery needle
tacking thread
needle
embroidery hoop*

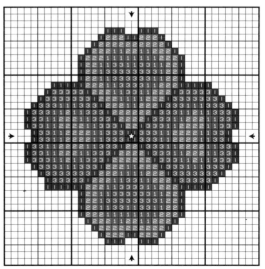

1

Turn under 6 mm / ¼ in round all sides
and machine stitch. Mitre the corners
and turn over a further 6 mm / ¼ in.
Hold the hem in place with running
stitch in dark blue going over and under
4 threads at a time.

2

Complete the border with rust-coloured
cotton. Tack a guideline round one
corner of the napkin, 3 cm / 1¼ in in
from the edge. Work the cross stitch
over 2 threads and press.

Anchor		
∎∎ 127	33	341
11 150		
22 326	☆	Middle point

Herb Decoration

This delightful little gingerbread man could be filled with a sachet of herbs or pot pourri.

1

Tack guidelines across the centre of one square of the linen in both directions and work the cross stitch using 2 strands of cotton over 2 threads. When complete, press on the reverse side.

2

To make up, cut the ribbon in half and pin to the top edge of one square 4 cm / 1½ in apart. Pin the 2 pieces of linen together with right sides facing, tucking the ribbon inside. Stitch round the sides leaving a 5 cm / 2 in gap at the bottom. Trim the seams and across the corners then turn through.

3

Cut 2 squares of wadding (batting) the size of the cushion and tuck inside together with a sachet of herbs. Slip stitch the gap closed. Tie a bow for hanging.

MATERIALS

2 16 cm / 6¼ in squares evergreen 28-count Belfast linen, Zweigart E3609
tacking thread
needle
stranded cotton DMC nos. 221, 310, 676, 729, 825 and 3823
tapestry needle
1 m / 1 yd of 2 cm / ¾ in gingham ribbon
scissors
pins
sewing machine
sewing thread
polyester wadding (batting)
dried herbs or pot pourri

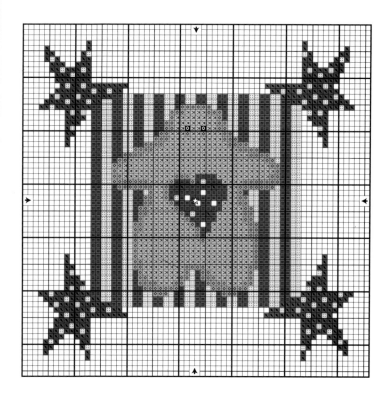

DMC						
▬	221	⋗	676	◣	825	☆ Middle point
⦂⦂	3823	◇	729	◯	310	

Patchwork Cushion

The motifs on this patchwork cushion are based on traditional North American samplers.

MATERIALS

9 13 cm / 5 in squares of different gingham fabrics with approximately 10 squares to 2.5 cm / 1 in embroidery hoop stranded cotton DMC nos. 304, 444, 801, 924, 3821 and 3830 embroidery needle pins sewing machine sewing thread 4 small pearl buttons scissors needle contrast backing fabric, 40 × 60 cm / 15 × 24 in 30 cm / 12 in cushion pad

1

Work the cross stitch using 3 strands of cotton over each small square. Stitch one orange basket and two of each of the other designs. Once complete, press on the reverse side and lay out the squares on a flat surface to check their positions.

DMC			
═ ═	444	◇ ◇	304
⋮ ⋮	3821	◥ ◣	801
⇥ ⇥	3830	▽ ▽	924

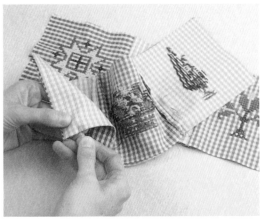

2

To make up, stitch 3 lots of 3 squares together with 1 cm/½ in seam allowances and press the seams open. Pin the rows together matching the seams, stitch and press again. Sew a button at each corner of the centre square.

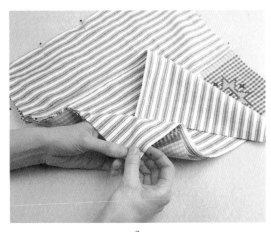

3

Cut the contrast backing fabric in half to make 2 30 × 40 cm (12 × 15 in) rectangles and sew a narrow hem lengthways along one side of each. With right sides together, pin one piece to the left side of the patchwork square and the second piece to the right side. Overlap the hems and sew round all 4 sides. Trim across the corners and turn through. Tuck the cushion pad inside to complete.

Kitchen Apron

Everyone will be happy to wear this big, bright apron with its cheery gingerbread men.

MATERIALS

large cook's apron
10-count waste canvas, 15 × 30 cm /
6 × 12 in
tacking thread

needle
coton perlé no.5 DMC no. 543
embroidery needle
6 small buttons

1

Tack the waste canvas onto the bib of the apron, positioning it about 8 cm/3 in down from the top edge. Work the cross stitch as shown through the waste canvas. Once complete, remove the tacking thread.

2

To make up, once complete, remove the canvas threads one at a time. You may find it easier to take out the shorter threads first. Press the embroidery on the reverse side. Sew on the buttons.

DMC coton perlé no.5
33 543

Hand Towel

Make this pretty border to sew on to a plain waffle towel and add your own initials.

MATERIALS

white waffle hand towel
homespun cotton gingham
with approximately
10 squares to 2.5 cm / 1 in
scissors
tacking thread
needle
stranded cotton DMC nos.
321, 815 and 3808
embroidery needle
pins
sewing machine (optional)
sewing thread

DMC	
⊥⊤ 3808	▐ Your
⊞⊞ 321	choice
— 815	

1

Wash both the towel and the gingham to check for shrinkage. Cut the gingham so that it measures 5 cm / 2 in wider than the towel. Tack guidelines across the centre of the gingham in both directions and work the cross stitch using 3 strands of cotton over each square. Stitch your choice of initials first, then work the hearts on either side.

2

To make up, press the embroidery on the reverse side. Trim the long edges so that there is 4 cm / 1½ in on either side of the cross stitch. Press under 1 cm / ½ in on all sides and pin to the end of the towel. Fold the short ends to the back and tack. Hand- or machine-stitch the gingham close to the edges using matching thread.

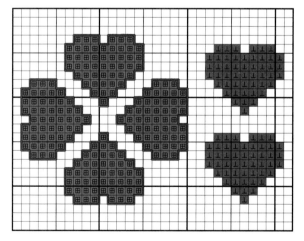

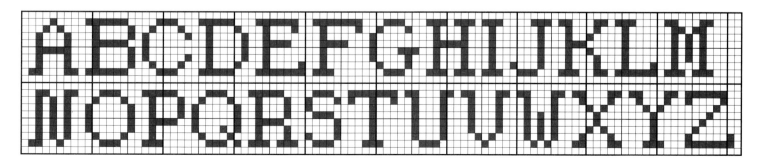

Wooden Spoon Mobile

Paint an old wooden spoon and make a charming kitchen decoration with some oddments of gingham and embroidery cotton.

MATERIALS

3 8 cm / 3 in squares of different gingham fabric
3 5 cm / 2 in squares of 14-count waste canvas
tacking thread
needle
6 10 cm / 4 in squares of contrast gingham
fusible bonding web, 8 × 25 cm / 3 × 10 in
scissors
Anchor Nordin nos. 13, 134 and 281
embroidery needle
sewing machine
sewing thread
polyester stuffing
wooden spoon
pencil
hand drill
yellow paint (Colourman 122)
paintbrush
adhesive tape
large-eye needle

1

Tack the waste canvas onto the small gingham squares and work one motif in the centre of each.

2

To make up, iron fusible bonding web on to the reverse side of the squares and trim them to 5.5 cm / 2¼ in. Remove the backing paper and iron the embroidered squares on to 3 squares of the contrast gingham. Work a row of tiny red running stitches round each small square to secure. Sew the backs on to the cushions with right sides facing, leaving open along one side. Trim the corners and turn through. Fill with stuffing and slip stitch to close.

Remove the waste canvas one thread at a time once the embroidery is finished and press lightly on the reverse side.

3

Lay the cushions under the spoon and mark the position of the holes. Drill small holes through the spoon and apply two coats of yellow paint.

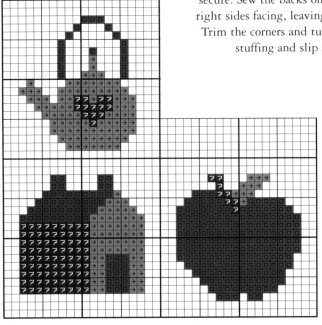

	Anchor
⁊⁊	134
☐☐	13
→→	281

4

Make a 60 cm / 24 in cord with Anchor Nordin no. 281. Cut it in 3 equal pieces and tape the ends to stop them unravelling. Thread a cord through each hole and sew the ends into one corner of each cushion.

Party Horse

Children love to role-play with this traditional folk art doll who is dressed in her Sunday best and ready for a tea-party.

1

Trace the apron template on to the white cotton. Tack the waste canvas in the middle of the lower half and work the cross stitch using 3 strands of cotton. Remove the waste canvas thread by thread and complete the back stitch as shown. Press the embroidery on the reverse side. Pin the broderie anglaise round the embroidered section of the apron.

2

Fold the apron in half with right sides together and stitch, leaving a gap on one side. Turn through and press. Pin the ribbon across the top of the apron and stitch all round close to the edge.

MATERIALS

white cotton fabric, 20 × 30 cm / 8 × 12 in
tracing paper
pencil
5 cm / 2 in square 14-count waste canvas
tacking thread
needle
stranded cotton DMC nos. 799 and 3347
embroidery needle
broderie anglaise, 30 cm / 12 in
pins

scissors
sewing machine
sewing thread
30 cm / 12 in of 6 mm / ¼ in white ribbon
40 cm / 16 in of 90 cm / 36 in wide natural linen or fine wool
polyester stuffing
2 6 mm / ¼ in black beads
25 cm / 10 in of 115 cm / 45 in wide blue cotton print

3

To make up, enlarge the templates and cut out the pattern pieces for the horse. Using 6 mm / ¼ in seam allowance, stitch the heads, ears, arms and legs together in pairs, leaving the short straight edges unstitched. Stuff all the pieces except for the ears. Turn the raw edges inside, pinch the bottom of each ear and hand sew on either side of the head seam.

4

For the eyes, stitch on one bead and take the thread through to the other side. Pull it taut to sink the eye slightly and sew on the second bead. Stitch the torso leaving open between the dots and at the top and bottom. Tuck the head inside and slip stitch securely. Attach the arms in the same way, then stuff the body firmly.

5

Pin the legs in place and backstitch through all layers along the bottom of the torso. Cut out the dress bodice and a 20 × 61 cm / 8 × 24 in rectangle for the skirt. Stitch the outer sleeve seam and the underarm seam. Sew a small piece of lace to the neck edge and hem the sleeve ends. Stitch the short ends of the skirt together to form a tube and gather round one end. Pin to the bodice and stitch. Fold under a narrow hem and stitch to complete.

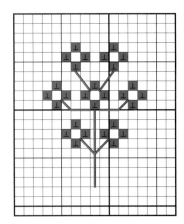

DMC
11 799
Backstitch
— 3347

CROSS STITCH

Guest Towel

Screw brass hooks to the back of a door or hang this unusual towel from wooden pegs.

1

Wash the towel and gingham before beginning to check for colour fastness and shrinkage. Cut the gingham 2.5 cm / 1 in wider than the towel. Fold the fabric in half crossways and mark this with a line of tacking. Beginning with the red flower, embroider the motifs 5 cm / 2 in up from the bottom of the fabric. Reverse the motifs for the other side.

MATERIALS

white waffle hand towel
30 cm / 12 in homespun check fabric with approximately 10 squares to 2.5 cm / 1 in
scissors
tacking thread
needle
coton perlé no. 5 DMC nos. 311, 400, 469, 726 and 814

embroidery hoop
embroidery needle
pins
sewing machine
sewing thread
40 cm / 16 in woven tape
2 pearl buttons

DMC		Backstitch
▦	726	—— 726
▦	400	—— 311
▦	814	
▦	311	☆ Middle
▦	469	point

2

To make up, with right sides together, stitch the bottom edge of the embroidered panel to the top of the hand towel. Fold and press under a 1 cm / ½ in seam allowance along the top edge. Fold the gingham in half with right sides together, stitch the side seams, trim and turn through.

3

Slip stitch the folded edge to the back of the towel. Cut the tape in half. Fold into loops and pin the raw edges to each corner of the embroidered panel. Stitch across the bottom of the loop, fold it over and stitch securely. Sew a button to the front of each corner as a trimming.

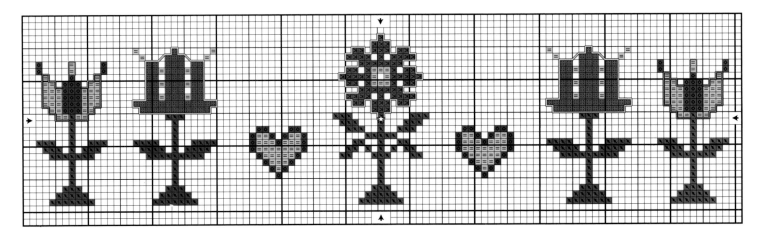

Folk Art Cow

Children will love this traditional folk art style cow and the bright, colourful border.

Tack guidelines across the middle of the Aida in both directions. Begin in the middle and work the cow picture. Leave 2 rows of Aida clear all round for the green ribbon. Next, work the patchwork border.

2

Pin the ribbon round the edge of the cross stitch and in the space left round the cow. Hem the ribbon to the Aida with tiny stitches.

3

Cut the mount board slightly larger than the outside ribbon edge. Stretch the embroidery over the board and put into a frame.

MATERIALS

white 14-count Aida,
36 × 40 cm / 14 × 16 in
tacking thread
needle
coton à broder DMC in
ecru and nos. 10, 444,
553, 603, 605, 702, 799,
827, 898, 954 and Anchor
no. 254
tapestry needle
1.5 m / 1 ⅝ yd of 3 mm / ⅛
in green satin ribbon
scissors
pins
sewing thread
30 × 36 cm / 12 × 14 in
mount board
craft knife
safety ruler
strong thread
frame

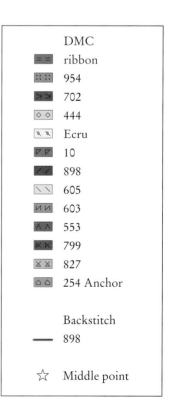

DMC	
==	ribbon
⠂⠒⠒	954
▶▶	702
◇◇	444
��	Ecru
▽▽	10
⁄⁄	898
＼＼	605
ИИ	603
∧∧	553
⊠⊠	799
✕✕	827
△△	254 Anchor

Backstitch
——— 898

☆ Middle point

Herbs on a Rope

Fill these five lovely bags with cinnamon sticks, chilli peppers or dried herbs.

MATERIALS

*white 16-count Aida,
10 × 15 cm / 4 × 6 in
scissors
stranded cotton DMC nos.
311 and 815
tapestry needle
dark blue denim,
12 × 20 cm / 4 ¾ × 8 in
pins
embroidery needle
pinking shears
5 15 × 20 cm / 6 × 8 in
rectangles in different red
and blue checks
all-purpose glue
sewing machine
sewing thread
cinnamon, chilli peppers
and other dried herbs
1 m / 1 yd heavyweight
cotton cord
2.5 cm / 1 in brass curtain
ring
coarse string*

1

Cut 5 4.5 cm / 1¾ in squares out of the Aida.
Work a cross stitch heart in the middle of each
piece using 3 strands of cotton and then
complete the red cross stitch squares
in the border.

2

To make up, cut 5 7 cm / 2¾ in denim squares
and pin the embroidered pieces to them. Work
the blue cross stitch through both layers. Fray the
edge of the Aida squares and trim the edges of
the denim with pinking shears. Glue each heart
motif to the centre of a check rectangle, 4 cm /
1½ in from the lower edge. Fold in half so that
the heart is on the inside and stitch the short
edges together. Position the seam at the centre
back and press flat. Stitch along the bottom edge,
trim the corners and turn through. Trim the tops
of the bags with pinking shears and work a row
of running stitches 4 cm / 1½ in from the top.

DMC		
▦ 815	☆	Middle point
▦ 311		

3

Fill with herbs, pull up the running stitches and
fasten securely. Thread the brass ring onto the
cord, fold it in half and bind the top with string
to secure. Tie the bags on to the double string at
intervals using short lengths of string.

Embroidered Laundry Bag

Embroider your own choice of initials in a similar style and make one of these big,
useful laundry bags for each member of the family.

50 cm / 20 in of 6 cm /
2 ½ in Aida band with red
border, Zweigart E7315
stranded cotton DMC no.
815
tapestry needle
white linen or a textured
woven cotton, 80 × 100 cm
/ 31 × 39 in
scissors
pins
sewing machine
sewing thread
quilting pencil
needle
2 m / 2 ¼ yd medium white
piping cord
safety pin
comb

1

Fold the Aida band in half crossways to find the
centre and work the cross stitch using 3 strands
of cotton.

2

To make up, cut the white fabric into 2
50 × 80 cm / 20 × 31 in rectangles. Pin, then
stitch the band to one piece, 20 cm / 8 in
from the lower edge.

3

With the embroidered band on the inside, pin
the 2 pieces together. Starting and finishing
20 cm / 8 in from the top, stitch round the sides
and along the bottom. Press the seams open and
flatten the corners to make a right angled point
at each end of the bottom seam. Measure
5 cm / 2 ½ in in from each point and mark a
diagonal line across each corner. Pin and stitch
across the corners to form a flat base.

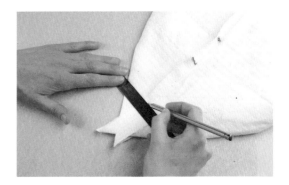

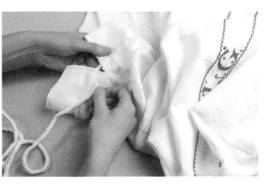

4

Fold over and stitch the seam allowance round
both top flaps. Fold in half to the inside and
stitch along the edge of the hem. Make a second
row of stitching 4 cm / 1 ½ in up from this to
form a drawstring channel. Cut the cord in 2 and
thread through opposite ends of the channel
using a safety pin. Knot the 2 ends of each cord
together 8 cm / 3 in from the end. Unravel the
ends to form a tassel, comb the ends out and
trim neatly.

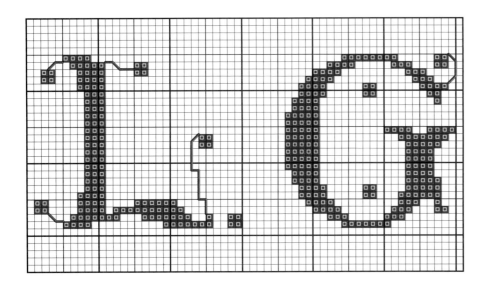

	DMC		Backstitch
□□	815	——	815

Pot Pourri Sachet

The beautiful white Austrian lace adds the finishing touch to this charming little cross stitch design.

2 13 × 15 cm / 5 × 6 in pieces of 14-count Aida stranded cotton DMC nos. 517 and 666 tapestry needle 1 m / 1 yd of 4 cm / 1 ½ in Austrian lace tacking thread needle and pins 15 cm / 6 in narrow red ribbon sewing machine sewing thread pot pourri sachet 2 10 × 13 cm (4 × 5 in) pieces of wadding (batting)

DMC

- 517
- 666

Backstitch

— 666

☆ Middle point

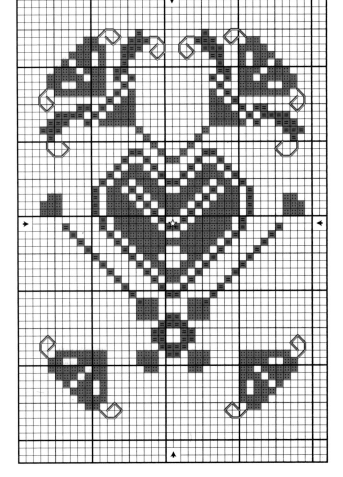

1

Find the centre of the Aida and work the cross stitch using 2 strands of cotton and the back stitch using one strand. Press on the reverse side.

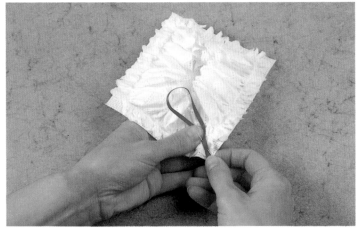

2

To make up: gather the lace and pin round the edge of the embroidered panel. Adjust the gathers and tack. Fold the ribbon in half and pin to a top corner with the loop facing inward.

3

With the embroidery and lace to the inside, stitch round 3 sides. Trim the seams and corners and turn through. Put the pot pourri sachet between the layers of wadding (batting) and insert into the cushion. Slip stitch the opening to finish.

Nightdress Case

Match the ribbon in the lace edging to the brilliant blue of the cornflowers and bow.

MATERIALS

1.5 m / 1 ²/₃ yd white cotton
fabric
12-count waste canvas,
10 × 13 cm / 4 × 5 in
tacking thread
needle
embroidery hoop
stranded cotton DMC nos.
798, 799 and 3347
embroidery needle
tailor's chalk
sewing machine
sewing thread
scissors
60 cm / 24 in white
crocheted lace with ribbon
insert
pins

1

Tack the waste canvas in the centre of the cotton fabric, 10 cm / 4 in from one end. Work the cross stitch through the waste canvas using 2 strands of cotton. The bow should be at the end of the fabric. Manipulate the canvas to loosen the threads and pull them out one by one. Press the embroidery on the reverse side.

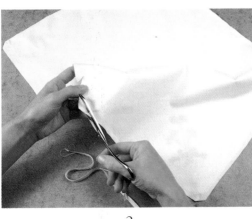

2

To make up, fold the fabric in half crossways and mark the triangular flap with tailor's chalk. With right sides together, stitch round the edge, leaving a gap on one side. Trim the seams and cut across the corners before turning through.

DMC	
▦ 798	
▤ 799	☆ Middle point
▨ 3347	

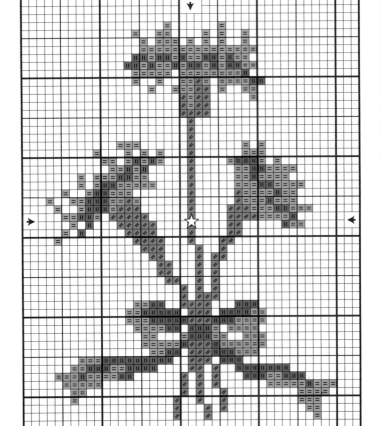

3

Ease out the corners and point of the flap and press on the reverse side. Pin and tack the lace along the edge of the flap and stitch it in place. Fold in the ends of the lace and hand sew. Slip stitch the side seams to finish.

Tablecloth and Napkin

This pretty table linen set with its colourful border will make
Sunday lunch a very elegant affair.

MATERIALS

115 cm / 45 in square of
white 28-count Jobelan
for the tablecloth
50 cm / 20 in square of
white 28-count Jobelan
for the napkin
tacking thread
scissors
needle
embroidery hoop
stranded cotton Anchor,
3 skeins each of 131 and
133, 1 skein each of nos.
35, 47, 110, 112, 211
and 297
tapestry needle
pins
sewing thread
sewing machine

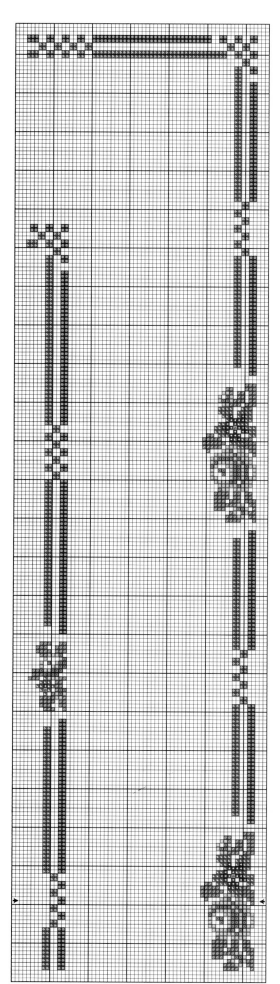

Tablecloth

Fold the fabric in half and tack a guideline about 20 cm / 8 in along one fold to mark the centre on each side. Tack a line across one of these sides, 16 cm / 6¼ in from the edge, as a starting-point. Work the cross stitch using 2 strands of cotton over 2 threads.

1

To make up, note that the chart shows one half of one side. Repeat the design on the other side, keeping the floral motifs facing in the same direction. Continue the cross stitch round the other sides of the tablecloth.

2

Press on the wrong side of the fabric when finished. Trim the fabric to a 95 cm / 37½ in square, mitre the corners and fold over a 2.5 cm / 1 in hem. Stitch close to the turned edge and slip stitch the mitred corners.

Napkin

Tack the centre line as before and mark the starting point 8 cm / 3 in in from the side. Work the cross stitch using 2 strands of cotton over 2 threads, repeating the design on all sides.

1

To make up, press the fabric on the reverse side when complete and trim to 45 cm / 18 in.

2

Mitre the corners and fold over a 2 cm / ¾ in hem. Finish in the same way as the tablecloth.

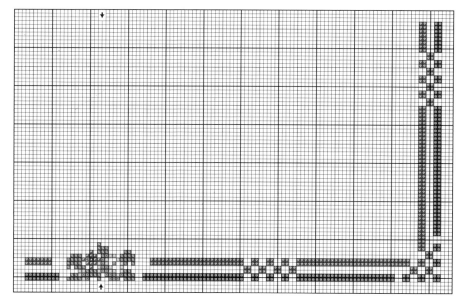

Anchor			
⑤⑤	297	∅∅	211
∞∞	133	◀◀	112
↖↖	131	◣◣	110
□□	47		
⊞⊞	35		

Floral Tie-backs

These tie-backs are quick and easy to make and would be ideal for the kitchen.

MATERIALS

*1.5 m / 1 ⅔ yd of
8 cm / 3 in raw linen band,
Zweigart E7272
scissors
tacking thread
needle
tapestry needle
stranded cotton DMC nos.
517, 518, 553, 554, 561,
562, 563 and 741
pins
4 2.5 cm / 1 in brass rings*

1

Cut the linen band into 4 equal pieces. Tack guidelines across one of the bands to mark the centre and work the cross stitch using 2 strands of cotton over 2 threads. Turn the band round and repeat the design at the other end.

2

To make up, press the band on the reverse side and fold over 6 mm / ¼ in at each end. Fold in the corners to make a point, then pin and tack. Finish a plain piece of linen band in the same way – this will form the backing.

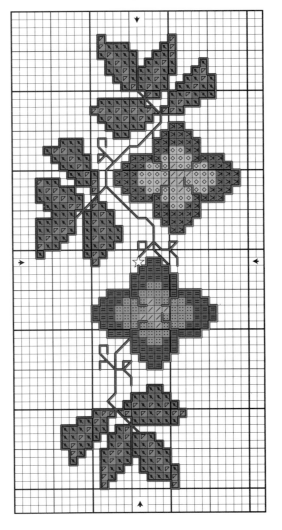

DMC	
▬▬	517
⣿	518
▶▶	553
◇◇	554
◤◤	562
▽▽	563
◿◿	741

Backstitch	
——	561
——	553
——	517
☆	Middle point

3

Pin the tie-back and its facing together, with the raw edges to the inside. Sew a decorative cross stitch every 1 cm / ½ in along the border to join the 2 pieces together. Slip a brass ring between the layers at each point and sew cross stitches on the point and at either side to secure. Make a second matching tie-back in exactly the same way.

Herb Box and Pot Stand

Keep the herb box on the windowsill filled with fresh herbs. The special heatproof glass inside the pot stand frame will protect the design.

MATERIALS

*60 cm / 24 in of 10 cm / 4 in wide plain bleached linen, Inglestone collection 900 / 100
tacking thread
needle
stranded cotton DMC in white and nos. 210, 211, 300, 310, 311, 318, 340, 349, 445, 472, 500, 562, 704, 726, 741, 742, 809, 966, 3607 and 3746
tapestry needle
scissors
30 cm / 12 in pinewood box
staple gun*

Herb Box

1

Tack guidelines across the centre of the linen band in both directions then work the cross stitch using 2 strands of cotton over 2 threads of the linen.

2

To make up, once complete, press the linen on the wrong side and then fit round the box. Turn under the ends and staple them to the back of the box.

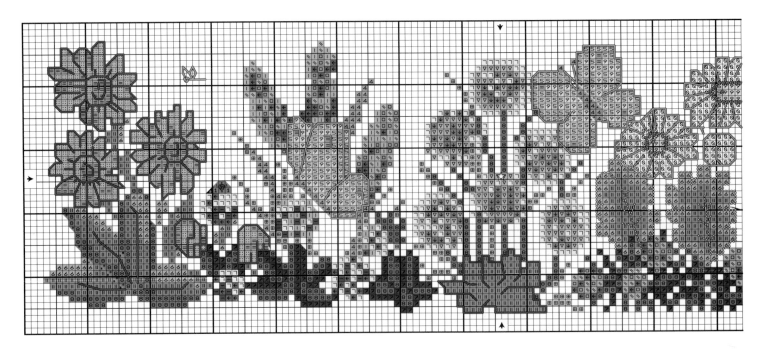

CROSS STITCH
·······················

MATERIALS

23 cm / 9 in square of white
18-count Aida
tacking thread
needle
scissors
tapestry needle
embroidery hoop
stranded cotton Anchor
nos. 120 and 122
hexagonal frame,
Framecraft WTS

Pot Stand

1

Work the cross stitch as for the Herb Box. Sew the back stitch outlines and press the work on the wrong side.

2

Follow the manufacturer's instructions to fit the embroidery inside the frame. The stand has a felt base to protect tables.

DMC		DMC	
◈◈	210	▫▫	809
77	211	⊞⊞	966
▬▬	311	↓↓	3607
▯▯	340	←←	3746
1 1	349	◎◎	white
22	310	▽▽	3607 +211
33	300		(1 strand each)
44	318		Backstitch
55	445	──	500
66	472	─♥	300
77	500	═══	472
88	562	∘∘∘∘	966
99	726	─♥	318
‖ ‖	704	──	310
══	741		
⁞⁞⁞	742	☆	Middle point

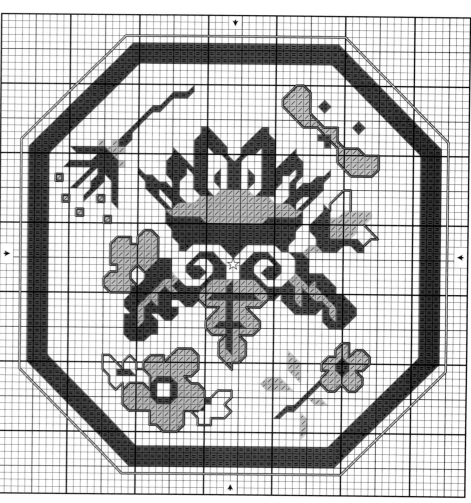

Anchor (in two strands)	Backstitch (in one strand)	Backstitch (in two strands)
══ 122	── 122	── 120
∕∕ 120		☆ Middle point

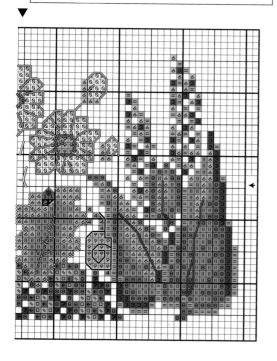

Embroidered Sheet and Pillow Case

This classic bed linen would look superb with a Victorian blue and white wash bowl and jug set on a marble washstand. You could use the same pattern to add a decorated band to a guest towel.

MATERIALS

8 cm / 3 in wide Aida band,
Fabric Flair BA7349
scissors
sheet and pillow case
stranded cotton Anchor:
2 skeins of 130 and 132
and 1 skein of 134
(pillow case); 6 skeins
of 130, 5 skeins of 132
and 3 skeins of 134
(single sheet)
tapestry needle
pins
sewing thread
sewing machine

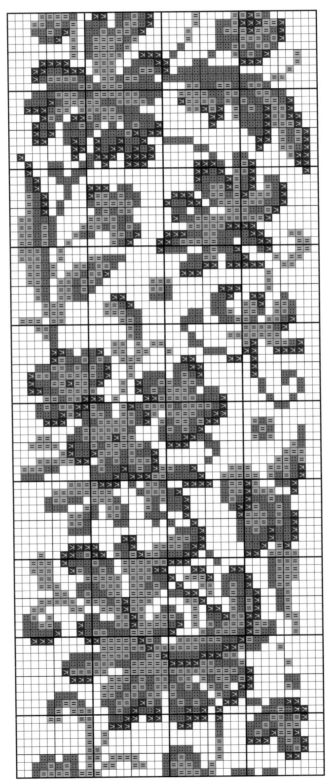

1

Measure the widths of the sheet and pillow case and cut the Aida band 10 cm/4 in longer. Work the cross stitch design using 2 strands of cotton, beginning 5 cm/2 in from one end.

2

To make up, once complete, press on the wrong side and pin to the sheet or pillow case 6 cm/2½ in in from the edge. Turn under the ends and stitch the band in place.

Anchor	
==	130
⋮⋮	132
▶▶	134

Embroidered Coathanger

Protect delicate negligées and sweaters with this pretty padded coathanger.

MATERIALS

30 × 60 cm / 12 × 24 in
fabric for the cover
scissors
5 × 25 cm / 2 × 10 in
10– count waste canvas
pins
tacking thread
needle
stranded cotton Anchor
nos. 19, 35, 118, 218,
302 and 304
embroidery needle
30 cm / 12 in polyester
wadding (batting)
wooden coathanger
sewing thread
double-sided tape
50 cm / 20 in fine cord

1

Cut the fabric for the cover in half lengthways and the waste canvas into 5 equal pieces. Pin and tack a square of waste canvas in the middle of the fabric.

2

Position the other pieces of canvas on either side, leaving a gap of 4 cm / 1½ in between them, and tack securely. Work the cross stitch using two strands of cotton. Once complete, loosen the threads of the waste canvas and pull them out one at a time. Press on reverse side.

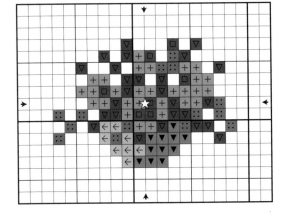

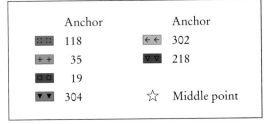

Anchor		Anchor	
⠿	118	← ←	302
+ +	35	▼ ▼	218
▫ ▫	19		
▼ ▼	304	☆	Middle point

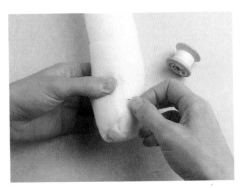

3

To make up, cut the wadding (batting) into 4 5 cm / 2 in strips and one of 10 cm / 4 in. Wrap the narrow bands round the coathanger and finish with the wider band. Oversew the ends.

4

Trim both pieces of fabric to a width of 11 cm / 4½ in, making sure that the cross stitch motifs are along the centre line. With right sides facing and a seam allowance of 1.5 cm / ¾ in, stitch the pieces together, leaving a small gap in the middle for the hook. Press the seam flat and place over the coathanger, feeding the hook through the gap. Turn under the front edge of the fabric, overlap at the bottom of the coathanger and slip stitch.

5

Fold in the fabric at the end of the coathanger and sew tiny running stitches close to the edge. Gather up the stitches and sew in to secure. Cover the hook with double-sided tape. Starting at the curved end, wrap the cord tightly round the hook and sew the end into the wadding of the coathanger to finish.

Cross Stitch Pincushion

A pincushion was an invaluable sewing aid for women who spent hours stitching for their families; pins could be plucked effortlessly from, or returned to, the pincushion without interrupting the sewing rhythm. Wool was used as a filling because its natural greases helped the pins glide in and out and protected them from rust.

Amish women had a particular need for pincushions as their strict dress code forbade the use of buttons and all their clothing was fastened with straight pins. Because they were practical objects, Amish pincushions were allowed some decoration – some were made from patchwork, others were embroidered and lace-trimmed and some, like the one in this project, were worked in needlepoint. Most had a loop at one corner so that they could hang from the wrist when working, and from a shelf hook when not in use.

MATERIALS

needlepoint canvas 20 cm / 8 in square, 10- or 11-mesh double-thread
soft-leaded pencil and ruler
tacking thread in contrasting colour
tapestry needle, size 24, and sewing needle
Persian yarn: 1 skein each in light green, mid-green, deep green, gold, grape, red and bottle green
2 pieces of dark green corduroy fabric, 11 × 20 cm / 4½ in × 8 in
matching sewing thread and top-stitching thread
sewing machine
scissors
polyester toy stuffing
small multicoloured beads

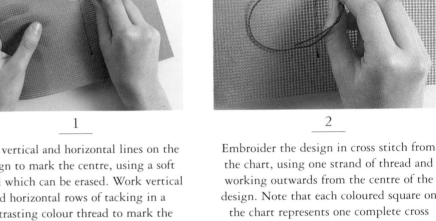

1

Rule vertical and horizontal lines on the design to mark the centre, using a soft pencil which can be erased. Work vertical and horizontal rows of tacking in a contrasting colour thread to mark the centre of the canvas.

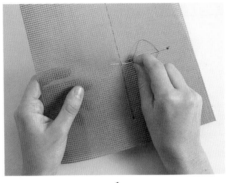

2

Embroider the design in cross stitch from the chart, using one strand of thread and working outwards from the centre of the design. Note that each coloured square on the chart represents one complete cross stitch worked over one canvas intersection. Work each cross stitch horizontally in individual rows.

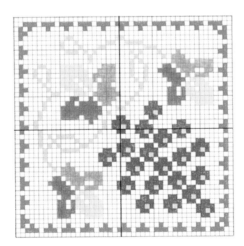

light green
mid green
deep green
gold
grape
red
bottle green

3

Place the corduroy pieces right sides together and make a seam along one edge, leaving an opening of about 10 cm / 4 in at the centre. Making sure the seam is in the centre, place the back and the finished embroidery right sides together and pin round the edge. Machine-stitch close to the last row of embroidery. Trim the seams, clip the corners and turn the work right side out through the opening. Stuff it firmly with polyester stuffing, then stitch up the opening.

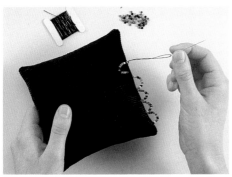

4

Using the top-stitching thread, stitch
groups of beads around the edge to make a
looped fringe. You will need about 15
beads for each loop. Work from the back of
the pincushion and tighten the thread after
each loop, securing it by making 2–3 small
stitches into the fabric. Secure the
beginning and the end of the thread
carefully so the beads do not work loose.

Sampler

There was a time when every little girl began her first sampler at about the age of five. She would work alphabets, numbers, motifs and a variety of stitches neatly in many different colours on a strip of linen. The final addition was her name, age and the date of her work's completion. There are some remarkably detailed pieces of work surviving which declare the maker to be just six years old.

Old samplers from England, Denmark, Germany, Greece, America and other countries are strikingly similar, not only in the regularity of the cross stitch pattern but also in their arrangement and the subjects they depict.

The project sampler takes some of the elements from an old Danish family tree sampler featuring hearts and birds, both symbols of love. Match the colours or make up your own colour scheme, but do buy all your silks at the same time to be sure that they are harmonious.

MATERIALS

*graph paper 10 squares to
2.5 cm / 1 in
coloured pencils or pens
11-count cream cross stitch fabric,
50 cm / 20 in square
tacking thread in a contrasting
colour
tapestry needle, size 26, and sewing
needle
stranded cotton: 1 skein each in
light pink, deep red, purple, light
blue, mid-blue, orange, light green and
deep green, and 2 skeins of mid-green
stiff piece of card
scissors
pins and button thread
picture frame*

1

Using the motifs and alphabets in the template section, sketch out your own design on graph paper using coloured pencils or pens, reversing the bird motifs as necessary.

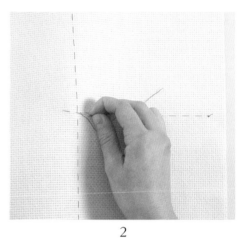

2

Mark the centre of the canvas with coloured thread.

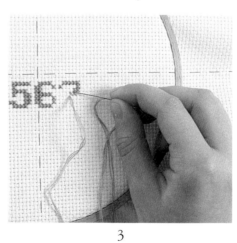

3

Work the sampler design in cross stitch, but remember that the top diagonal stitches of each cross should always slant in the same direction, usually from bottom left to top right. Centre the piece of card over the wrong side of the finished embroidery.

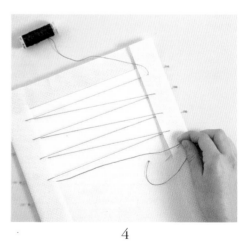

4

Cut away the surplus fabric, leaving a margin of about 5 cm / 2 in all round. Fold over the fabric at the top and bottom of the card, secure with pins, then take long stitches between the two fabrics using the button thread. Repeat along the other sides. Mount in the frame.

Country Throw

50%

Heart

Grapes

Hand

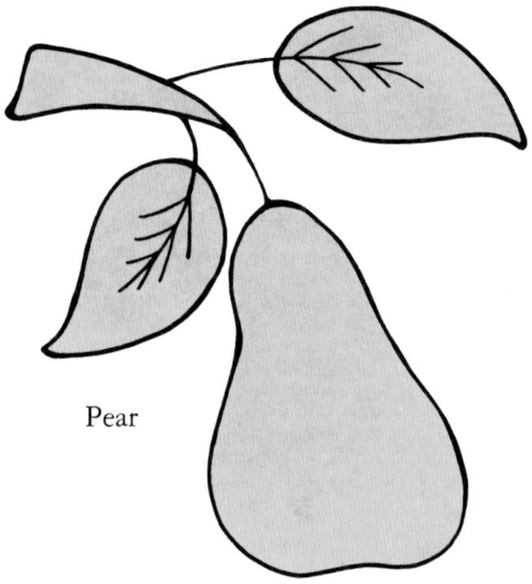

Pear

Bird 2

Bird 1

Flower

Strawberry

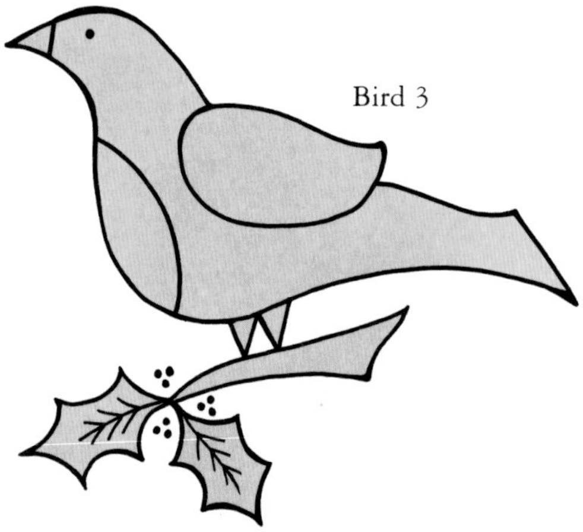

Bird 3

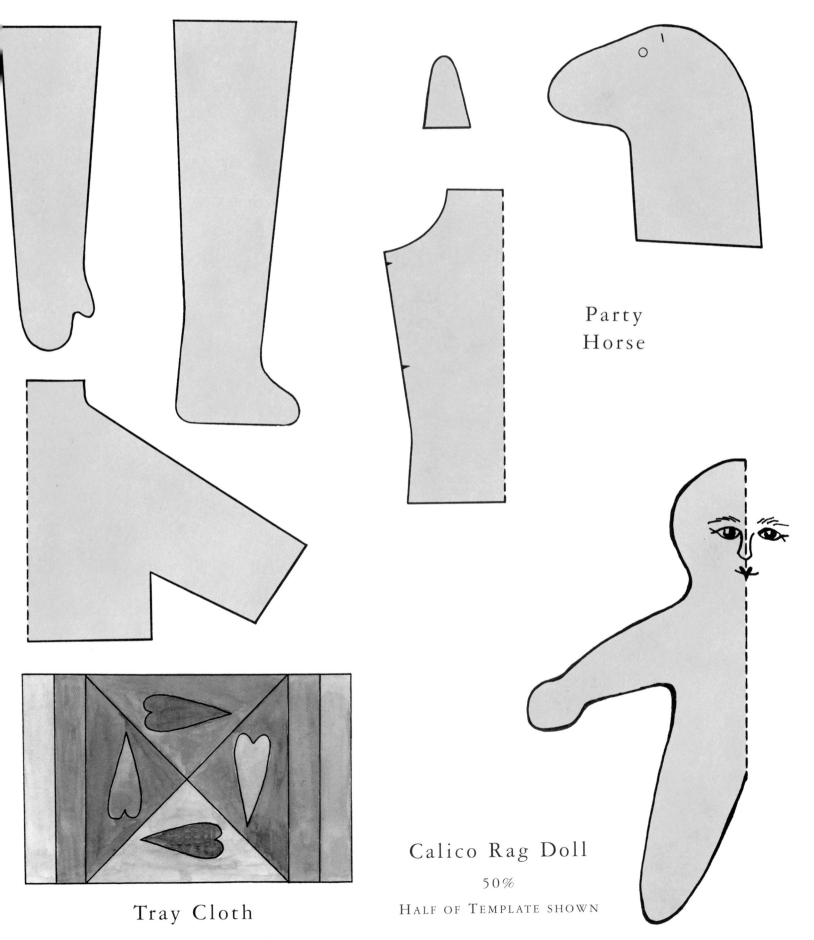

Party
Horse

Calico Rag Doll

50%

HALF OF TEMPLATE SHOWN

Tray Cloth

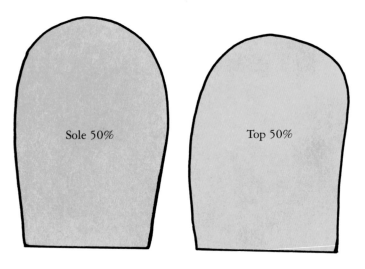

Crazy Patchwork Bootees

Nine Star Picture

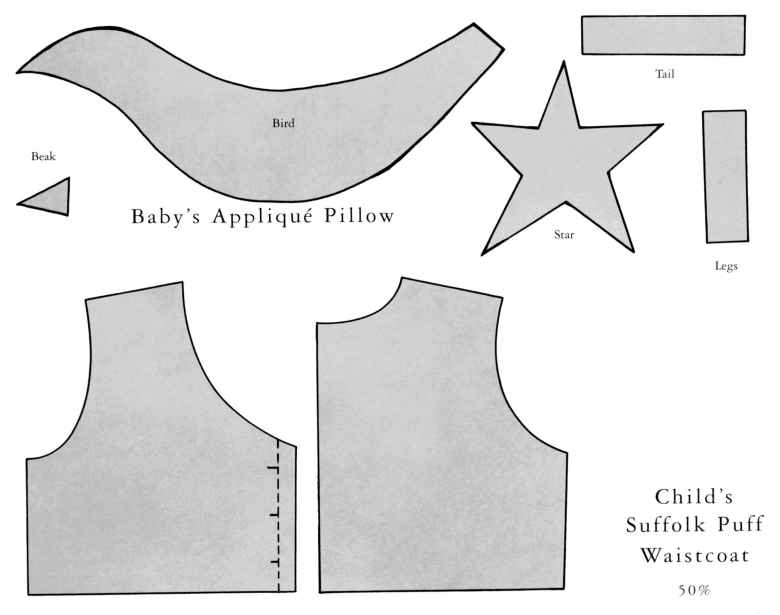

Baby's Appliqué Pillow

Child's
Suffolk Puff
Waistcoat

50%

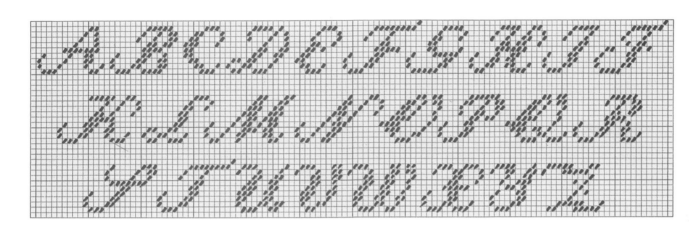

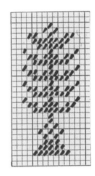

Sampler

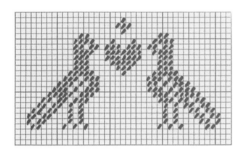

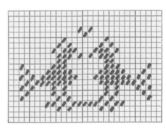

Alphabet Cot Quilt

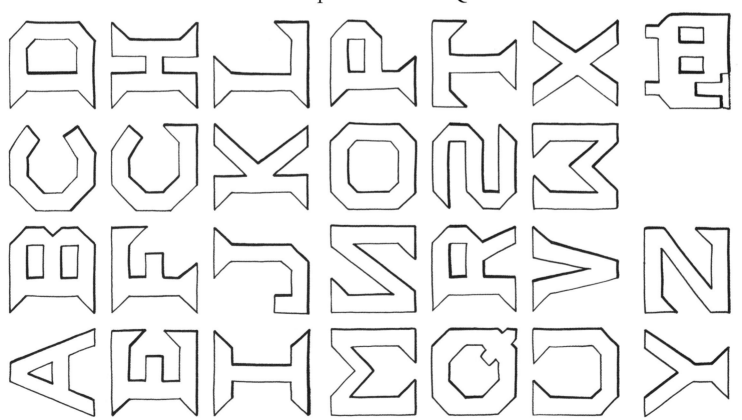

COUNTRY
Crafts and Flowers

Fresh from the Fields

....

Nothing captures the mood of the season better than bringing a little of the outdoors inside. Glean flowers, herbs and greenery from your own garden, the hedgerows, the fields, and even the market-place; gather together a few simple containers to put your treasures in; and then enjoy the abundance of seasonal colours, textures and aromas.

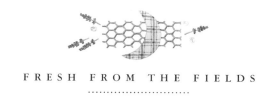
Bringing Outdoors Inside

One of the easiest ways of bringing the country into the home is to use fresh flowers and foliage. Whatever the season, there is always plenty of material to create beautiful arrangements.

The vagaries of fashion have had their impact on flower arranging just as they have on most other aspects of life. However, one discernible long-term trend has been a relaxation of the formal approach of twenty years or more ago when flowers sometimes looked as though they had been beaten into submission! Nowadays, the straitjacket of formality has been replaced by an emphasis on the flowers themselves creating the impact in a natural way.

No longer restricted by a set of rigid rules, the flower arranger is free to take inspiration from anything that triggers the creative process – it may be the decor of a room or a particular type of container, but equally it could just be the mood of the moment or even the state of the weather! Of course, modern flower arranging still relies on the basic principles of colour, scale, proportion and balance but it uses these to create more adventurous designs in exciting colour combinations and textures. It is also concerned with simplicity, and today the flower arranger is as likely to create a successful display with daffodils in a jam jar as with an opulent arrangement on a pedestal.

Contemporary flower arranging has become the art of understanding the materials and getting the best out of them with the minimum complication. One of the single most important factors in allowing the flower arranger more creative freedom has been the enormous improvement in the availability and good quality of commercially grown cut flowers. The flower arranger is no longer restricted by the seasonal availability of the majority of popular cut blooms and has an ever-growing range of flowers to work with. Further, modern growing techniques have improved the quality and increased the life span of cut flowers, for example the few days' cut life of sweet peas has been extended to a week or more.

All of these improvements give today's flower arranger more options in terms of choice of materials, colour palette and arranging techniques.

To some people, flower arranging is an all-consuming passion but to many it remains a mystery. In reality, it is an activity in which most people can, to a greater or lesser extent, participate successfully. All you need is a working knowledge of the basic rules and techniques of flower arranging coupled with a little determination, some imagination and lots of practice. The important thing to remember is that flower arranging is a creative, not just a physical, process.

LEFT: *This Summer Basket Display makes the best possible use of fresh garden flowers to create an appealing display that will last for at least a week.*

CLOCKWISE FROM TOP LEFT: *Stems of contorted willow are an unusual contrast with arum lilies. The warm pinkish-red of tulips makes a lovely pomander, while raffia adds a rustic touch to a fruit swag. Simplicity and spontaneity make for highly successful displays.*

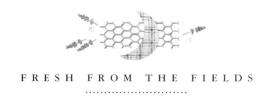
Care of Cut Flowers

CONDITIONING

Conditioning is the term for the process of preparing flowers and foliage for use in arranging.

The general rules are: remove all lower leaves to ensure there is no soft material below the water level where it will rot, form bacteria and shorten the life of the arrangement; cut the stem ends at an angle to provide as large a surface area as possible for the take-up of water; and, finally, stand all materials in cold water for a couple of hours to encourage the maximum intake of water. For many varieties of flower and foliage this treatment is perfectly adequate; for some, however, there are a number of additional methods to increase their longevity.

BOILING WATER

The woody stems of lilac, guelder rose and rhododendron, the sap-filled stems of euphorbia and poppy, even roses and chrysanthemums, will benefit from having their stem ends immersed in boiling water.

Remove all lower foliage, together with approximately 6 cm/2½ in of bark from the ends of woody stems. Cut the stem ends at an angle of 45 degrees and, in the case of woody stems, split up to

approximately 6 cm/2½ in from the bottom. Wrap any flowerheads in paper to protect them from the hot steam.

Carefully pour boiling water into a heatproof container to a depth of approximately 6 cm/2½ in and plunge the bottoms of the stems into the hot water, leaving them for two to three minutes before removing and plunging them into deep cold water. The heat of the boiling water will dispel air from the stems to enable the efficient take-up of cold water and will destroy bacteria on the stem ends.

Wilted roses can also be revived by having their stems recut and given the boiling water treatment, and then left standing in cold water for two hours.

SEARING

Searing is a method of extending the lives of plants such as euphorbia and poppies which contain a milky sap, the release of which affects the water quality. It involves passing the stem end through a flame until it is blackened, then placing it in tepid water. This forms a layer of charcoal to seal the stem end, preventing sap leakage but still allowing the take-up of water.

HOLLOW STEMS

Delphiniums, amaryllis and lupins have hollow stems and the best method of conditioning them is to turn them upside-down and literally fill them with water. To keep the water in the stem, form a plug from cotton wool or tissue and carefully bung the open stem end. Tie a rubber band around the base

of the stem to avoid splitting, then stand the stem in tepid water. The water trapped inside the stem will keep it firm and the cotton wool will help draw more water up into it.

FOLIAGE

Generally the rules for conditioning foliage are the same as for flowers. It is vital to strip the lower leaves and cut the stem base at an angle. Depending on the stem structure and size, other special techniques may well apply. It is also important to scrape the bark from the bottom 6 cm/2½ in of the stem and split it to further encourage the take-up of water.

WRAPPING TO STRAIGHTEN STEMS

Some flowers, such as gerbera, have soft, flexible weak stems and other flowers may simply have wilted. There is a technique for strengthening such material: take a group of flowers and wrap the top three-quarters of their stems together in paper to keep them erect, then stand them in deep cool water for about two hours. The cells within the stems will fill with water and be able to stand on their own when the paper is removed.

ETHYLENE GAS

Ethylene is an odourless gas emitted by such things as household rubbish, exhaust fumes, fungi and ripening fruit. It has the effect of accelerating the rate at which some flowers mature which in turn causes non-opening and dropping of buds and yellowing of leaves. Particularly susceptible are carnations, freesia, alstroemeria and roses. Be aware of this when using fruit in a flower arrangement.

LEFT: *Cut flowers for arranging in the early morning, before the sun can begin to fade the fresh colours.*

CLOCKWISE FROM TOP LEFT: *A pinholder and glass nuggets are ideal for holding cut stems. Straighten bent stems by wrapping them in damp newspaper for a while. Remember that although fruit introduces wonderful colour and and texture to arrangements, it can give off ethylene gas and thus hasten the rate at which cut flowers mature.*

FRESH FROM THE FIELDS

Hyacinth Bulb Vases

Bulbs can be grown in water as well as in soil. This technique and some long-term planning make it possible to give a fresh look to the commonplace hyacinth.

There are vases expressly made for water-growing bulbs, some particularly attractive. A simple jam jar, with a twig frame to support the bulb, will do the job just as well, however.

This particular arrangement is a grouping of both types of container, which are as important to the overall success of the display as the flowers themselves.

If you are using bulb vases, simply fill each one with water and place the bulbs on the top with their bases sitting in the water. Top up the water occasionally, taking care not to disturb the roots. Then just wait until the hyacinth bulbs root, grow and flower!

3 bulb vases
2 jam jars
4 thin sturdy twigs
raffia
scissors
5 hyacinth bulbs

1
———

The use of a jam jar requires making a square frame to sit on top of the jar.

2
———

Use thin but sturdy twigs firmly tied together with raffia to form the frame. Trim the stem ends and the raffia when you have established that the frame fits the jar neatly, then position the bulb on the frame so that its base is in the water.

Spring Napkin Decoration

The combination of gold and white in this pretty and delicate napkin decoration would be perfect for a special lunch or an occasion such as a wedding. In addition to their exquisite scent, the tiny bells of lily-of-the-valley visually harmonize with the pure white of the cyclamen.

The slender stems of both flowers enable each decoration to be made into a tied sheaf. The splayed stems echo the shape made by the flowers.

MATERIALS

napkins
small-leaved ivy trails
scissors
pot lily-of-the-valley
pot tiny cyclamen (dwarf
Cyclamen persicum)
gold cord

1

Fold the napkin into a rectangle, then roll into a cylindrical shape. Wrap an ivy trail around the middle of the napkin. Tie the stem firmly in a knot. Take 4–5 stems of lily-of-the-valley, 3 flowers of cyclamen on their stems and 3 cyclamen leaves. Using both flowers, create a small, flat-backed sheaf in your hand by spiralling the stems.

2

Place one leaf at the back of the lily-of-the-valley for support and use the other 2 around the cyclamen flowers to emphasize the focal point. Tie at the binding point with gold cord. Lay the flat back of the sheaf on top of the napkin and ivy and wrap the excess gold cord around the napkin, gently tying it into a bow on top of the stems.

Fresh Herbal Wreath

In many parts of Europe a herb wreath hung near the entrance of a house is a sign of welcome, wealth and good luck. This wreath will stay fresh for two or three weeks because the stems of the herbs are in water, but even if it dries out it will continue to look good for some time.

MATERIALS

30 cm / 12 in plastic foam
wreath frame
scissors
2 branches bay leaves
2 bunches rosemary
stub wires
6 large bulbs garlic
6–7 beetroot
40 stems flowering
marjoram
40 stems flowering mint

1

Soak the wreath frame thoroughly in cold water. Create the background by making a foliage outline using evenly distributed bay leaves and sprigs of rosemary. To ensure an even covering, position the leaves inside, on top and on the outside of the wreath frame.

2

Wire the garlic bulbs and beetroot by pushing 2 wires through their base so that they cross, then pull the projecting wires down and cut to the correct length for the depth of the foam. Decide where on the wreath they are to be positioned and push the wires firmly into the foam.

3

Infill the spaces in the wreath, concentrating the marjoram around the beetroot and the mint around the garlic.

Spring Blossom Urn

The explosion of plant life in the spring is visually depicted in this arrangement. Heavily flowered heads of white lilac are the focal blossoms of the display, set against the dark stems of pussy willow and cherry. The starkness of these stems is softened by the pink cherry blossom and the silver pussy willow buds.

MATERIALS

urn
cellophane
block plastic foam
scissors
stub wires
reindeer moss
15 stems pussy willow
10 stems white lilac
15 stems pink cherry
blossom

1

Line the urn with cellophane and wedge in the water-soaked block of plastic foam. Trim away the excess cellophane.

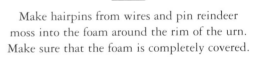

2

Make hairpins from wires and pin reindeer moss into the foam around the rim of the urn. Make sure that the foam is completely covered.

3

Arrange the pussy willow in the urn to establish the height and width of a symmetrical outline. Press the pussy willow stems firmly into the plastic foam to secure the arrangement.

4

Distribute the lilac throughout the pussy willow. Look carefully at the way lilac flowers hang from their stems and try to exploit their natural attitude in the arrangement. You will find there is no need to position the stems at extreme angles.

5

Position the pink cherry blossom throughout the display to reinforce the overall shape and to provide a link between the slender stems of pussy willow and the large heads of the flowering lilac.

Hyacinth Bulb Bowl

This novel approach to the display of developing hyacinth bulbs takes them out of their pots and into organic containers, which become feature elements in the design.

The bulbs' roots, along with their soil, are simply wrapped in leaves and then grouped together, sitting in water in a glass bowl. The bulbs take up the water and happily grow from these attractive green spikes through to full flowers.

MATERIALS

*8 sprouting hyacinth bulbs
24 leaves
raffia
scissors
glass bowl*

1

Carefully remove the hyacinth bulbs from their pots, keeping the soil tightly packed around the roots. Wrap a leaf underneath the root ball and soil of each bulb, with 2 more leaves around the sides. Leave the majority of each bulb exposed as it would be in a pot.

2

Secure the leaves in position by tying around with raffia. Group the wrapped hyacinths in the glass bowl and fill to approximately 5 cm/ 2 in deep with water. Remember to top up regularly. The bulbs will continue to grow and will eventually bloom.

Napkin Tie

This beautiful alternative to a napkin ring is easy to make. Its appearance can be changed to suit many different occasions or even to reflect the dishes you are serving.

1

Find a suitable length of rosemary, to wrap around the rolled napkin once or twice. Tie the stem securely.

2

Gently push the geranium leaves and the mint through the knot in the binding stem of rosemary.

The method is simply to use any reasonably sturdy trailing foliage to bind the napkin and then to create a focal point by the addition of leaves, berries or flower heads of your choice. If a firm fixing is required, wire the leaves and flowerheads before attaching them to binding material. The materials listed below are sufficient for one tie.

MATERIALS

napkin
scissors
long, thin, flexible stem rosemary
3 lemon geranium leaves
2–3 heads flowering mint

Fruit and Flower Swag

The colour and content of this decorative swag make it especially suitable for a kitchen but, if it was made on a longer base, the decoration could be a mantelpiece garland or even extended to adorn the balustrade of a staircase.

The component parts have to be wired, but otherwise the swag is simple to construct. Do remember that although lemons and limes will survive in this situation, grapes and cut flowers will need regular mist spraying with water.

MATERIALS

stub wires
4 limes
9 lemons
4 bunches black grapes
4 bunches sneezeweed
(Helenium)
bundle tree ivy
scissors
straw plait, about
60 cm / 24 in long
raffia
bunch ivy trails

1

First, all the fruit has to be wired. Pass a wire through from side to side just above the base of the limes. Leave equal lengths of wire projecting from either side, bend these down and twist together under the base. If the lemons are heavier than the limes, pass a second wire through at right angles to the first, providing four equal ends to be twisted together under their bases.

2

Group the grapes in small clusters and double leg mount with stub wires. Then form 12 small bunches of sneezeweed mixed with tree ivy and double leg mount these on stub wires.

3

Starting at its bottom end, bind 3 wired lemons to the plait with raffia. Then in turn bind a bunch of flowers and foliage, a lime, grapes and a second bunch of flowers and foliage.

4

Continue to add materials until almost at the top. Secure by wrapping the remaining raffia tightly around the plait.

5

Make a bow from raffia and tie to the top of the swag. Trim off any stray wire ends. Twine the ivy trails around the top of the swag.

Pink Phlox Arrangement in a Pitcher

A simple-to-arrange pitcher of flowers and foliage brings an explosion of late summer colour and scent into the house.

The colour collision between a mass of pink phlox flowerheads and the vibrant autumn reds of Virginia creeper gives this arrangement its visual impact and is a simple, yet effective arrangement to create.

MATERIALS

scissors
15 stems pink phlox
'Bright Eyes'
pitcher
5 trails of Virginia creeper
in autumn tints

1

Cut the stems of phlox to a length proportionate to the container. Arrange the phlox evenly with taller stems towards the back.

2

Place the cut ends of Virginia creeper trails in the pitcher of water and weave them through the phlox, spreading them out evenly.

Candle Ring

Filled with a heady combination of fennel, rosemary, lemon geranium, hyssop and violas, this would be perfect for a country supper table.

The floral ring is simply placed over the candlestick to create this simple but effective decoration. Never leave a burning candle unattended and do not allow it to burn down to within less than 5 cm / 2 in of the foliage.

MATERIALS

15 cm / 6 in diameter plastic foam ring candlestick scissors small quantities of rosemary, lemon geranium leaves, fennel, hyssop and violas

1

Soak the plastic foam ring in cold water and place it over the candlestick. Start the arrangement by making a basic outline in the plastic foam with stems of rosemary and geranium leaves, positioning them evenly around the ring. Try to arrange the leaves at different angles so that they completely cover the foam.

2

Infill the gaps evenly with the fennel and hyssop. Finally add a few violas for colour.

All-foliage Arrangement

If the garden is void of flowers, your budget is limited or you simply fancy a change, then creating an arrangement entirely from different types of foliage can be both challenging and rewarding. Whatever the season, finding three or four varieties of foliage is not difficult. Anything from the common privet to unusual shrubs can be used.

MATERIALS

2 blocks plastic foam
shallow bowl large enough
for the plastic foam blocks
florist's adhesive tape
scissors
stub wires
bun moss
5 stems grevillea
10 stems shrimp plant
(Beloperone guttata)
10 stems ming fern
(cultivar of Boston fern)
10 stems pittosporum
5 stems cotoneaster

1

Tape the soaked foam in the bowl.

2

Make hairpin shapes from stub wire and pin clumps of bun moss around the rim of the bowl by pushing the wires through the moss into the plastic foam. This conceals the plastic foam where it meets the edge of the bowl.

3

Start arranging the grevillea from one side, to establish the maximum height, and work diagonally across with progressively shorter stems, finishing with foliage flowing over the front of the bowl. Arrange the shrimp plant in a similar way along the opposite diagonal, but make it shorter than the grevillea and emphasize this line by adding ming fern.

4

Strengthen the line of grevillea by interspersing it with the broader leafed pittosporum. Finally, distribute the cotoneaster evenly throughout the whole arrangement.

Old-fashioned Garden Rose Arrangement

The beautiful full-blown blooms of these antique-looking roses give a wonderfully evocative and romantic feel to a very simple combination of flower and container.

This arrangement deserves centre stage in any room setting. The technique is to mass one type of flower in several varieties whose papery petals will achieve a textural mix of colour and scent.

MATERIALS

watertight container, to put inside plant pot
low, weathered terracotta plant pot
pitcher
selection of short- and long-stemmed garden roses
scissors

1

Place the watertight container inside the terracotta plant pot and fill with water. Fill the pitcher as well. Select and prepare your blooms and remove the lower foliage and thorns.

2

Position the longer stemmed blooms in the pitcher with the heads massed together. This ensures that the cut stems are supported and so can be simply placed directly into the water.

3

Mass shorter, more open flowerheads in the glass bowl inside the plant pot with the stems hidden and the heads showing just above the rim of the pot. The heads look best if kept either all on one level or in a slight dome shape. If fewer flowers are used, wire mesh or plastic foam may be needed so that the positions of individual blooms can be controlled.

Blue and Yellow Bud Vases

The bud vase is possibly the most common form of table decoration, but that does not mean that it has to be dull. These delightful examples demonstrate that, with just a little imagination, it can be just as exciting as a more elaborate container.

When deciding on a bud vase and its contents, consider both the size of the table and the proportion of flowers to the container to be used. Generally, bud vases are used on small dining-tables and therefore must not be too large and obtrusive. A small container with tall flowers is unstable, too, and likely to be knocked over.

MATERIALS

2 bud vases
3 stems sneezeweed
(Helenium)
scissors
5 Virginia creeper leaves
3 stems delphinium
2 stems campanula
3 small vine leaves
raffia

1

Fill the vases approximately three-quarters full with water. Measure the stems of your helenium next to your chosen vase in order to achieve the correct height, then cut the stems at an angle and place in the vase. Position Virginia creeper leaves around the top of the vase to frame the helenium.

2

Use 2–3 flowered stems of delphinium and also use the delicate tendrils of buds, which are perfect for small arrangements. Prune the relatively large leaves of the campanula before adding. Finally, position the vine leaves around the base of the flowers in the neck of the vase, and finish off each vase with a raffia tie.

Summer Basket Display

The lovely scents, luscious blooms and vast range of colours available in summer provide endless possibilities for creating wonderful displays. This arrangement – a bountiful basket overflowing with seasonal summer blooms – is designed for a large table or sideboard but could be scaled up or down to suit any situation.

Keep this display well watered and it should go on flowering for at least a week. The lilies should open fully in plastic foam and new phlox buds will keep opening to replace the spent flowerheads.

MATERIALS

basket
cellophane
scissors
2 blocks plastic foam
florist's adhesive tape
10 stems Viburnum tinus
15 stems larkspur
in 3 colours
6 stems lily, such as
'Stargazer'
5 large ivy leaves
10 stems white phlox

1

Line the basket with cellophane to prevent leakage, and cut to fit. Then soak the two blocks of plastic foam and secure them in the lined basket with the florist's adhesive tape.

2

Arrange the viburnum stems in the plastic foam to establish the overall height, width and shape. Next, strengthen the outline using the larkspur, making sure that you use all of the stems and not just the flower spikes.

3

Place the lilies in a diagonal line across the arrangement. Position the large ivy leaves around the lilies in the centre of the display. Arrange phlox across the arrangement along the opposite diagonal to the lilies.

Tulip Topiary Tree

The flowers used to make this stunning decorative tree are unlike conventional tulips, which have only one layer of petals. These tulips have layer upon layer of different sized petals which together create a very dense, rounded head, reminiscent of a peony.

To get the best result from the flowerheads, they have been spread open. This increases their visual impact and means fewer blooms are needed

MATERIALS

*block plastic foam for dried flowers
knife
basket
raffia
5 30 cm / 12 in cinnamon sticks
scissors
glue gun and glue
stub wires
reindeer moss
plastic foam ball, approximately 15 cm / 6 in diameter
open tulip heads*

1

Cut and fit the block of dry plastic foam into the basket base. Depending on its stability, the container may need to be weighted with wet sand, stones, or plaster of Paris, for example. Using the raffia, tie the cinnamon sticks together at both top and bottom and push the resulting tree trunk into the foam to approximately 4 cm/1½ in, securing with glue.

2

Make hairpins out of the wires and pin the reindeer moss into the foam at the base of the tree, completely covering the foam.

3

Soak the plastic foam ball in cold water. Carefully apply a small amount of hot glue to the top end of the cinnamon stick trunk and push the wet foam ball approximately 4 cm/1½ in on to it.

4

Make sure that the flowerheads are as open as possible by holding the flower in your hand and gently spreading the petals back, even to the extent of folding those at the edge inside out.

5

Cut the tulip heads with a stem length of approximately 4 cm/1½ in and push them into the soaked foam ball, covering the surface evenly. Handle the flowerheads with care to avoid crushing.

Hydrangea Basket Edging

Mature hydrangea heads, some autumn leaves and a little imagination transform an old wicker basket into a delightful container. Whether you fill it with fruit or pot pourri, this basket will make a decorative and long-lasting addition to your home.

Hydrangea heads, together with autumn leaves, have been used in a floral decoration that can evolve from fresh to dry and remain attractive.

MATERIALS

*30 autumn leaves
stub wires
scissors
30 fresh late hydrangea
heads
basket
silver reel wire*

1

Wire the leaves by stitching and mounting on wires.

2

Wire clusters of hydrangea by mounting on wires.

3

Secure the wired hydrangea clusters and leaves alternately around the basket edge by stitching through the gaps in the basket with silver reel wire. Keep the clusters tightly together to ensure a full edging.

4

When the entire basket edge is covered, finish by stitching the reel wire through several times. If the arrangement is placed in an airy position, the hydrangea heads will dry naturally and prolong the basket's use.

Autumn Crocus Trug

Although one expects to see crocuses in the spring, this autumn variety is a welcome sight as its flowers push up determinedly through the fallen leaves. Of course, they do not have to be confined to the garden.

Bring the outdoors inside by planting up an old trug with autumn-flowering crocus bulbs in soil covered in a natural-looking carpet of moss and leaves.

MATERIALS

trug
cellophane
soil or compost
6 autumn-flowering crocus bulbs
bun moss
autumn leaves
raffia
scissors

1

Line the trug and plant the bulbs in soil.

2

Ensure the bulbs are firmly planted and watered. Arrange the bun moss on top of the soil, then scatter the leaves over the moss.

3

Tie raffia into a bow on each side of the trug.

Autumn Candle Display

The autumn fruits of Chinese lanterns, crab apples and baby pumpkins are put to good use in this charming and compact candle decoration. The rich colours of the fruits and hypericum buds complement beautifully the soft apricot of the spray roses.

Beeswax candles have an attractive texture and natural honey colouring, which are the perfect accompaniment for this seasonal rustic display. Never leave burning candles unattended and do not allow them to burn down to within 5 cm/2 in of the display height.

MATERIALS

block plastic foam
metal candleholder
6 crab apples
small pumpkin
3 Chinese lantern
heads
stub wires (medium gauge
and fine)
scissors
hypericum buds
2 stems spray roses
beeswax candle

1

Soak the foam in water and cut it into small pieces to fit into the candleholder drip tray. Wedge the pieces firmly in place.

2

Wire the crab apples and pumpkin on medium wires and Chinese lantern heads on fine wires. All wires should be about 4 cm/1½ in long.

3

By pushing wires into the foam, position the pumpkin, 2 groups of 3 crab apples and a group of 3 Chinese lantern heads, spacing them equally around the drip tray.

4

Arrange the hypericum foliage between the fruits by pushing short stems into the plastic foam to create the outline shape of the display.

Cut flowerheads from the spray roses on stems long enough to push into the plastic foam among the foliage and fruits. Use rose buds towards the outside edge of the arrangement and more open blooms towards the centre. Remember to make sure that there is enough space left to accommodate the beeswax candle.

Blue and Yellow Arrangement in a Pitcher

The sunny yellow faces of sneezeweed become almost luminous when set against the electric blue colour of 'Blue Butterfly' delphinium, a brave colour combination guaranteed to brighten any situation. The easy-to-make, hand-tied spiral bunch is designed to look as though the flowers have just been cut and loosely arranged.

The container is a major element in this design. The yellow pitcher gives the display a country look, but the same arrangement would look more sophisticated if a modern glass vase were used.

MATERIALS

10 stems 'Blue Butterfly'
delphinium
2 bunches sneezeweed
(Helenium)
3 stems dracaena
raffia
scissors
pitcher

1

Lay out the materials for ease of working. Build the display by alternately adding stems of different material while continuously turning the growing bunch in your hand so that the stems form a spiral.

2

Continue the process until all materials are used and you have a full display of flowers. At the binding point – i.e. where all the stems cross – tie firmly with raffia. Trim the stem ends to the length dictated by the container.

Large Dahlia Arrangement

The complex and precise geometry of the dahlia flowerheads means that, even with the informality of the bright red rosehips and softness of the campanulas, this arrangement retains a structured feel. The dark campanula leaves are a wonderful foil for the vibrant dahlias.

Dahlias bloom vigorously all through the summer, until the first frosts of autumn, offering dazzling variations of colour and shape for the flower arranger. These beautiful golden dahlias have clean, long straight stems, which make them easy to arrange in a large display.

MATERIALS

*large, watertight pot
15 stems campanula
scissors
10 stems long-stemmed
rosehips
30 stems pompon dahlias*

1

Fill the pot three-quarters full with water. Create the basic domed outline and the structure using the leafy campanula.

2

Cut and strip the thorns from the stems of the rosehips and arrange in among the campanula, varying the heights as required to follow the domed outline.

3

Cut the pompon dahlias to the required heights and add to the arrangement, distributing them evenly throughout. The aim is to achieve a smooth dome.

Mantelpiece Arrangement

The mantelpiece offers a prominent position for a floral display. The challenge is to create not just a visual balance, but a physical balance, too. The mantel shelf is relatively narrow, and flowers must be carefully positioned to avoid them toppling forwards. So, as you build, ensure stability by keeping the weight at the back and as near the bottom of the display as is practicable. The delicate stems of butcher's broom and euphorbia are light in relation to their length and thus ideal for this type of arrangement. Their trailing habit means they can be positioned to give width along the shelf and length over its front edge, and, together with birch twigs, they give the display its structure. The strongly coloured flowers bring the arrangement alive.

On its own, or combined with a fireplace arrangement (pictured opposite and featured over the page), this mantelpiece arrangement creates a stunning focal point to a room.

1

Soak the block of plastic foam in cold water and securely tape into the plastic tray with florist's adhesive tape. Position the tray at the centre of the mantelpiece.

2

Arrange the birch twigs and butcher's broom in the foam to establish height and width. Take advantage of the natural curving habit of the broom to trail over the container.

3

Add the scarlet plume to emphasize the trailing nature of the display. Distribute the amaranthus throughout the display to reinforce the established shape.

MATERIALS

*block plastic foam
plastic tray for plastic foam
florist's adhesive tape
5 stems birch twigs
6 stems butcher's broom
5 stems* Eupohorbia fulgens
*7 stems straight amaranthus
5 stems spray chrysanthemums
5 stems alstroemeria
7 stems eustoma*

4

The spray chrysanthemums are the focal flowers and should be roughly staggered to either side of the vertical axis at the centre of the display. The alstroemeria stems add strength and, by recessing one or two of them, depth to the arrangement.

5

A stem of good quality eustoma has two to three side stems. Split these off to make the most of the flowers. Use budded stems towards the outside of the display and more open blooms towards its centre, making sure some are recessed to give visual depth.

Fireplace Arrangement

A fireplace is the focal point of a room, but without a fire, an empty grate can
be an eyesore. Turn this to your advantage by filling the hearth with an arrangement
of flowers. In the absence of real flames, this display substitutes the bright, fiery reds,
oranges and yellows of scarlet plume, alstroemeria, tulips, lilies and chrysanthemums.
The colour is given depth and richness by the purple eustoma. The butcher's broom
and stark birch twigs define the architecture of the arrangement.

MATERIALS

2 blocks plastic foam
plastic-lined basket
florist's adhesive tape
scissors
10 stems butcher's broom
6 stems birch twigs
10 stems Euphorbia
fulgens
5 stems orange lilies
5 stems red alstroemeria
5 stems spray
chrysanthemums
10 stems orange tulips
10 stems eustoma

1

Soak the plastic foam in water and secure in
the basket using florist's adhesive tape. Place
the basket in the grate of the fireplace.

2

Arrange the butcher's broom and birch to
create the outline, taking advantage of the
broom's natural curves to give a flowing effect.

3

Use the scarlet plume to reinforce the outline
and define the height of the display. The lilies
are the focal flowers and should be arranged to
follow roughly a diagonal through the display.
The alstroemeria should be positioned to
follow the opposite diagonal. Decrease the
length of the stems of both flowers from the
rear to the front.

4

Arrange the spray chrysanthemums,
approximately following, and thus reinforcing,
the line of lilies. Again reduce the
chrysanthemum stem height from rear to front.
Finally, distribute the tulips and eustoma
evenly through the arrangement, using the
most open of the eustoma blooms towards the
centre and the buds at the sides.

Arum Lily Vase

Pure in colour and form, elegant and stately, the arum lily has the presence to be displayed on its own, supported by the minimum of well-chosen foliage. Here it is arranged with the wonderfully contorted Peking willow and the large, simple leaves of aucuba. The willow and the aucuba serve as a backdrop to the arum.

1

Fill the vase to approximately three-quarters with water. Arrange the willow stems in the vase to establish the overall height of the arrangement. (When cutting a willow stem to the right length, cut the base at a 45° angle and scrape the bark off to approximately 5 cm/2 in from the end, then split this section to aid take-up of water.)

The choice of container is of great importance, the visual requirement being for simple unfussy shapes, with glass and metal being particularly appropriate. The chosen vase should complement the sculptural impact of the arum.

MATERIALS

vase
scissors
branches of Peking willow
6 arum lilies
2 bushy branches aucuba
'Gold Dust'

2

Arrange the arum lilies at different heights to achieve a visual balance. The willow stems will help support the blooms.

3

Give visual substance to the display by adding stems of aucuba to provide a dark backdrop to throw the arum blooms into sharp relief.

Orange Arrangement

The matt green of gaultheria tips creates the perfect background for the spectacular zesty orange colour of the three different flowers used in this display.

There are two points worth remembering. First, the tulips will continue to grow and straighten in the plastic foam, so make allowance for this in your dome shape; second, any buds on the lilies will open, so give them the space to do so.

wire basket
reindeer moss
cellophane
block plastic foam
knife
florist's adhesive tape
scissors
10 stems Gaultheria shallon *tips*
7 stems orange lily
10 stems orange tulip
20 stems marigold

1

Line the basket with a layer of reindeer moss, about 3 cm/1½ in thick, and line the moss with cellophane. Cut a block of water-soaked foam to fit the basket and tape in place.

2

Push the gaultheria tips into the plastic foam to create a dome-shaped foliage outline in proportion with the container. The tips have relatively large rounded leaves, which generally should be used sparingly to avoid overwhelming the flowers. However, the strength of the colour and shape of the flowers in this particular arrangement works well with the large, bold leaves.

3

Cut the lily stems to a length to suit the foliage framework and add evenly throughout the arrangement to reinforce the overall shape.

4

Distribute the tulips evenly through the display, remembering that as they continue to grow their downward curve will straighten.

5

Add the marigolds last,
positioning them evenly
throughout the display.
Remember that marigold
stems are soft, so take care
when pushing them into the
plastic foam.

Decorated Vase with Calla Lilies

A novel and simple way to transform a container is to decorate its outside with organic material. This example uses lichen-covered twigs, which, with careful handling, can be kept on the vase for the next display.

By making the twigs project above the top of the vase, they become an integral part of the arrangement and provide helpful support for the flowers. An alternative look could be created by gluing the heads of dried flowers, such as sunflowers, all over a plain glass vase.

MATERIALS

*selection of lichen-
covered twigs
glass vase
raffia
scissors
10 red antirrhinums
15 calla lilies
3 calla lily leaves*

1

The twigs have to be fixed securely to the vase. To do this, make 2 lengths of bundles of raffia and lay on these sufficient twigs to go around the circumference of the vase. Place the vase on its side, on the twigs, and tie firmly with the lengths of raffia. Trim the twigs level with the base of the vase and make sure they are straight.

2

Stand the vase upright and three-quarter fill with water. Begin with the red antirrhinums, placing them towards the back to establish the height and width of the arrangement.

3

Distribute the calla lily blooms evenly throughout the arrangement, varying their heights to achieve a visual balance and a good profile. Add the calla lily leaves diagonally through the arrangement, reducing their height from the back to the front. This will visually emphasize the depth of the arrangement.

Winter Twigs Arrangement

Cut flowers can be expensive during the winter months but this does not mean flower arranging has to stop. This display is created from the types of winter growth found in domestic gardens. It is simple to arrange and offers a scale suitable to decorate a large space. Delicate lichen softens the otherwise rough branches of larch, while the winter-flowering viburnum adds a touch of spring. Finally, the stems of red-barked dogwood provide a strength of colour that will persist throughout the life of the display.

1

Cut the larch twigs so that most are at the maximum height of the display, and arrange to the outline shape. The container should be about one-third of the overall height.

Cut the red-barked dogwood and arrange among the larch twigs so that the stems at the rear of the display are at their maximum height, becoming shorter towards the front.

As a general rule when using twigs, remember to strip the stem ends of bark and lichen otherwise they will rot, accelerate the formation of bacteria, shorten the life of the display and very quickly cause the water to smell.

MATERIALS

*5 stems lichen-covered
larch twigs
scissors and secateurs
large ceramic pot
5–10 stems red-barked
dogwood* (Cornus alba)
10 stems Viburnum X
bodnantense *'Dawn'*

3

Add the flowering viburnum, again varying its length from tall at the rear to shorter at the front. To avoid rotting, be sure to strip off all bark and flowers from the stem ends in the water and to split any thick woody stems to encourage water take-up.

Herb Obelisk

This colourful pillar of herbs and vegetables looks wonderful on its own but is even more striking if you make two obelisks. This arrangement is particularly suitable for a buffet table decoration but can also be used simply as a decorative object.

The urn container gives the obelisk a grand look, but a less formal, more rustic feel can be achieved by using a terracotta plant pot or mossy basket.

MATERIALS

ruler
pencil
block plastic foam
sharp knife
suitable container
7 radishes
8 button mushrooms
9 small, clean new potatoes
stub wires
scissors
dill
curry plant
marjoram
mint
bay leaves

1

Using a ruler and pencil, score the cutting lines on the block of plastic foam. Carve the block to the required shape using a sharp knife. Soak the carved plastic foam shape and secure firmly in your chosen container.

2

Wire all the vegetables by pushing a stub wire through from one side to the other, leaving sufficient wire projecting on both sides to allow you to pull down and out of the base to approximately 4 cm / 1½ in. Mushrooms are very fragile and particular care must be taken when wiring these. Having decided on the order you want to use the vegetables, work from the bottom of the obelisk upwards, pushing the wires into the plastic foam to position the vegetables in horizontal, concentric rings around the shape decreasing the diameter towards the top.

3

Fill in the gaps between rings of vegetables, using a different herb for each ring. Finally, select a quantity of bay leaves of similar size and insert them into the plastic foam under the bottom layer of vegetables to create a formal border. Wire the bay leaves if necessary so that they visually balance the display.

Provençal Herb Hanging

Fix bunches of fresh herbs to a thick plaited rope, add tiny terracotta pots to give the design structure and then fill it in with garlic and colourful chillies to make a spicy, herbal gift full of Provençal flavour, for anyone who loves to cook.

MATERIALS

*hank of seagrass string
scissors
garden string
florist's wire
fresh sage
fresh thyme
fresh oregano
2 small flowerpots
6 florist's stub wires
2 garlic heads
hot glue gun and glue sticks (optional)
large dried red chillies*

1

Cut six lengths of seagrass string about three times as long as the desired finished length of the hanging. Take two lengths, fold them in half and place them under a length of garden string. Pass the cut ends over the string and through the loop of the fold, thereby knotting the seagrass on to the garden string. Repeat twice with the remaining four seagrass lengths. Divide the seagrass into three bundles of four lengths and plait them to form the base of the herb hanging.

2

Finish the end of the plait by binding it with a separate piece of seagrass string.

3

Using florist's wire, bind the herbs into small bundles and tie each one with garden string. Use this to tie them to the plaited base.

4

Wire the flowerpots by passing two stub wires through the central hole and twisting the ends together.

5

Wire the pots to the base by passing a stub wire through the wires on the pots, passing it through the plait, and then twisting the ends together.

6

Tie garden string around the garlic heads and tie these to the base. Wire or glue the chillies into position, and fill the pots with more chillies.

Fresh-flower Fruit Bowl

Make the prettiest summer fruit bowl by arranging trailing flowers and foliage through a wire basket, topping it with chicken-wire and a pretty plate, and then piling on the fresh fruit. This is a delightful touch for outdoor entertaining.

MATERIALS

jam jar
wire basket
fuchsia flowers or
similar trailing blooms
secateurs
chicken-wire to fit the diameter
of the basket
attractive plate to fit the
diameter of the basket
selection of colourful fruit

1

Fill the jam jar with water and place it in the centre of the basket.

2

Trim the flower stems with secateurs and arrange them all round the basket by threading the stems through the wire and into the jar of water. Continue until the flowers and foliage provide a delicate curtain of colour around the basket.

3

Cut the chicken-wire to fit over the basket and fix it by bending it around the rim. Place a plate on this chicken-wire, and then fill the plate with colourful summer fruits.

Vegetable Centrepiece

The flower stall is not the only source of material for centrepieces — the vegetable stall provides great pickings, too. Here, a still-life of ornamental cabbages — complemented by a simple cut-open red cabbage and some artichokes — makes a flamboyant focal-point for the table. The theme is carried through by adding an ornamental cabbage leaf to the cutlery bundle at each setting.

MATERIALS

dyed raffia
painted wooden basket
2 ornamental cabbages in pots
lichen moss
1 set of cutlery and napkin
per person
baby-food jar
painted trug
red cabbage, halved
globe artichokes

1

Tie a bow of dyed raffia around the handle of the wooden basket. Remove several perfect cabbage leaves and place the cabbages in their pots in the basket.

2

Cover the tops of the pots with silvery-grey lichen moss.

3

Tie up each cutlery bundle with a napkin and an ornamental cabbage leaf. Finish the arrangement by putting a few more leaves into a baby-food jar and tying dyed raffia around it. Fill a garden trug with the red cabbage halves and the globe artichokes.

Wild at Heart

Often, the simplest arrangements are the most appealing. Here, flowers are arranged very simply in little glass jars wound around with blue twine and carefully grouped to make a delightful still life.

MATERIALS

blue twine   *scabious*
2 jam jars   *anemones*
garden shears   *glass plate*

1

Wrap the blue twine around the jars and tie securely. Fill the jars with water.

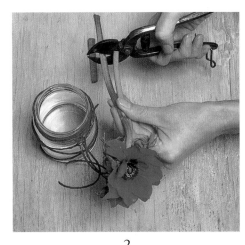

2

Fill one jar with scabious and another with anemones, cutting the stems to the right lengths as you go.

3

Fill the plate with water.

4

Cut one of the flower stems very short and allow the bloom to float in the plate. This is a delightful solution for any heads of flowers that have broken off during transit.

Autumn Fruitfulness

*The sheer beauty of autumn produce makes it difficult to resist. It's too good
to be left in the larder. Gather together all the softly bloomed purple fruits
and pile them into a rich seasonal display for a side table or centrepiece.*

MATERIALS

*metal urn
filling material, such as
bubble-wrap, newspaper or
florist's foam
several varieties of plums
black grapes
hydrangea heads
globe artichokes
blueberries*

1

Unless you have a huge abundance of fruit,
fill the bottom of the urn with bubble-wrap,
newspaper or florist's foam.

2

Arrange as many different varieties of plums
as you can find on the filling, saving a few
for the final decoration.

3

Add a large bunch of black grapes, draping
them over the rim of the urn. Finish the
arrangement with hydrangea heads,
artichokes, scattered plums and blueberries.

Autumn Gold

The golds of autumn can be gathered into a fabulous display, using even the humblest of containers. Here, the dahlias have simply been put into a store-cupboard Kilner jar and given a seasonal necklace of hazelnuts.

MATERIALS

hazelnuts
seagrass string
secateurs
dahlias
Kilner jar
pumpkins
branches of pyracantha
with berries

1

Tie the hazelnuts on to the seagrass string
to make a 'necklace'.

2

Cut about 1 cm / ½ in off the end of each
dahlia stem and place the stems in the
Kilner jar filled with water.

3

Tie the hazelnut 'necklace' around the jar.
Finish the arrangement with pumpkins
and pyracantha branches.

Springtime Garland

*Garlands of fresh flowers make delightful decorations for any celebration.
This pretty little hanging of pansies and violas has a woodland feel that can be
re-created at any time, because these flowers are available in
most months of the year.*

*secateurs
chicken-wire the desired length of
the garland and three times the
desired width
scissors
black plastic bin liner
about two pansy plants for every
15 cm / 6 in of garland
about six viola plants for every
15 cm / 6 in of garland
florist's stub wires
moss*

1

Using secateurs, cut the chicken-wire to size
and then form it into a flattened roll.

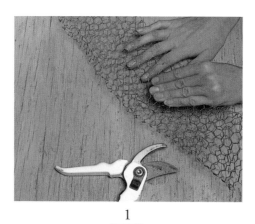

2

Cut the bin liner into squares large enough
to cover the rootballs of the pansies
and violas.

3

One by one, unpot each plant, gently remove
any loose soil and place the rootball in
the centre of a square of bin liner.

4

Gather the plastic around the rootball and
fix it in place by winding stub wires loosely
round the top, leaving a short length free
to fix to the garland.

5

Fix the bagged-up plants to the garland
using the free end of wire.

6

Finish off by covering any visible plastic with
moss, fixing it with short lengths of florist's
stub wire bent hairpin-style.

Tied Posy

Flowers are at their most appealing when kept simple. Just gather together some garden cuttings and arrange them in a pretty posy that the recipient can simply unwrap and put straight into a vase, without further ado.

MATERIALS

secateurs	scabious
roses	brown paper
eucalyptus	ribbon

1

Using secateurs, cut each flower stem to approximately 15 cm / 6 in long.

2

Gather the flowers together, surrounding each rose with some feathery eucalyptus, and then adding the scabious.

3

Wrap the posy with paper and tie it with a pretty ribbon bow.

Tussie Mussie

*Traditionally, tussie mussies were bouquets of concentrically arranged aromatic
herbs that were carried around as a personal perfume. This one combines the
blue-greens of sage and thyme with the soft blues of lavender and scabious flowers.*

MATERIALS

*6 scabious
fresh thyme
fresh lavender
fresh sage
dyed raffia*

1

Encircle the scabious blooms
with fresh thyme.

2

Arrange a circle of lavender around this,
making sure the piece keeps its circular shape.

3

Add a circle of sage, then tie with a
generous bundle of dyed raffia.

Everlasting Treats

....

Nature offers many exquisite textures and colours
that have natural everlasting qualities – or
that can be encouraged to have them – so scour the
countryside, dried-flower stockists, and even
your own store-cupboard for flowers, leaves, grasses
and dried whole spices; collect richly textured
strings, raffias and twines; and then transform
them into delightfully lasting natural gifts.

New Ways with Dried Flowers

Dried flowers used to be thought of chiefly as a winter substitute for unavailable fresh blooms. But improvements in the technology of preserving plant materials have resulted in an increase in types of dried flowers and the introduction of vibrant new colours. The astonishing range of materials and colours now available has heralded a new dawn of possibilities in dried flower arranging and made it possible to create displays for every occasion.

Today's approach to dried flower displays is to emphasize colour and texture by using massed materials so that the collective strength of their qualities creates the impact. Even where a number of varieties are incorporated in a display they should be used in clusters to extract the maximum effect. It is wise to avoid using individual stems of a particular material because this will make for rather bitty looking displays.

To get the best out of dried plant material, do not be afraid to integrate other materials with them: dried fruits, gourds, seashells, roots and driftwood can all add an extra dimension to a display. To create a richer, more luxurious effect, bunches of dried herbs and spices and varieties of dried and preserved mosses can be added and groups of filled terracotta pots may be attached. With all this choice, today's dried flower display is a far cry from the fading brown and orange dust traps of the past.

Impressive though improvements in preserving plant materials may be, the ravages of time, sunlight, moisture and dust still take their toll on dried flowers. Do not make the mistake of believing dried arrangements will last for ever. A useful life of around six months is the best that can be expected before dried flowers begin to look dusty and faded.

However, by taking a few simple common sense precautions, the life of a dried arrangement can be maximized. To avoid fading, keep the arrangement out of direct sunlight. Do not allow dried flowers to become damp and particularly be aware of condensation in bathrooms and on window ledges. To prevent the build-up of dust give the arrangement an occasional blast with a hair-dryer set on slow and cool. When the arrangement is new, spray it with hair lacquer to help prevent the dropping of grass seeds and petals, but do not use hair-spray on dust-covered dried flowers.

A potentially rewarding aspect of dried flower arranging is drying and preserving the plant material yourself. It takes patience and organization but with application you will be able to preserve materials not commercially available and, since some dried flowers can be expensive, you will save yourself money.

There are different methods of preservation to suit different plant materials. In the following pages, these methods are clearly explained. There is also a list of materials with the appropriate drying method for each. The list is not exhaustive so if the material you want to preserve is not included, then assess its characteristics, find a similar type and try the method recommended for that. One of the joys of working with dried flowers is that no one method is wrong. Experiment with techniques and materials as much as you wish.

LEFT: *Starfish, which are available in dried flower shops if you do not live sufficiently near the sea to find your own, combine surprisingly well with the pretty peach rose buds.*

ABOVE: *Dried apple is a striking contrast with the delicate peony flowers in this subtly coloured arrangement. Cinnamon sticks are both attractive and fragrant. Florist's foam is available in spheres and can be used instead of the traditional orange to make pretty pomanders.*

Drying Techniques

AIR DRYING

Probably the simplest method of preserving plant material is to air dry it. Air drying is the generic term for a number of techniques but fundamentally it is the preservation of plant materials without the use of chemicals or desiccants. The ideal environment for air drying will be dark, warm, clean, dust-free, well ventilated and dry. Typically, these conditions are found in attics, boiler rooms or large airing-cupboards.

HARVESTING MATERIALS

If you are preserving material you have grown yourself, be sure it is as dry as possible when you harvest it. Choose a dry day after the morning dew has disappeared and before the damp of evening begins to settle.

It is also important to harvest materials at the right point in their development, to ensure colours remain vibrant and petals do not drop. Experience will teach you about any variations from plant to plant, but in general the time to harvest is when the material is neither too young nor too mature – when the flowers have developed from bud to open bloom but are still young, fresh and firm. Seed pods and grasses must be just fully developed – any more and the seeds may drop.

If you buy commercially grown materials to dry yourself, bear in mind the general principles of harvesting when you select them, and remember, drying must take place as soon as possible after harvesting or purchasing the plant materials.

AIR DRYING BY HANGING

In most instances the foliage on flowers does not dry as well as the blooms so, when your materials are fresh, remove the leaves from the lower half of the stems before drying.

As a rule plant materials are bunched together in groups of not more than 10 stems and each bunch should contain only one plant variety. Stems should be all around the same length with all their heads at the same level. Do not pack the heads too tightly together as this will inhibit the circulation of air around them and may distort their final dried shape.

Secure the stem ends together with twine, raffia or a rubber band. The stems will shrink as they dry so a rubber band is probably most practical because it will contract with them to maintain a firm hold. Hang the bunches in a suitable environment in a safe position, high enough so that they will not be disturbed and with their heads down and stems vertical.

Drying rates vary from plant to plant and are subject to factors such as atmospheric conditions, bunch sizes and temperatures but it is essential that

LEFT AND RIGHT: *Selecting the right drying method for a plant comes with experience. The weight of the flowerheads help keep the stems straight.*

you make sure the materials are thoroughly dried before using them. This will be when the thickest part of the flowerhead has dried and when bending the stem causes it to snap. Any moisture retained in plant materials will cause mould, resulting in drooping and shrivelling.

It should be noted that some materials which can be dried with this method should not be hung with their heads down. In particular physalis, with its pendulous orange Chinese lanterns, would look unnatural if dried upside-down. Instead, hook individual physalis stems over a horizontal length of twine in their upright growing attitude.

AIR DRYING ON A RACK

Some plants such as *Daucus cariba* (Queen Anne's lace) can be air dried, but their florets will curl up if they are hung upside-down. Instead, make a rack from a piece of small mesh wire, place it in a suitable environment, and drop the stem down through the mesh so that it is held by its bloom. With the flower facing upwards, it will dry well.

Hydrangea heads and gypsophila can both be air dried with their stems in water.

AIR DRYING

This is the method of preservation for those types of flowers which have a tendency to wilt before the drying process is completed. It is sometimes called the 'evaporation technique' and is particularly suitable for hydrangea, allium and heather.

Cut the bottoms of stems at an angle of 45 degrees and place them in a container with a depth of about 7.5 cm/ 3 in of water and place the container in a suitable environment. This slows down the drying process to give the plant material time to dry fully in a natural position and without deterioration in the condition of the blooms.

AIR DRYING IN A 'NATURAL' ATTITUDE

Some materials benefit from being dried in an upright position so that they retain a more natural shape. Simply stand the material in the sort of container in which you might make an arrangement, place it in a suitable environment and it will dry in its natural shape. Grasses and stems of

mimosa are suitable for this method.

However, with some material this method can produce extraordinary results. The normally straight stems of bear grass (*Xerophyllum tenax*) will, when placed in a short container, form themselves into attractive ringlets as they dry. A simple alternative method for drying grasses is to lie them flat on paper in a suitable environment and they will retain a satisfactory shape.

USING A DESICCANT

A particularly effective method of preservation is drying by the use of a desiccant such as sand, borax or, best of all, silica gel. The desiccant absorbs all the moisture from the plant material. This can be a time-consuming process but it is well worth the effort because the result is dried materials with colour and form nearer their fresh condition than can be achieved by almost any other method of preservation.

This method is essential for the preservation of fleshy flowerheads that cannot be successfully air dried. Flowers such as lilies, tulips, freesias, pansies and open garden roses all respond well to desiccant drying and provide the flower arranger with a wealth of preserved materials not generally commercially available.

For the flower arranger there is little point in using this method for flower materials that air dry well because on a non-commercial scale desiccant drying is only suitable for small amounts of material and silica gel is expensive.

Flowers to be preserved by this method must be in perfect, healthy condition and harvested preferably after a few hours in the sun, with as little surface moisture as possible.

It is important to choose a drying method which will allow the plant material to retain its original colour and form.

Wiring flowers for desiccant drying

Desiccant drying is normally only used for flowerheads as the process weakens stems to the extent that they become virtually unusable. Also, it should be remembered that the flowerheads themselves will become very fragile. Indeed, if you are going to make wire stems it should be done while the flowers are still fresh before beginning the desiccant process.

Flowers with hollow stems, like zinnias, are wired by inserting the wire through their natural stem and pushing it into the flowerhead. Be careful not to push it too far because the flowerhead will shrink as it dries and this might expose an unsightly wire. Heavy petalled flowers like dahlias have to be dried face up, so only provide them with short-wired stems. These stems can be extended after the flowers have been dried. Flowers which have woody, tough or very thin stems may be wired through the seed box (calyx) at the base of the flowerhead from one side to the other. Bring the projecting wire ends down and form them into a mount.

During the drying process the flower and stem will shrink, so a double or single leg mount will become loose and slide off unless its wire has been securely pushed into the stem while the flower was still fresh. Remember that you still need to make the gauge of wire used for a mount compatible with the weight of the fresh flower.

DRYING WITH SILICA GEL

Nowadays silica gel is considered a superior material to borax or sand for desiccant drying. Sand and borax are heavy and great care must be taken to avoid damaging flowers dried in these materials. Silica gel on the other hand is lightweight and can be crushed very fine so it can be worked into complicated petal configurations without causing damage.

Flowers dry very quickly in silica gel, five to ten days being the usual time necessary for most plant material. Borax and sand are much slower and it can take up to five weeks to dry some materials! Use an airtight container when using silica gel as it absorbs moisture from the air, whereas sand and borax can be used in any container provided it has a lid. The method for sand and borax is generally the same as for silica gel.

Some silica gel crystals are blue and this changes to pink as they absorb moisture which will help you measure the progress of the drying process.

Since each flower type will probably require a different time to dry, check progress at regular intervals. Flowers left too long in a desiccant will eventually disintegrate. When you start using this method, there will, of course, be an element of trial and error before you are able to establish the time necessary for each flower type.

Some flowers with a deep cupped shape, such as tulips, should be dried individually in a plastic cup of crystals sealed with clear film to ensure they keep their shape. After you remove the dried flowers from the silica gel, they will probably still have powder on them and this must be removed very carefully with a fine, soft paintbrush. You can, of course, re-use the silica gel over and over again. All you need to do is spread it out on a tray and leave it in a warm oven until it is dry. This will be easy to recognize in the coloured silica because it will become blue again.

When you have prepared your silica gel crystals place a layer approximately 5 cm/2 in deep in the bottom of your container. Place the flowerheads in the crystals face down or if the petals are complex face up. If their stems are wire mounted, bend them as necessary to fit the flowers into the container.

When all flowerheads are in position, spoon a second 5 cm/2 in deep layer of silica gel over them to cover completely. Be sure to fill all parts of the flowerhead with crystals. If it has complex petals, lift them carefully with a toothpick and gently push the crystals into every crevice. Put the lid on the container and tape around to make airtight.

LEFT AND RIGHT: *There are flowers and materials from every season suitable for drying. Silica gel is especially suitable for drying flowers with delicate and highly coloured petals.*

Microwave method

The silica gel process can be accelerated by using a microwave oven. Remember, however, that you must not put wired materials in a microwave oven. Any wiring will have to be done after drying which may be difficult given the fragility of the dried blooms. Bury the material in silica gel in a container, but do not put a lid on it. Instead, place the uncovered container in the microwave oven with about half a cup of water next to it.

Set the microwave timer according to the type of flower you are drying. Delicate blooms may take less than two minutes while more fleshy flowers will, of course, take longer. The time required will also vary according to the weather – in midsummer it will take only seconds, but on a damp autumn day it will take much longer. You will need to experiment with your timing to get accurate settings. After the process is ended leave the silica to cool before removing the flowers.

STORAGE OF DESICCANT DRIED MATERIALS

To keep desiccant dried materials in good condition store them in an airtight container, packed loosely with layers of tissue paper in between. Place a small pouch of silica gel in the container to absorb any moisture, but take care that you do not allow the powder to come into direct contact with the flowers.

PRESERVING WITH GLYCERINE

Foliage in particular does not respond well to air drying. Its green colours fade and the result is tired-looking, brittle material. Happily the use of glycerine works well for many varieties of foliage. This method enables plant material to replace the moisture which has evaporated from its stems and leaves by absorption of a solution of glycerine and water.

Because this process relies on the ability of plant material to draw up the solution, it is not suitable for autumn foliage which has, of course, already died. Indeed, it is important that materials to be treated with glycerine are harvested in the middle of their growing season, when the leaves are young but developed and are full of moisture. Foliage that is too young and is soft and pale green does not respond to glycerine.

The stem ends of material to be treated should be cut at an angle of 45 degrees and the lower leaves stripped. Peel the bark off the bottom 6 cm/2½ in of the stem and split the end up to about 10 cm/4 in to ensure efficient absorption of the solution.

Mix one part glycerine with two parts hot water and pour the solution into a substantial container to a depth of about 20 cm / 8 in. The size of container will depend on the amount of material to be treated. Stand the stems of foliage in the solution for anything from two to six weeks, depending on the size and texture of the leaves, to achieve full absorption. Always keep an eye on the amount of solution in the container and top it up whenever necessary to maintain the level.

If you are treating individual leaves they can be completely submerged in the solution, but a thicker half-glycerine, half-water mixture should be used. It

will take two to three weeks for leaves to be properly treated, after which time remove them from the solution and wipe off any excess with a clean, soft cloth.

Glycerine treatment works best for mature, sturdy plant material such as beech, hornbeam, magnolia and elaeagnus. Surprisingly it is also successful with less robust material like *Molucella laevis* (bells of Ireland) and trails of ivy.

As materials are preserved their leaves will change colour to a variety of shades of brown. When all the leaves have changed colour you will know the process is complete. The visual results on materials of treatment with glycerine may vary even for the same material but with increasing experience of the technique you will become better able to predict what you are likely to achieve. Berried foliage can also be preserved with glycerine, but the berries will shrink slightly and change colour. An advantage of glycerine-preserved foliage is that it remains malleable, and dusty leaves can simply be wiped with a damp cloth.

ABOVE LEFT AND RIGHT: *Include in your dried flower arrangements natural materials that you find in the country. Pine cones, grasses and seed heads are beautifully coloured and will introduce texture and form into your displays. Glycerine is especially suitable for sturdy leaves, and it imparts a wonderful gloss to the plant material preserved in this way.*

Peony and Apple Table Arrangement

This delicate arrangement, which is suitable for a small table, can be made for a specific occasion and kept to be used again and again, whenever a special decoration is called for. The construction of the decoration is relatively simple, involving the minimum of wiring.

Peonies can be dried either in a desiccant such as silica gel or by air drying. Remember that the dried petals are fragile, so handle them carefully.

MATERIALS

block plastic foam for dried flowers
knife
terracotta bowl
florist's adhesive tape
scissors
10 stems preserved (dried) eucalyptus
18 slices preserved (dried) apple
stub wires
2 large heads dried hydrangea
10 pale pink dried peonies
20 deep pink dried roses
20 dried peony leaves
10 stems ti tree

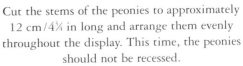

1

Cut the block of plastic foam so that it wedges into the bowl and hold it securely in place with the florist's adhesive tape. Cut the eucalyptus stems to about 13 cm/5 in, making sure that the cut ends are clean of leaves, and arrange them evenly around the plastic foam to create a domed foliage outline to the display.

2

Group the slices of preserved (dried) apple into 3s and double leg mount them with stub wires. Push the 6 groups of wired apple slices into the foam, distributing them evenly throughout the display. The apple slices should be slightly shorter than the eucalyptus when in place.

3

Break each hydrangea head into 3 smaller florets and push them into the foam, distributing them evenly throughout the display and recessing them slightly as you work.

4

Cut the stems of the peonies to approximately 12 cm/4¾ in long and arrange them evenly throughout the display. This time, the peonies should not be recessed.

5

Cut the dried rose stems to approximately
13 cm/4¾ in long and push them into
the plastic foam throughout the other materials
in the arrangement.

6

Arrange the dried peony leaves evenly among
the flowers. Cut the ti tree into stems of
approximately 13 cm/4¾ in long and distribute
them throughout the display.

Rose and Starfish Wreath

The design of this visually simple wall decoration involves massing a single type of flower and framing them with a halo of geometric shapes, in this case stars. The prettiness of its soft peach colours makes it suitable for a bedroom wall.

The construction of this wreath involves a small amount of wiring but is otherwise straightforward.

MATERIALS

10 small dried starfish
stub wires
scissors
florist's adhesive
plastic foam ring for
dried flowers, 13 cm / 5 in
diameter
45 shell-pink dried rose
heads
velvet ribbon

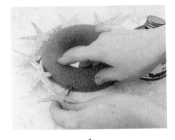

1

Double leg mount the starfish as an extension of one of their arms with a stub wire. Cut the wire to about 2.5 cm / 1 in and apply florist's adhesive to both the tip of the starfish arm and wire. Push the wired arm into the outside edge of the plastic foam ring. Position all the starfish evenly around the ring. Leave a gap of 3 cm / 1¼ in for attaching the velvet ribbon loop.

2

Cut the stems of the rose heads to about 2.5 cm / 1 in and put florist's adhesive on their stems and bases. Push the glued stems into the plastic foam to form a ring around its outside edge on top of the starfish. Working towards the centre of the ring, continue to form circles of rose heads until the ring is covered, apart from a gap for the ribbon.

3

Pass the ribbon through the centre of the ring and position it so that it sits in the gap between the roses and starfish to cover the foam. This can be used to hang up the wreath or just tied in a bow for decoration.

Peony and Shell Display

This display cleverly mixes sea shells with flowers in a lovely pink, mauve and green arrangement. The result is a stunning compact dome. The beautifully patterned rose-pink conical sea shells are echoed by the colour and texture of the cracked glazed ceramic container.

This arrangement would be perfect for a bathroom, as long as it is not allowed to become too damp.

MATERIALS

*knife
block plastic foam for dried flowers
ceramic bowl
florist's adhesive tape
scissors
12 stems dried pale pink peonies
3 dried heads hydrangea
7 pink conical shells*

1

Cut the plastic foam so that it fits snugly into the container and secure it in place with the florist's adhesive tape. Strip the leaves from the peony stems and cut the stems to about 9 cm / 3½ in long. Push the stems into the foam to create a regular dome shape. Arrange the peony leaves liberally throughout the display.

2

Break each hydrangea head into 3 clusters and push them into the foam, distributing them among the peony heads. Distribute the sea shells throughout the display by pushing their wider bottom ends between the flowers so that they are held in place by the mass of blooms (secure with glue if necessary).

Summer Displays

*Most people who pick fresh summer flowers think of doing no more
than informally arranging them in a vase or pitcher of water. These two matching
displays in similar pitchers are loosely arranged in what is almost the dried flower
equivalent of this informal approach to flower arranging. The two displays are
characterized by their use of summer flowers in typical summer colours: purple and
pink larkspur, blue globe thistle, deep pink peonies and green amaranthus. Creating
the displays requires only the most relaxed approach to dried-flower arranging – you
just need to consider carefully the visual balance of the materials to their containers.*

Use the displays in a pair to
achieve the maximum
impact. Before you begin,
cut the stems of the purple
larkspur and amaranthus so
that they are three times the
height of the pitchers.

MATERIALS

*10 stems dried purple
larkspur
2 pitchers
10 stems dried pink
larkspur
10 stems blue globe thistle
(small heads)
10 stems dried green
amaranthus (straight)
16 stems dried deep pink
peonies
scissors*

1

Split the materials into 2 equal groups. Arrange
5 stems of purple larkspur loosely in each
pitcher. Cut the stems of the pink larkspur to a
similar length to the purple larkspur.

2

Arrange the pink larkspur in each pitcher.
Break off any offshoots on the globe thistle
stems to use separately. Cut the main globe
thistle stems to 3 times the height of the
pitchers and arrange in each. Place the
offshoots of globe thistle in the pitchers.

3

Place 5 stems of amaranthus in each pitcher.

4

Cut the peony stems to different heights, the
tallest being 2.5 cm / 1 in shorter than the
larkspur, and the shortest being 20 cm / 8 in
shorter than the larkspur. Arrange the peonies
evenly throughout the other materials.

Summer Table Display

This delicate and pretty little display is designed as a centrepiece for a table laden with summer foods — and whether your dinner party is inside or outside, this display is perfect. The materials in the arrangement — peach-pink spray roses and the misty pale green honesty seed heads and phalaris — combine to create a soufflé of summer colours. Enhance the seasonal feel of this delightful display by sprinkling it with summer scented oil.

All the materials have relatively fragile stems, which require careful handling, especially when they are being pushed into the plastic foam.

MATERIALS

knife
block plastic foam for dried flowers
small basket, approximately 12.5 cm / 5 in diameter
florist's adhesive tape
scissors
5 stems natural dried honesty
20 stems dried spray roses
50 stems natural dried phalaris heads
ribbon

1

Cut the plastic foam to fit the basket so that it projects 2 cm / ¾ in above its rim, and tape it into place using florist's adhesive tape.

2

Cut off the small offshoots of dried honesty seed heads and use these seed heads on stems cut to about 8 cm / 3¼ in to create the outline.

3

Cut the dried spray roses to a stem length of approximately 8 cm / 3¼ in and arrange them evenly and densely in the plastic foam.

4

Cut the phalaris stems to about 8 cm/3¼ in and distribute them evenly in the foam.

5

Once all the materials have been used up, tie the ribbon around the basket.

Massed Arrangement in Blue and Yellow

This contemporary arrangement uses simple massed materials in strong contrasting colours to achieve a strikingly bold display. The polished texture of the silver-grey galvanized bucket provides an ideal visual foundation on which to build the domed cushion of deep yellow achillea with contrasting spiky, blue globe thistles. No special techniques are required to construct the display but you must make sure the materials are massed to achieve the surface density necessary.

This table decoration would complement a modern kitchen or dining-room.

Before you begin, wedge the blocks of foam in the bucket and use florist's tape to hold the foam securely in place.

MATERIALS

galvanized shallow bucket, 30 cm / 12 in diameter
2 blocks plastic foam for dried flowers
florist's adhesive tape
scissors
25 large dyed blue globe thistle heads
35 dried natural heads yellow achillea

1

Cut the globe thistle stems to around 12 cm / 4¼ in and arrange in the foam. Use the smaller heads around the outside.

2

Cut the achillea stems to about 12 cm / 4¼ in and arrange them between the globe thistles, massing them carefully so that no gaps are visible.

Globe Thistle and Mussel Shell Ring

If you were wondering what to do with all those shells you collected during last year's seaside holiday, this decoration may be the answer. The spiky globe thistles contrast with the smooth, hard surface of the mussel shells, but probably the most memorable feature of the display is its beautiful blue colouring.

1

Position 3 groups of 3 slightly overlapping mussel shells at equidistant points around the ring. Glue them to the plastic foam and to each other, taking great care when using the glue gun, which will be very hot.

2

Cut the globe thistle stems to around 2.5 cm / 1 in long, put a small blob of glue on the stem and push them into the plastic foam. Continue this process until all areas of the plastic foam not covered with shells are filled.

The material content of this display is strongly evocative of the seaside, and the ring would look wonderful displayed in either a bathroom or a kitchen.

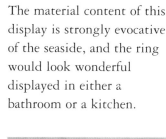

MATERIALS

plastic foam ring for dried flowers, 13 cm / 5 in diameter
glue gun and glue
9 half mussel shells
65 globe thistle heads of various sizes
scissors

Artichoke Pinholder Display

This otherwise traditional line arrangement is unusual in that dried materials are used on a pinholder. Dried stems are hard and it is not easy to push them on to the spikes of a pinholder. There is also the heaviness of the artichokes to consider, and they have to be carefully positioned to avoid disrupting the physical balance of the arrangement. Make sure that all the stems are firmly pushed on to the pinholder's spikes.

Use naturally trailing stems of hazel at the front of the pinholder and bring it down over the pedestal to the right of its centre line to create a natural trailing effect.

MATERIALS

pedestal stand
pinholder
scissors
6 stems contorted hazel
9 stems dried artichoke
heads
25 stems dried poppy seed
heads

1

Push the hazel stems, cut to 45 cm/18 in, on to the spikes of the pinholder, positioning the tallest stem at the back.

2

Arrange the artichoke heads throughout the hazel. Use the smallest head on the longest stem centrally at the back. Work away from this with progressively shorter stems. Position the largest artichoke head about two-thirds down from the top of the display.

3

Arrange the poppy seed head stems throughout the display. Position the longest stem at the back, making sure it is shorter than the tallest hazel stem but taller than the tallest artichoke. Work away from this point with progressively shorter stems, with some stems trailing over the front to the right of centre.

Small Candleholder Display

There are many containers in the average household that, because of their colour, shape or material content, are suitable for a flower arrangement. This display was inspired entirely by the small, crown-shaped, brass candleholder in which it is arranged. An elevated position on, for example, a mantelpiece, would be perfect for such a small, neat display. Indeed, it could be used as a wedding-cake decoration.

Making the display is straightforward and the method is applicable to any arrangement in a similarly small container.

1

Cut a piece of plastic foam so that it can be wedged firmly into the candle holder, and sits about 2 cm / ¾ in below its top edge.

2

Cut the stems of the poppy seed heads to 9 cm / 3½ in and push them into the foam, distributing them evenly to create a domed shape.

3

Cut the dried rose stems to 9 cm / 3½ in and push them into the foam between the poppy seed heads, to reinforce the domed outline.

MATERIALS

knife
block plastic foam for dried flowers
crown-shaped candleholder
scissors
15 stems poppy seed heads
20 stems dried pink roses

Edging Basket in Blue

Tired household containers can be decorated to give them a new lease of life. This might simply be a fresh coat of paint or, as in the case of this basket, a dried-flower edging around its rim. The display uses the blues and mauves of marjoram, floss flower (ageratum), lavender, globe thistle and sea holly to create a decoration with colour and texture.

Dried flowers transform this plain wire-mesh and cane basket into an attractive object you would happily put on display in your house.

MATERIALS

*scissors
33 stems globe thistle
stub wires
24 stems sea holly
medium-weight silver wire
bunch floss flower
bunch marjoram
60 stems lavender
florist's tape
silver reel wire
wire-mesh and
rectangular
cane basket*

1

Cut the globe thistle stems to 2.5 cm/1 in long and double leg mount each with stub wires. Cut the sea holly stems to 2.5 cm/1 in and double leg mount each with medium weight silver wire. Split the floss flower and the marjoram into 20 small clusters of each on stems 5 cm/2 in long and double leg mount them individually with silver wire. Cut the lavender stems to about 5 cm/2 in long, group in 3s and double leg mount each group with silver wire. Cover all the wired elements with florist's tape.

2

Lay a wired stem of sea holly on the edge of the basket and attach it by binding it in place with a length of silver reel wire. Slightly overlap the sea holly with a cluster of floss flower, binding in place with silver reel wire.

3

Overlap the floss flower with a globe thistle head, the globe thistle with the marjoram and the marjoram with the lavender, binding all of them to the basket with the same continuous length of reel wire. Repeat the sequence of materials around the edge of the basket. When the entire edge is covered, stitch the reel wire through the basket several times to secure.

Peony and Globe Thistle Candle Decoration

This beautiful arrangement of dried flowers in a terracotta pot is designed to incorporate a candle. The massed flowerheads give a rich, full look to the display, which has the stunning colour combination of deep pink peonies and bright blue globe thistles surrounding a dark green candle and finished with a lime green ribbon. Simple to construct, you could make several arrangements, using different colours and display them as a group. Alternatively, you could use a larger container and more flowers and incorporate more than one candle.

The effect of this display relies on the peonies being tightly massed together. Never leave burning candles unattended and do not allow the candles to burn down below 5 cm/2 in of the display.

MATERIALS

*knife
block of plastic foam for
dried flowers
terracotta pot, 15 cm/6 in
diameter
wide candle
10 dried deep pink
peonies
15 stems dried small blue
globe thistle
scissors*

1

Cut a piece of plastic foam to size and wedge it firmly into the terracotta pot. Push the candle into the centre of the plastic foam so that it is held securely and sits upright.

2

Cut the peony stems to 4 cm/1½ in and the globe thistle stems to 5 cm/2 in. Push the stems of the peonies into the foam. Push the stems of the globe thistle into the foam among the peonies.

3

Make sure that the heads of all the flowers are at the same level. Wrap a ribbon around the top of the terracotta pot and tie a bow at the front. Shape the ends of the ribbon to avoid fraying.

Summer Pot Pourri

The traditional pot pourri is based on rose petals because when fresh they have a powerful fragrance, some of which is retained when they are dried. Today's pot pourri does not rely entirely on the fragrance of its flowers since there is a wide range of scented oils available, and materials can be used for their visual qualities. This pot pourri is traditional in that it uses dried roses, but it has been brought up to date by the inclusion of whole buds and heads.

1

Break the stems off the lavender, leaving only the flower spikes. Place all the dried ingredients in the glass bowl and mix together thoroughly. Add several drops of pot pourri essence to the mixture of materials – the more you add, the stronger the scent. Stir thoroughly to mix the scent throughout the pot pourri, using a spoon. As the perfume weakens with time it can be refreshed by the addition of more drops of essence, in an appropriate fragrance.

Predominantly pink and purple, the look of this pot pourri, and its scent, will enhance any home throughout the summer months. The sea holly heads, apple slices and whole lemons are used entirely for their appearance.

MATERIALS

20 stems lavender
15 preserved (dried) apple slices
5 dried lemons
handful cloves
20 dried pale pink rose heads
2 handfuls dried rose buds
handful hibiscus buds
10 sea holly heads
large glass bowl
pot pourri essence
tablespoon

Bathroom Display

Though a steamy environment will cause dried flowers to deteriorate, if you accept the shorter life span, such arrangements are an opportunity to add an attractive decorative feature to a bathroom. The starfish in this arrangement evoke images of the sea, while the soft pastel colours – shell-pink, apricot, blue, pale green and cream – give it a soft summery look. Oval shaped, in a rectangular wooden trug, the display is a traditional full arrangement, which can be viewed in the round and used anywhere in the house where its pastel shades would look appropriate. The scale and colour of the arrangement is designed to show off the faded blue container.

Before you begin to arrange the dried flowers, cut the blocks of plastic foam so that they fit tightly inside the trug. Use florist's tape to hold the foam in place.

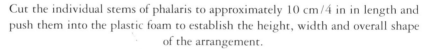

1

Cut the individual stems of phalaris to approximately 10 cm/4 in in length and push them into the plastic foam to establish the height, width and overall shape of the arrangement.

MATERIALS

2 blocks plastic foam for dried flowers
knife
pale coloured wooden trug
florist's adhesive tape
scissors
50 stems natural phalaris
40 stems shell-pink roses
20 stems cream-coloured helichrysums
150 stems dried lavender
15 small dried starfish
stub wires

2

Cut the stems of the roses to approximately 10 cm/4 in and push them into the plastic foam, distributing them evenly throughout.

3

Cut the stems of the helichrysum to a length of about 10 cm/4 in and push them into the foam among the roses and phalaris, recessing some. Cut the dried lavender to 11 cm/4½ in and, by pushing into the foam, arrange it throughout the display in groups of 5 stems.

Wire all the starfish
individually by double leg
mounting one of the arms
with a stub wire. Cut the wire
legs of the starfish to a length
of about 10 cm/4 in and
push the wires into the foam,
distributing them evenly
throughout the display.

Textured Foliage Ring

*Some types of foliage can be successfully air dried but many others cannot
and need to be glycerine preserved. This decoration mixes both types of
foliage to create a feast of textures and subtle colours.*

Very easy to construct from
commercially available
materials, this foliage ring
makes a wonderful autumn
wall decoration for a hall or,
if protected from the
weather, a front door.

MATERIALS

scissors
*10 stems dried natural
coloured honesty*
*5 branches glycerine-
preserved beech leaves*
*5 branches glycerine-
preserved adiantum*
*60 cm / 24 in length dried
hop vine*
*twisted wicker wreath
ring, approximately
30 cm / 12 in diameter*
twine

1

Cut all the foliage stems to
around 12 cm/4¾ in long.
You will need 21 lengths of
each type of foliage to cover
your ring. Start by securely
tying a group of 3 stems of
honesty to the wicker ring
with twine.

2

Making sure it slightly
overlaps the honesty, bind on
a group of 3 glycerined beech
stems with the same
continuous length of twine.
Repeat this process with a
group of 3 stems of hops
followed by a group of 3
stems of glycerined adiantum.

3

Continue binding materials to
the ring in the same sequence
until the ring is completely
covered. Cut off any untidy
stems and adjust the materials
to achieve the best effect if
necessary. Finally, tie off the
twine in a discreet knot at the
back of the ring.

Wall Hanging Sheaf

The rustic charm of this delightful hand-tied sheaf is difficult to resist, especially since it is so easy to make once you have mastered the ever-useful stem-spiralling technique. The focal flowers are large, round, orange globe thistle heads, the creamy-white papery flowers of the helichrysum and country green of linseed and amaranthus. The green carthamus, with its curious orange tufts, acts as a visual bridge between the other materials.

1

Set out the materials so that they are easily accessible. Divide each of the bunches of linseed and helichrysum into 10 smaller bunches. Break off the side shoots from the main stems of the carthamus and the globe thistle to increase the number of individual stems available.

2

Take the longest stem of amaranthus in your hand and, to either side of it, add a stem of carthamus and a bunch of linseed making sure all the material is slightly shorter than the amaranthus. The stems of the materials should be spiralled as they are added. Add materials to the bunch to maintain a visual balance between the bold forms of the globe thistle and helichrysum and the more delicate linseed and carthamus.

The sheaf shape makes a feature of the stems as well as the blooms. Finished with a green ribbon, this decoration would look lovely hung in a country-style kitchen.

MATERIALS

1 bunch dried linseed
1 bunch white
helichrysum
10 stems dried carthamus
8 stems large dried orange
globe thistle
10 stems dried green
amaranthus (straight)
twine
scissors
green paper ribbon

3

When all the materials have been incorporated, tie with twine at the binding point. Trim the ends of the stems.

4

Make a paper ribbon bow and attach it to the sheaf at the binding point with its tails towards the flowerheads.

Red Display in a Glass Cube

This display uses dried oranges to create a coloured base within the glass container itself on which an arrangement using only shades of red is built. The arrangement is a dome of massed materials with contrasting textures: the spikes of globe thistles, the velvet cushions of achillea, and the papery petals of roses. The materials and colours are classical and the container allows the shapes and textures to be seen.

The display is easy to make but clever in that the mechanics of its construction are hidden when it is completed.

1

Three-quarter fill the glass cube with dried oranges. Cut the plastic foam block so that it fits into the glass cube snugly above the oranges. Only about a third of the depth of the block should be inside the container. Hold the plastic foam securely in place by taping over it and on to the glass (no more than 2.5 cm / 1 in down its sides).

2

Cut the bottlebrush stems to 10 cm/4 in and create the overall outline of the display by pushing their stems into the plastic foam.

MATERIALS

20 cm / 8 in glass cube
20 dried oranges
knife
block plastic foam for dried flowers
florist's tape
scissors
2 bunches dried bottlebrush
2 bunches dried red-dyed achillea
2 bunches dried red-dyed globe thistle
2 bunches dried red roses

3

Cut the dried achillea to a stem length of 10 cm/4 in and evenly distribute through the bottlebrush by pushing the stems into the foam.

4

Cut the globe thistle stems to 10 cm/4 in and position evenly throughout the display, pushing their stems into the foam to secure them.

5

Cut the dried rose stems to 10 cm/4 in in length and, in groups of 3, fill the remaining spaces by inserting them evenly throughout the display.

Dried Mantelpiece Display

When a fireplace is not in use it can lose its status as the focal point of a room but decorating its mantelpiece and grate with dramatic floral arrangements will ensure it remains a major feature. The material contents of this mantelpiece arrangement give it a high summer look; it incorporates bright yellow sunflowers, green amaranthus and green hops with corn cobs used as the focal material. Construction is relatively straightforward provided you maintain the physical as well as visual balance of the display. To prevent the arrangement falling forwards, make sure the majority of the weight is kept at the back.

Using dried flowers is more practical than a fresh display because the arrangement will last far longer and require little maintenance.

1

Cut the block of plastic foam in half, position one half at the centre of the mantelpiece and secure it in place with adhesive tape. If using a plastic tray, secure the foam to the tray with tape, then tape the tray to the mantelpiece.

2

Lie the string of hops along the full length of the mantelpiece and secure it to the ends of the shelf with adhesive tape. The hops on the vine should lie on and around the plastic foam without covering it completely.

3

Push the stems of beech into the plastic foam, distributing them evenly to create a domed foliage outline that also trails into the hops. Push the three stems of the corn cobs into the foam towards the back, one at the centre with a slightly shorter cob at either side.

4

Distribute the sunflowers evenly throughout the plastic foam following the domed shape. Place longer stems toward the back and shorter stems towards the front. Arrange the amaranthus throughout the other materials in the plastic foam to reinforce the outline shape.

Dried Fireplace Arrangement

Fill the black hole of an empty grate with a bright display of dried flowers and foliage such as this informal arrangement. The display incorporates the cheery faces of sunflowers with the soft textures of bright green amaranthus and the delicate white flowers of the ti tree, all set against the rust tints of beech to create a sunny decoration for a small fireplace. The plastic foam in this display has been secured by firmly wedging it into the grate. For a larger fireplace the foam will need to be mounted in a separate tray. Do remember that a fireplace display is generally arranged to project outwards, and preventing it from falling forwards will be a major problem.

Using dried materials means you can make this display at any time of the year.

MATERIALS

1½ blocks plastic foam for dried flowers
scissors
8 branches glycerined beech
10 stems dried green amaranthus (straight)
10 stems dried sunflowers
10 stems natural ti tree

1

Wedge the plastic foam into the grate. Cut the stems from the branches of glycerined beech and push them into the foam to create a fan-shaped foliage outline that projects out of the grate and forms a curved profile to the front.

2

Push the stems of amaranthus into the foam, distributing them evenly throughout the beech stems to reinforce their outline.

3

Push the sunflower stems into the foam, distributing them evenly in the other materials.

4

Push the stems of ti tree in to the foam to reinforce the overall shape.

302

Hydrangea Circlet

Hydrangea heads remain beautiful when dried, but they do not necessarily dry well when hung in the air. Thus, while it might seem a contradiction in terms, it is best to dry hydrangea while they are standing in shallow water. This slows down the process and stops the hydrangea florets shrivelling. Hydrangea flowers range from white through pinks, greens, blues and reds to deep purples, and most keep these colours when dried.

1

Break down each hydrangea head into five smaller florets. Double leg mount each one individually with stub wire.

2

Take a long length of silver reel wire and attach a hydrangea floret to the vine circlet by stitching the wire around one of the vines and the wired stem of the hydrangea, pulling tight to secure. Using the same continuous length of wire, add consecutive hydrangea florets in the same way, slightly overlapping them until the front surface of the vine surface is covered.

This circlet is a celebration of the colours of dried hydrangeas and is a perfect decoration for a bedroom.

MATERIALS

*12 full dried heads
hydrangea
scissors
stub wire
silver reel wire
1 vine circlet, about
35 cm / 14 in diameter*

3

Finish by stitching the silver reel wire around the vine.

303

Massed Star-shaped Decoration

This display has a huge visual impact of massed colour and bold shape with the added bonus of the delicious scent of lavender. Built within a star-shaped baking tin, the combination of lavender and rosebuds gives the arrangement a traditional feel.

The decoration is simple to make, although it does call for a substantial amount of material.

MATERIALS

*2 blocks plastic foam for
dried flowers
knife
star-shaped baking tin
scissors
50 stems dried lavender
100 stems dried yellow roses*

1

Cut the plastic foam so that it fits neatly into the star-shaped baking tin and is recessed about 2.5 cm/1 in down from its top. Use the tin as a template for accuracy.

2

Cut the lavender stems to 5 cm/2 in and group them into 5s. Push the groups into the plastic foam all around the outside edge of the star shape to create a border of approximately 1 cm/½ in.

3

Cut the dried roses to 5 cm/2 in. Starting at the points of the star and working towards its centre, push the rose stems into the foam. All the heads should be level with the lavender.

Fruit and Fungi Basket Rim Decoration

Creating a dried flower embellishment for the rim of an old and damaged wicker basket gives it a new lease of life by transforming it into a resplendent container for the display of fruit.

The decoration is full of the bold textures and rich colours of sunflowers, oranges, lemons, apples and fungi. The principles of this design can be used to decorate a wicker container of any type and shape.

1

Group the orange slices in 3s and double leg mount each group with stub wires. Repeat with the lemon and apple slices. Cut the sunflower stems to about 2.5 cm/1 in and individually double leg mount them on stub wires. Double leg mount the individual pieces of fungi with stub wire. Finally, completely cover all the wires with florist's tape.

2

Starting at one corner of the basket, bind a group of orange slices to its rim by stitching silver reel wire through the wicker and around the stem. With the same wire, stitch on the apple slices, the sunflower heads, the lemon slices and the fungi. Repeat this sequence until the rim is covered. Stitch the wire around the last stem and the basket.

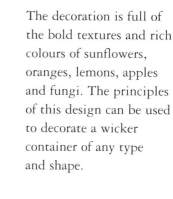

MATERIALS

45 slices dried orange
45 slices dried lemon
45 slices preserved (dried)
apple
stub wires
18 sunflower heads
16 small pieces dried
fungus
florist's tape
scissors
old wicker basket,
without a handle
silver reel wire

Autumnal Orange Display

Warm autumn colours dominate this display both in the floral arrangement and in its container. The lovely bulbous terracotta pot is a feature of the display, and the arrangement is domed to reflect the roundness of the container. Indeed, in order to focus attention on the pot, the container unusually takes up half the height of the finished display. The autumnal red and burnt-orange colours of globe thistle, bottlebrush, oranges and adiantum contrast with the green of the carthamus, the orange tufts of which act as a colour link. Texturally varied, the display incorporates tufted flowers, spiky flowers, feathery foliage and recessed leathery skinned fruits. The arrangement involves simple wiring of the oranges but is otherwise straightforward and just requires a good eye and a little patience in arranging the materials.

This is designed as a feature display that would be particularly effective positioned where it could be viewed in the round such as on a low coffee table.

MATERIALS

*3 blocks plastic foam for
dried flowers
terracotta pot, 30 cm /
12 in high
florist's adhesive tape
10 stems glycerine-
preserved adiantum
stub wires
9 dried split oranges
10 stems dried carthamus
10 stems orange-dyed
globe thistles
10 stems dried bottlebrush*

1

Pack the blocks of plastic foam into the terracotta pot and secure in place with florist's adhesive tape. The surface of the foam should be about 4 cm/1¼ in above the rim of the pot.

2

Create a low domed foliage outline using the adiantum stems at their length of about 25 cm/10 in. Wire the dried oranges with stub wire.

3

Bend down the wires projecting from the bases of the oranges and twist together. Arrange the oranges throughout the adiantum by pushing their wire stems into the foam.

4

Cut the carthamus stems to approximately 25 cm/10 in and push them into the plastic foam throughout the display to reinforce the height, width and overall shape.

5

Cut the globe thistle stems to a length of approximately 25 cm/10 in and push them into the foam evenly throughout the display. These are the focal flowers.

6

Finally, cut the stems of bottlebrush to a length of 25 cm/10 in and push them into the plastic foam to distribute them evenly throughout the display.

Pink Basket Display

The natural deep pink hues of these roses, papery helichrysum and velvet-spiked amaranthus have survived the preservation process and here work together to produce a richly-coloured dense textural display of dried flowers. The arrangement, mounted in an oval basket, is a low dome and thus would be good as a table arrangement, but its formal appearance would make it an appropriate display to place in any reception room in the house.

Helichrysum is one of the most useful of all dried flowers. Sprays, dyed in every imaginable shade, are available in all dried flower shops and also in many florist's shops.

MATERIALS

*knife
block plastic foam for
dried flowers
oval basket, about 20 cm /
8 in long
florist's adhesive tape
scissors
20 stems dried red
amaranthus (straight)
20 stems dried deep pink
roses
20 stems deep pink
helichrysum*

1

Cut the foam to fit snugly into the basket and fix it in place with adhesive tape.

2

Cut the amaranthus to an overall length of 14 cm/5¾ in and push them into the foam to create a dome-shaped outline.

3

Cut the stems of dried roses to 12 cm/4¾ in and push them into the foam, distributing them evenly among the amaranthus.

308

Cut 10 of the helichrysum
stems to approximately
12 cm/4¾ in in length and
push them into the foam
evenly throughout the display.
Cut the other 10 stems to
approximately 10 cm/4 in in
length and push them into the
foam evenly throughout the
display, so that they are
recessed to give visual depth
to the arrangement.

Lavender Basket

A basket decorated with bunches of dried lavender makes an exquisitely pretty aromatic linen store. It could also be kept on the kitchen dresser, filled with freshly laundered tea towels ready on hand when you need them.

MATERIALS

dried lavender (2 bunches for the handle plus about 1 bunch for every 10 cm / 4 in of basket rim)

florist's wire
scissors
willow basket

hot glue gun and glue sticks
blue paper-ribbon
blue twine

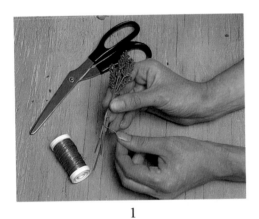

1

Wire up enough small bundles of about six lavender heads to cover the rim of the basket generously. Arrange the heads so they are staggered to give fuller cover. Trim the stalks short.

2

Wire up the remaining lavender into 12 larger bunches of about 12 lavender heads for the handles, leaving the stalks long.

3

Form a 'star' of three of the larger bunches and wire them together. Repeat with the other nine so you have four largish star-shaped bunches of lavender.

4

Fix the small bunches to the rim of the basket, using either wire or hot glue in a glue gun. Start at one end and work towards the handle. Use the bunches generously so they overlap each other to cover the width of the rim.

5

Once the rim is fully covered, glue on individual heads of lavender to cover any spaces, ugly wires or stalks. Pay particular attention to the area near the handles, because you will have finished up with quite a few bare stalks there.

6

Wind blue paper-ribbon around the handle. Wire the longer lavender bunches to the handles, leaving the stalks long but trimming to neaten them. Cut the stalks on the inside of the handle shorter to fit the space. Bind the wired joints with blue twine.

Flower Topiary

Dried flowers look fabulous when given the sculptural form of faux topiary.
These strawflowers and larkspur set into a tall cone make a stunning everlasting
display. Wrap the pot in a co-ordinating fabric to finish off the arrangement.

MATERIALS

small flowerpot
square of fabric to cover the pot
knife
small florist's dry foam cone
4 florist's stub wires
florist's dry foam cone,
about 18 cm / 7 in tall
scissors
bunch of dried blue larkspur
florist's wire, if necessary
bunch of dried
yellow strawflowers

1

Stand the pot in the centre of the fabric and
tuck the corners into the pot. Tuck in any
other loose portions of fabric.

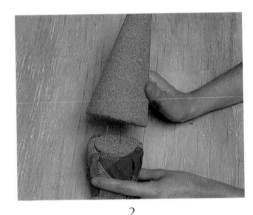

2

Cut down the small foam cone to fit the
inside of the pot. Position four stub wires
so they project above the foam. Use these
for attaching the top cone.

3

Snip the florets off the larkspur, leaving the
small stalks to push into the foam. Make four
rows of larkspur down the length of the cone
to quarter it; then fill in either side of these
rows to create broad blue bands. Many of the
florets' stalks will be strong enough to pierce
the foam. If not, wire the florets with
florist's wire. Finally, fill in the panels
with the strawflowers.

E V E R L A S T I N G   T R E A T S

....

Leaf and Petal Decorations

Decorations are so much more appealing when made from all things natural.
These, made from preserved oak and beech leaves and dried hydrangea flowers,
are easy to do, and they make delightful tree or table decorations.

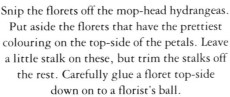

MATERIALS

scissors
dried mop-head hydrangeas
(about two for every ball)
hot glue gun and glue sticks
florist's dry foam balls, about
7.5 cm / 3 in in diameter
glycerined beech leaves
glycerined or dyed, dried
oak leaves
picture framer's wax gilt

1

Snip the florets off the mop-head hydrangeas.
Put aside the florets that have the prettiest
colouring on the top-side of the petals. Leave
a little stalk on these, but trim the stalks off
the rest. Carefully glue a floret top-side
down on to a florist's ball.

2

Continue to glue the florets face downwards
until the ball is completely covered.

3

Put a tiny spot of glue on the back of each of
the petals of a reserved floret. Fix this,
top-side up, on to the ball – over the base
covering of petals. If you leave a little stalk
on the florets you set aside for the top layer,
this can be used to help attach it to the ball.
Let the glue work just where the petals touch
the ball, allowing them to curl naturally at
the edges to provide texture. Continue until
the ball is covered. To make the leaf balls,
first gild the beech leaves with wax gilt.
Stick the beech and oak leaves over the ball,
overlapping them slightly to cover the foam.

Hydrangea Pot

Dried materials can be used to make the simplest, yet most exquisite, gifts.
Here's an easy but effective idea, using a single hydrangea head.

MATERIALS

glue
dyed, dried oak leaf
small flowerpot
dyed raffia
scissors
dried mop-head hydrangea

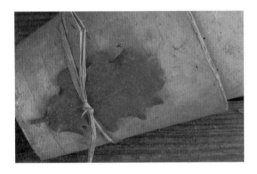

1

Use a spot of glue to attach the leaf to the pot,
and then tie it on with raffia. Secure the raffia
tie at the back with another spot of glue.

2

Cut the hydrangea stalk short enough so that
the head rests on the pot. Place the head
in the pot.

Spice Pots

For a cook, make a cornucopia of culinary flavourings by putting different dried
herbs and spices into terracotta pots and packing the pots in a wire basket.

MATERIALS

cinnamon sticks
dried bay leaves
garlic
dried red chillies
small flowerpots
wire basket
wire
raffia

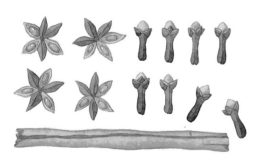

1

Place the herbs and spices in the pots and
place the pots in the basket.

2

Bend a piece of wire into a heart shape and
bind it with raffia. Leave a long end free
before starting to bind. When binding is
complete, the end can be used to tie the heart
to the basket. Finish with a bow.

Everlasting Christmas Tree

*This delightful little tree, made from dyed, preserved oak leaves and decorated with
tiny gilded cones, would make an enchanting Christmas decoration. Make several
and then group them to make a centrepiece, or place one at each setting.*

MATERIALS

knife
bunch of dyed, dried oak leaves
florist's wire
small fir cones
picture framer's wax gilt
flowerpot, 18 cm / 7 in tall
small florist's dry foam cone
4 florist's stub wires
florist's dry foam cone,
about 18 cm / 7 in tall

1

Cut the leaves off the branches and trim the
stalks. Wire up bunches of about four leaves,
making some bunches with small leaves,
some with medium-sized leaves and others
with large leaves. Sort the bunches into piles.

3

Prepare the pot by cutting the smaller foam
cone to fit the pot, adding stub-wire stakes
and positioning the larger cone on to this.
Attach the leaves to the cone, starting at the
top with the bunches of small leaves, and
working down through the medium and
large leaves to make a realistic shape. Add
the gilded cones to finish.

2

Insert wires into the bottom end of each
fir cone and twist the ends together.
Gild each cone by rubbing on wax gilt.

Fruity Tree

Glycerined leaves make a perfect foundation for any dried topiary. You can buy them in branches, ready glycerined for use, or glycerine your own garden prunings. Here, they have been wired into bunches for a fabulous, full look.

MATERIALS

secateurs
3 branches of glycerined
beech leaves
florist's stub wires
dried pear slices
florist's dry foam ball, about
13 cm / 5 in diameter
flowerpot, 18 cm / 7 in tall

1

Cut the leaves off the branches and trim the stalks short. Wire up small bunches of four or six beech leaves and twist the ends of the wires together.

2

Pass a stub wire through the top of each pear slice and twist the ends together.

3

Completely cover the portion of the ball that will show above the pot with beech leaves.

4

Add the pear slices and put the ball into the pot.

Dried-flower Pot

Dried flowers always look their best when the blooms are massed and the stalks not too prominent. Here's a charming treatment: roses and lavender tucked into a tiny terracotta pot, and then tied around with raffia.

MATERIALS

knife
small florist's dry foam cone
small 'long Tom' flowerpot
dried rosebuds
scissors or secateurs
dried lavender
dyed raffia
hot glue gun and glue sticks

1

Trim the foam to fit the pot. Place the rosebuds around the edge of the pot.

2

Cut the lavender stalks to about 1 cm / ½ in and use them to fill the centre of the arrangement. Tie a dyed raffia bow around the pot and secure it at the back with a spot of glue.

Everlasting Basket

*Hydrangeas look fabulous dried, providing a flamboyant display that can simply
be massed into a basket. They're also about the easiest flowers to dry at home.
Just put the cut flowers in about 1 cm / ½ in of water and leave them.
The flowers will take up the water and then gradually dry out.*

MATERIALS

*knife
florist's dry foam
painted wooden basket
dried mop-head hydrangeas
dried globe artichokes
ribbon*

1

Cut the florist's foam to fit and fill the
basket, and then arrange the hydrangeas
to cover the top of the basket.

2

Add the dried globe artichoke at one end
for texture.

3

Tie a ribbon to the handle of the basket
to finish.

Dried-herb Wreath

A dried-herb wreath based on lavender makes a wonderful, textural, aromatic wall hanging. This one also incorporates mugwort, tarragon, lovage and large French lavender seedheads.

MATERIALS

scissors
florist's wire
dried lavender
dried mugwort
dried lovage
dried tarragon
hot glue gun and glue sticks
small wreath base
French lavender seedheads

1

Wire all the dried herbs and flowers, except the French lavender seedheads, into small bunches.

2

Using a glue gun, fix a bunch of lavender to the wreath base.

3

Next, glue a bunch of mugwort to the wreath base.

4

Work round the base, adding a bunch of lovage.

5

Continue all round the wreath, interspersing the different bunches of herbs to cover it completely, using the tarragon to add a feathery look.

6

Finally, for structure, add the individual French lavender seedheads.

COUNTRY
Gifts

Tokens to Treasure

What can bring more pleasure than gifts inspired by country traditions? They have a quality that acknowledges the seasons and withstands the test of time. Gather together all the natural materials you can find – shells, papers, natural fabrics, wire, and even chicken-wire – and turn them into something very special.

Sleep Pillow

Many people still swear by sleep pillows, which are traditionally filled with chamomile and hops. Since hops are related to the cannabis plant, they induce a feeling of sleepy well-being, while chamomile helps you to relax. Either buy ready-prepared sleep mix, or make up your own with chamomile, lemon verbena and a few hops. Stitch a pillow filled with these relaxing herbs to keep on your bed, and look forward to some good night's sleep.

MATERIALS

*linen muslin, 2 m × 20 cm /
80 × 8 in (this can be made up
of two or more shorter lengths)
pins, needle and thread
scissors
pure cotton fabric, 50 × 25 cm /
20 × 10 in
herbal sleep mix
1 m / 39 in antique lace
1 m / 39 in ribbon,
1 cm / ½ in wide
4 pearl buttons*

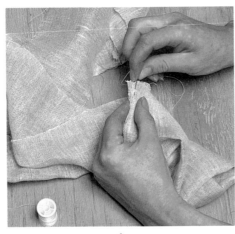

1

Prepare the linen muslin border by stitching together enough lengths to make up 2 m / 80 in. With right sides facing, stitch the ends together to form a ring. Trim the seam. Fold the ring in half lengthways with wrong sides facing and run a line of gathering stitches close to the raw edges.

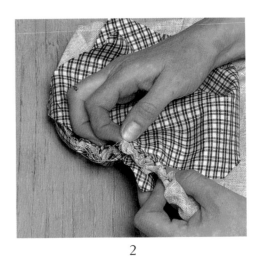

2

Cut two pieces of cotton fabric into 25 cm / 10 in squares. Pull up the gathering threads of the muslin to fit the cushion edge. Pin it to the right side of one square, with raw edges facing outwards, matching the raw edges and easing the gathers evenly round the cushion. Put the second square on top and pin the corners. Stitch the seams, leaving a gap for stuffing. Trim the seams.

3

Turn the cushion right-side out and fill it with herbal sleep mix. Stitch the gap to enclose the border.

4

Using tiny stitches, sew the lace to the cushion about 2.5 cm / 1 in away from the border.

5

Stitch the ribbon close to the lace, making a neat diagonal fold at the corners.

6

Finish by sewing a tiny pearl button to each corner.

Herb Pot-mat

Protect tabletops from hot pots and pans with an aromatic mat, filled with cinnamon, cloves and bay leaves. The heat of the pot immediately releases the piquancy of its contents, kept evenly distributed with mattress-style ties.

MATERIALS

scissors
ticking, at least 62 × 55 cm /
25 × 22 in
pins, needle and thread

spice mix to fill, e.g. dried bay
leaves, cloves, cinnamon sticks
heavy-duty upholstery needle
cotton string

1

First make the hanger by cutting a strip of ticking 5 × 30 cm / 2 × 12 in. With right sides facing, fold this in half lengthways. Stitch the long side, leaving the ends open. Trim the seam. Turn right side out and press. Fold in half to form a loop. Cut two rectangles from the fabric measuring about 62 × 50 cm / 25 × 20 in.

2

Place the cushion pieces on a flat surface, right sides facing, and then slip the hanging loop between the layers, with the raw edges pointing out towards a corner.

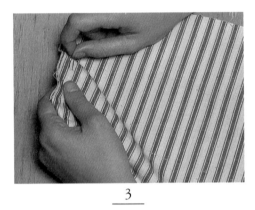

3

Pin and stitch the cushion pieces together, leaving about 7.5 cm / 3 in open. Trim the seams. Turn right side out.

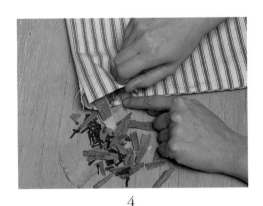

4

Fill the cushion with the spices.

5

Slip-stitch to close the opening.

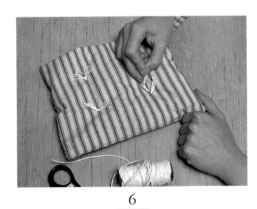

6

Using a heavy-duty upholstery needle threaded with cotton string, make a stitch about a third in from two sides of the cushion, clearing the spices inside the mat away from the area as you go. Untwist the strands of the string for a more feathery look. Repeat with three other ties to give a mattress effect. Make a simple knot in each to secure the ties.

Lavender Sachets

*Use fabric scraps to appliqué simple motifs on to charming chequered fabrics,
and then stitch them into sachets to fill with lavender and use as drawer-
fresheners. Inspired by traditional folk art, these have universal appeal.*

MATERIALS
*scissors
fabric scraps
paper for templates
pins, needle and thread
stranded embroidery thread in
different colours
loose dried lavender
button*

1

Cut two pieces of fabric into squares about
15 cm / 6 in. If you are using a checked or
striped fabric, it is a good idea to let the
design dictate the exact size. Scale up the
template and use it as a pattern to cut bird
and wing shapes from contrasting fabrics.
Pin and tack the bird shape to the
right side of one square.

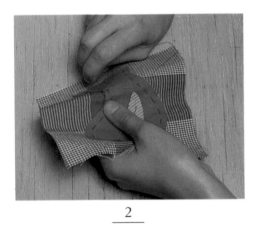

2

Neatly slip-stitch the bird shape to the
sachet front, turning in the edges as you go.
Repeat with the wing shape.

3

Using three strands of embroidery thread
in a contrasting colour, make neat running
stitches around the bird and its wing.

4

Make long stitches on the tail and wing to
indicate feathers, graduating them into a
pleasing shape. Sew in the button eye.

5

With right sides facing, stitch the front and
back of the sachet together, leaving a
5 cm / 2 in gap. Trim the seams. Turn it
right-side out and press. Fill with dried
lavender, and then slip-stitch to close the gap.

Lacy Lavender Heart

Evocative of the Victorian era, this exquisitely pretty heart-shaped lavender bag is made from simple, creamy muslin, and trimmed with antique lace and satin ribbon. The chiffon ribbon at the top is tied into a loop for hanging on coat hangers with favourite garments.

MATERIALS

paper for template
scissors
silky muslin, about
60 × 20 cm / 24 × 8 in

pins, needle and stranded
embroidery thread
pearl button
loose dried lavender

50 cm / 20 in antique lace
50 cm / 20 in very narrow
satin ribbon
50 cm / 20 in medium ribbon

1

Make a heart-shaped paper template about 15 cm / 6 in high and use this as a pattern. Cut four heart shapes from muslin. Tack the hearts together in pairs so each heart is a double thickness of muslin.

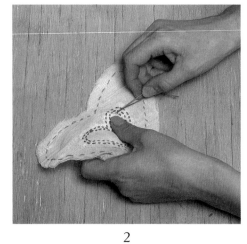

2

Cut a smaller heart shape from muslin. Carefully stitch this to the centre front of one of the larger heart shapes, using two strands of embroidery thread and a running stitch. Make another row of running stitches inside this.

3

Sew the button to the top of the smaller heart.

4

Stitch a third row of running stitches inside the other two. Allow the edges of the smaller heart to fray. With right sides facing, stitch all around the edge of the two large double-thickness muslin heart shapes, leaving a gap of 5 cm / 2 in. Trim the seams, snip into the seam at the 'V' of the heart and snip off the bottom point within the seam allowance. Turn the heart right-side out. Fill it with lavender and slip-stitch to close the gap. Don't despair if the heart looks pretty miserable and misshapen at this stage!

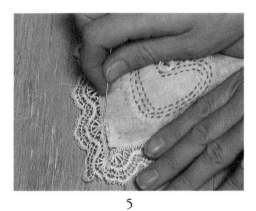

5

Carefully slip-stitch the lace around the edge of the heart.

6

Stitch the satin ribbon over the lower edge of the lace.

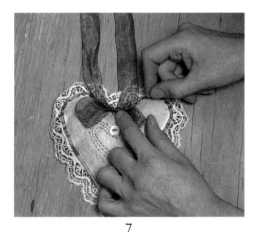

7

Finish with a ribbon bow, arranging it so the long tails are upwards as these can then be joined to form a loop for hanging on coat hangers in the wardrobe.

Lavender Bag

Stars are frequently found in patchwork, and the LeMoyne Star is a popular pattern. To achieve this tricky eight-seam join, which meets in the centre of the star, work slowly and carefully.

MATERIALS

*tracing paper and pencil
thin card
craft knife
scraps of silk organza in 3 colours
rotary cutter (optional)
scrap of lining silk
dressmaker's pins
sewing machine and matching thread
needle and matching thread
dried lavender
ribbon*

LeMoyne Star

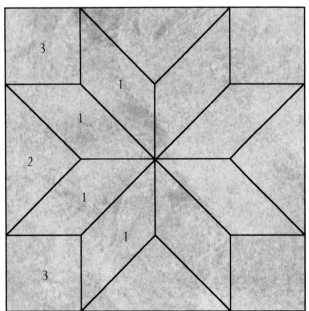

1

Trace the star and make the templates. For each star (you will need 2) cut out 8 pieces from template 1 in 2 colours and 4 pieces each from templates 2 and 3 in the third colour. Use a rotary cutter if you wish.

2

To make the star, with right sides facing, pin together 2 piece 1s that are in different colours, and stitch them together. Make another pair to match. Press the seams flat but not open, to reduce bulk.

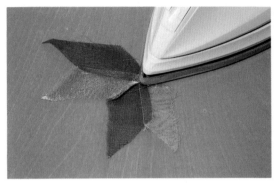

3

Join the 2 pairs together, carefully matching the centre seams, pin and stitch. Press the seams flat. Make the other half of the star in the same way.

4

To set in a square 3, swivel the square to match the corner points and pin to the angled edge. To set in a triangle 2, match the corner points and pin to the angled edge. Stitch and press.

5

Set in 3 more triangles to make the patch. Make a second patch in the same way. Measure one side and cut 2 pieces of organza to this length but 5 cm/2 in wide. Stitch one to the top of each patch and press. Right sides facing, stitch around the base and sides of the bag and turn through. Fold a 1 cm/½ in hem around the top of the bag, press and top stitch. Fill the bag with dried lavender and tie with a ribbon bow.

Little House Key Ring

Keep your keys safe on this pretty key ring. The little house is made from tiny patched pieces which are appliquéd on to the fob.

MATERIALS

tracing paper, paper and pencil
dressmaker's scissors
red and blue gingham and red fabric scraps
needle and tacking thread
iron
cream cotton fabric, 10 × 32 cm / 4 × 13 in
wadding (batting), 10 × 15 cm / 4 × 6 in red, cream and blue sewing threads
key ring

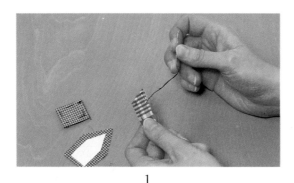

1

Trace the design on to paper and cut out 2 windows, 2 walls, 2 chimneys, a roof and a door. Cut out in scraps of fabric with a 6 mm / ¼ in seam allowance. Tack to the backing papers and press.

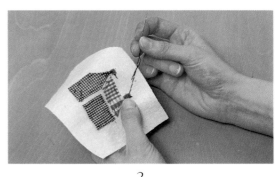

2

Cut 2 main pieces from cream cotton fabric and 2 from wadding (batting). Tack the house in sections to one piece of cotton fabric, removing the paper as you go. Slip stitch the pieces in position with matching thread.

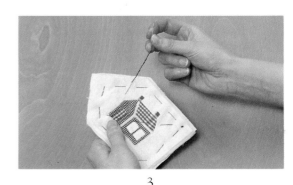

3

Sandwich the wadding between the appliquéd and plain fabrics, and tack through all the layers to secure.

4

Cut 3 bias strips in gingham. Press under 6 mm / ¼ in turnings and bind the raw edges leaving 2.5 cm / 1 in free either side of the point. Thread the ends through the key ring and slip stitch together.

Key fob and motif template

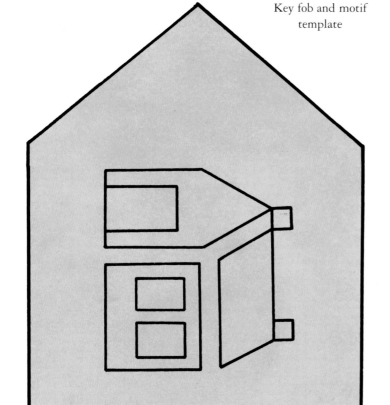

Patchwork Cards

Patchwork designs like this Northumberland star can be used to make unusual gift cards. Work out a design on paper and trace the design on to the bonding web.

MATERIALS

tracing paper and pencil
ruler
iron-on fusible bonding
web
iron
assortment of fabric scraps
dressmaker's scissors
coloured card
metallic marker pen

1

Cut out the shapes. Iron the shapes on to the back of the fabric scraps and cut out without a seam allowance.

2

Lay the shapes on the card to make up the design. Cover with a clean cloth and iron. Outline the design with the marker pen.

Photo Frame

Blue and white checked fabrics make a fresh-looking border for a favourite photo.

Cut out a centre square from one piece of the card, leaving a 5 cm / 2 in border. Cut 4 gingham border strips 27 × 10 cm / 11 × 4 in. Cut 4 7 cm / 3 in squares of cream fabric and press under the raw edges to make 5 cm / 2 in squares. Iron bonding web to the reverse of the fabric scraps and cut out 4 flower shapes and 4 pairs of leaves.

MATERIALS

2 pieces of thick card,
22 cm / 8 in square
craft knife
scraps of blue and white
gingham and checked
fabric
dressmaker's scissors
scraps of cream fabric
iron
iron-on fusible bonding
web
assorted scraps of fabric for
the flowers
green and navy embroidery
threads
crewel needle
dressmaker's pins
needle and matching
thread
fabric glue
double-sided tape

1

Pull off the backing from the bonding web and iron a flower and leaves motif to the corner of each cream square, as shown. Embroider the stems in green thread. Cut 4 narrow strips of checked fabric 27 cm / 11 in long and press under the long edges. Pin and stitch along the centre of the gingham borders.

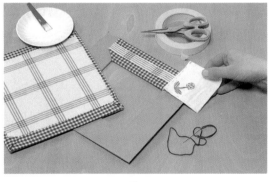

2

Glue the cream squares to the corners of the frame, with the flowers facing outwards. Work large stab stitches round the squares in navy thread. Fold the border fabric to the back of the frame and secure with tape. Cover the other piece of card with fabric, then slip stitch the 2 pieces together round 3 sides, leaving one side open.

Gift Tag

This gift tag would also look very pretty hanging from the wardrobe door key.

MATERIALS

*8 cm / 3 in square of
18-count Rustico, Zweigart
E3292
stranded cotton DMC nos.
500, 550, 552, 554,
3363, 3364 and 3820
tapestry needle
15 cm / 6 in square of
natural handmade paper
craft knife
safety ruler
scissors
all-purpose glue
single hole punch
two reinforcing rings*

DMC	
⚌	552
⠿	554
⧓	3820
◈	3363
⧄	3364

Backstitch

— 550

— 500

☆ Middle point

1

Beginning in the centre of the canvas, work the cross stitch design using two strands of cotton, and the backstitch using a single strand.

2

To make up, cut 2 tag shapes out of the handmade paper, and with the craft knife, cut an opening in one. Stick the embroidered panel in the window and trim the edges of the fabric. Glue the back of the label in place.

3

Once the glue has dried, punch a hole at the end of the tag and stick the reinforcing rings on either side. Plait a length of dark green, gold and purple threads together and loop them through the hole to finish off the tag.

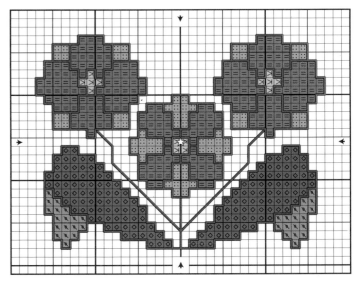

Greetings Card

1

Tack the fine calico to the back of the silk and fit into a hoop. Tack the waste canvas onto the middle of the fabric, keeping the canvas in line with the grain of the fabric. Mark the centre of the canvas. Stitch the design using 2 strands of cotton. When complete, fray and pull out the canvas threads one at a time. Press on the reverse side and trim to fit behind the opening.

2

To make up, stick tape round the inside edge of the opening and position the embroidery on top. Stick the backing card in position. Use double-sided tape to assemble because glue tends to buckle the card.

MATERIALS

20 cm / 8 in square of fine calico
20 cm / 8 in square of cream silk dupion (mid-weight silk)
tacking thread
needle
embroidery hoop
13 × 15 cm / 5 × 6 in 14-count waste canvas
stranded cotton DMC nos. 221, 223, 224, 744, 3362 and 3363
embroidery needle
scissors
craft card with an 8 × 12 cm / 3 × 4¾ in aperture
double-sided tape

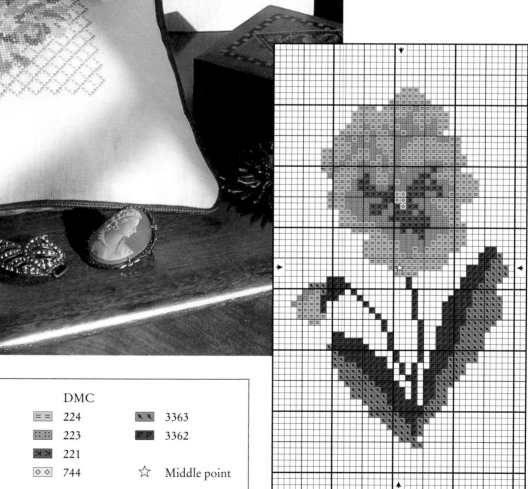

DMC		
═ ═ 224	◣ ◥	3363
⋰ ⋰ 223	◪ ◪	3362
► ► 221		
◇ ◇ 744	☆	Middle point

Handkerchief Case

*No more scrabbling in the drawer – this pretty and practical pouch with its
dainty trellis pattern will keep all your hankies tidy.*

MATERIALS

*two 53 × 20 cm / 21 × 8 in
pieces of white 36-count
evenweave linen
tacking thread
needle
embroidery hoop
stranded cotton DMC nos.
221, 223, 224, 225, 501,
502, 503, 832, 834, 839,
3032 and 3782
tapestry needle
pins
sewing machine
sewing thread
scissors
1 m / 1 yd wine-coloured
piping*

1

Tack a guideline crossways 10 cm / 4 in from one
end of the linen. Mark the centre of this line and
begin the cross stitch. The bottom of the design
is the side nearest the raw edge.

2

Work the design using a single strand of cotton
over 2 threads of linen. When the embroidery
is complete, press on the reverse side.
A magnifying glass might help.

DMC		DMC	
– –	501	5 5	225
1 1	502	7 7	839
1 1	503	9 9	832
2 2	221	II II	834
3 3	223	◇ ◇	3032
4 4	224	⚅ ⚅	3782

☆   Middle point

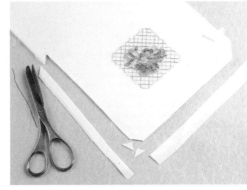

3

To make up, pin the 2 linen panels together with
the embroidery to the inside. With a 2 cm / ¾ in
seam allowance, sew all round, leaving a gap on
one side for turning. Trim the seams and across
the corners, then turn through.

4

Fold the panel in 3 and tack along the fold
lines. Pin the piping to the inside of the front
flap and down both sides as far as the second
fold line. Turn under the ends and slip stitch
the piping in place. Slip stitch the side seams
to complete the case.

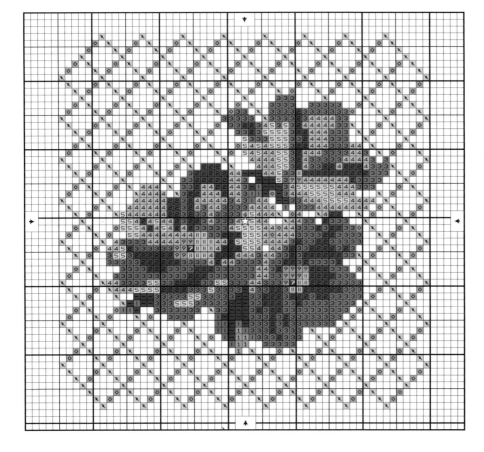

Birth Keepsake

This gift has a practical use as a pincushion but could be filled with lavender instead.

MATERIALS

*15 cm / 6 in square of white
25-count Lugana, Zweigart
E3835
tacking thread
needle
embroidery hoop
stranded cotton DMC nos.
350, 47 and 3326
tapestry needle
118 small pink beads
scissors
15 cm / 6 in square of white
backing fabric
sewing machine
sewing thread
2 14 cm / 5 ½ in squares of
wadding (batting)
pins
75 cm / 30 in white
crocheted lace edging
(dipped in weak tea to
colour slightly)*

1

Tack guidelines in both directions across the centre of the linen. Work the cross stitch using 3 strands of cotton over 2 threads. Once complete, sew a bead over the top of each stitch in the pink hearts. Use a double length of thread and begin with a secure knot.

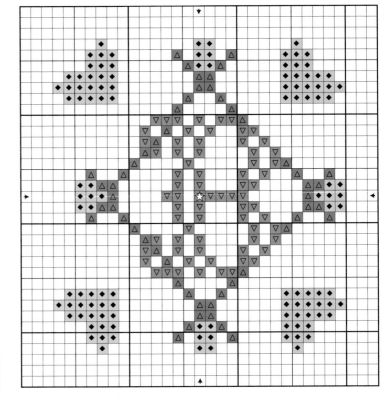

DMC	
▽▽	350
△△	472
◆◆	3326

☆ Middle point

2

To make up, block the design if necessary and trim away the excess fabric leaving 4 cm / 1½ in round the cross stitch. Cut the backing fabric to match and stitch the embroidery and backing fabric together, with right sides facing, leaving a gap along one side. Trim the seams and across the corners to reduce bulk.

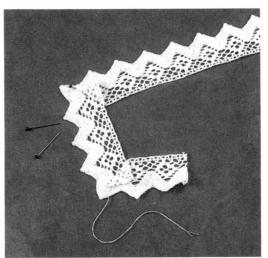

3

Tuck the wadding (batting) into the cushion and slip stitch to close. Mitre the corners of the lace one at a time by folding and stitching diagonally on the wrong side. Each side should be about 13 cm / 5 in long. Join the lace ends and pin round the cushion 1 cm / ½ in in from the edge. Stitch neatly in place.

Baby Birth Gift

Celebrate a baby's birth by giving the parents this very pretty arrangement in an unusual but practical container. The display incorporates double tulips, ranunculus, phlox and spray roses, with small leaves of pittosporum.

The choice of soft, subtle colours means that the arrangement is suitable for either a boy or a girl. There is also the added bonus of the beautiful scents of the phlox and dried lavender. Since the arrangement has its own container, it is particularly convenient for a recipient in hospital, avoiding, as it does, the need to find a vase. Finally, the container can be kept and used again after the life of the display.

MATERIALS

block plastic foam
scissors
small galvanized metal bucket
bunch pittosporum
15 stems pale pink 'Angelique' tulips
5 stems white spray roses
10 stems white ranunculus
10 stems white phlox
bunch dried lavender
ribbon, purple and white check

1

Soak the plastic foam in water, cut it to fit the small metal bucket and wedge it firmly in place. Cut the pittosporum to a length of 12 cm/4¾ in and clean the leaves from the lower part of the stems. Push the stems into the plastic foam to create an overall domed foliage outline within which the flowers can be arranged.

2

Cut the 'Angelique' tulips to a stem length of 10 cm/4 in and distribute them evenly throughout the foliage. Cut individual off-shoots from the main stems of the spray roses to a length of 10 cm/4 in, and arrange throughout the display, with full blooms at the centre and buds around the outside.

3

Cut the ranunculus and phlox to a stem length of 10 cm/ 4 in and distribute both throughout the display. Cut the lavender to a stem length of 12 cm/4¾ in and arrange in groups of 3 stems evenly throughout the flowers and foliage. Tie the ribbon around the bucket and finish in a generous bow.

Planted Basket for Baby

This display of pot plants in a basket makes a lovely gift to celebrate the birth of a baby. It is easy to make and is a long-lasting alternative to a cut-flower arrangement.

The combination of two simple and delicate white plants, baby cyclamen and lily-of-the-valley, gives the design charm and purity, indeed everything about it says 'baby'.

MATERIALS

*wire basket
2 handfuls Spanish moss
cellophane
scissors
3 pots miniature white
cyclamen
3 pots lily-of-the-valley
paper ribbon*

1

Line the wire basket with generous handfuls of Spanish moss, then carefully line the moss with cellophane. Trim the cellophane so that it fits neatly around the rim of the basket.

2

Remove the plants from their pots carefully. Loosen the soil and the roots a little before planting them in the basket, alternating the cyclamen with the lily-of-the-valley and adding more moss if necessary.

3

Make sure that the plants are firmly bedded in the basket. Make two small bows from the paper ribbon, smoothing open the ends, and attach one to each side of the basket at the base of the handle.

Herb Bath-bag

Enjoy a traditional herbal bath by filling a fine muslin bag with relaxing herbs, tying it to the taps and letting the hot water run through. This draw-string design means it can be re-used time after time, if you keep refilling it with new herbs. Chamomile and hops are relaxing; basil and sage are invigorating.

MATERIALS

silky muslin, about 30 × 40 cm / 12 × 16 in
pins, needle and thread

scissors
fabric scraps, for casing
1 m / 39 in narrow ribbon

safety pin
herb bath-mix or any combination of dried herbs

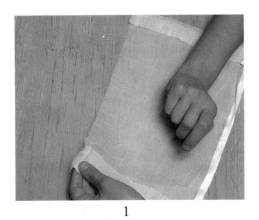

1

With right sides facing, fold over about 5 cm / 2 in of the silky muslin at both short ends, pin and stitch each side. Trim the seams. Turn right-side out.

2

Turn in and hem the raw edges of the folded-over ends.

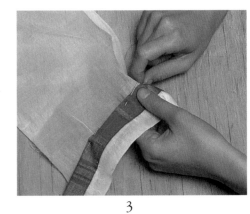

3

Cut two strips of cotton fabric about 2.5 cm / 1 in wide and as long as the width of the muslin, with about 5 mm / ¼ in extra for turnings all round. Iron a hem along both long edges. Turn in and hem the ends, then pin one casing on the right side of the muslin so the bottom edge of the casing lines up with the hem line. Neatly stitch the casing in place along both long seams. Repeat with the other casing.

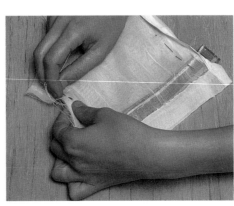

4

With right sides together, fold the muslin in half so the casings line up. Stitch the side seams from the bottom edge of the casing to the bottom edge of the bag. Trim the seams.

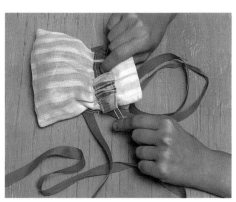

5

Cut the ribbon in half, attach a safety pin to one end and use this to thread the ribbon through the casing so both ends finish up at the same side. Remove the safety pin.

6

Attach the safety pin to one end of the other piece of ribbon and thread it through the casing in the other direction so the ends finish up at the other side. Fill with herbs ready for use.

Shell Pot

Decorate a flowerpot with shells and some old netting, and then use it to hold plants, pencils, paintbrushes, strings, ribbon, or any paraphernalia that needs to be kept in check. It's a pretty and inexpensive way to make a very special container.

MATERIALS

small net bag
flowerpot, 18 cm / 7 in tall
scissors
hot glue gun and glue sticks
thick string
small cowrie shells
cockle shells
starfish or similar central motif

1

Slip the net bag over the flowerpot and trim the top edge. Secure it by gluing on a length of string.

2

Using a glue gun, position a row of cowrie shells along the top edge.

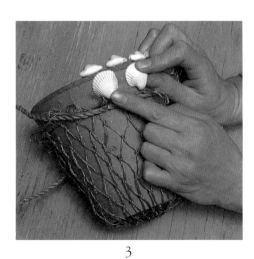

3

Glue cockle shells around the rim; position the starfish and four cockle shells at the front.

Shell Box

A simple brown-paper box takes on a South-Seas feel when decorated with half-cowries. Available from craft shops, their flattened bottoms make them easy to stick to surfaces. Here, some have also been strung together to make a toggle for fastening.

MATERIALS

MATERIALS

*hot glue gun and glue sticks
raffia
small buff box
half-cowrie shells
upholstery needle*

1

Glue a loop of raffia from the bottom of the box, up the back and along the top.

2

Tie half-cowries into a bunch on a length of raffia, tying each one in separately. Leave a short length of raffia free. Pierce the front of the box with an upholstery needle and thread the raffia through. Knot it on the inside.

3

Glue on a pattern of half-cowries to decorate the outside of the box.

Shell Candle Centrepiece

An old flowerpot, scallop shells gleaned from the fishmonger or kitchen and smaller shells picked up from the beach make up a fabulous, Venus-inspired table-centrepiece. Either put a candle in the centre, as here, or fill it with dried fruits or flowers.

MATERIALS

hot glue gun and glue sticks
8 curved scallop shells
flowerpot, 18 cm / 7 in tall
bag of cockle shells
4 flat scallop shells
newspaper, florist's foam or
other packing material
saucer
candle
raffia

1

Generously apply hot glue to the inside lower edge of a large curved scallop shell. Hold it in place on the rim of the pot for a few seconds until it is firmly stuck. Continue sticking shells to the top of the pot, arranging them so they overlap slightly, until the whole of the rim has been covered.

2

In the same way, glue a cockle shell where two scallops join. Continue all around the pot.

3

Place another row of cockles at the joins of the first row. Glue flat scallop shells face upwards to the bottom of the pot, first at the front, then at the back, and then the two sides, to ensure the pot stands straight.

4

Fill the pot with packing material and place a saucer on top of this. Stand a candle on the saucer.

5

Tie raffia around the pot where it joins the stand.

6

Decorate the stand with a few more cockles, if you like. Stand a few more curved scallop shells inside the original row to create a fuller, more petalled shape.

Shell Mirror

The subtle rose-pinks of ordinary scallop shells, picked up from the fishmonger, make for an easy, eye-catching mirror surround that's also environmentally friendly. Here, four large ones have been used at the corners with smaller ones filling in the sides.

MATERIALS

sandpaper
mirror in wooden frame
paint
paintbrush
4 large flat scallop shells
hot glue gun and glue sticks
10 small flat scallop shells
seagrass string
2 metal eyelets

1

Sand down and paint the mirror frame with the colour of your choice.

2

Position the large scallop shells at the corners of the mirror, using the hot glue.

3

In the same way, glue three of the smaller scallop shells to each side of the mirror.

4

Attach two of the smaller scallop shells to the top of the mirror and two to the bottom.

5

Plait three lengths of seagrass string to make a hanger.

6

Screw metal eyelets into each side of the frame at the back, and tie the hanger on to these.

354

Filigree Leaf Wrap

Even the most basic brown parcel-paper can take on a very special look. Use a gilded skeletonized leaf and gold twine in combination with brown paper: chunky coir string would give a more robust look.

MATERIALS

picture framer's wax gilt
large skeletonized leaf
brown paper
sticky tape
gold twine
hot glue gun and glue sticks,
if necessary

1

Rub wax gilt into the skeletonized leaf.

2

Wrap the parcel in the brown paper and rub gilt wax on to the corners. Tie the parcel with gold twine, bringing the two ends together and tying a knot. Fray the ends to create a tassle effect. Slip the leaf under the twine, securing it with glue at each end if necessary.

Fruit and Foliage Gift-wraps

Here, gilded brown parcel-paper provides a fitting background for a decoration of leaves and dried fruit slices.

MATERIALS

brown paper
sticky tape
picture framer's wax gilt
seagrass string
hot glue gun and glue sticks
dried fruit slices
preserved leaves

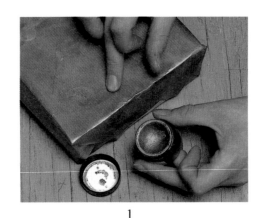

1

Wrap the parcel with brown paper and rub in gilt wax, paying special attention to the corners.

2

Tie the parcel with seagrass string, and then glue a different dried fruit or leaf to each quarter.

Tissue Rosette Gift-wrap

*Tissue papers make a fabulous foundation for any gift-wrapping; they come in
a glorious array of colours, and they softly take to any shape.*

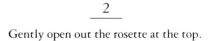

*tissue paper in 2 shades
co-ordinating twine*

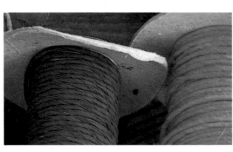

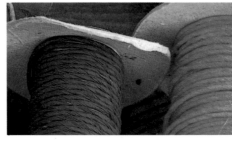

1

Place a cylindrical gift in the centre of two
squares of tissue, one laid on top of the other.
Gather the tissue up and tie it with twine.

2

Gently open out the rosette at the top.

Lavender Tissue Gift-wrap

*Bunches of lavender add a real country touch to tissue gift-wrap,
and become part of the gift.*

*dried lavender
twine
tissue paper in 2 shades
sticky tape
glue*

1

Make two bunches of lavender and tie them
with twine to form a cross.

2

Wrap the parcel in the darker toned tissue
paper, and then wrap it with the paler tissue,
cut to form an envelope. Glue the lavender
to the front of the parcel.

Dried Flower Gift Wrap

To make a present extra special why not make the wrapping part of the gift? The display is effectively a dried flower corsage but used to embellish gift wrapping.

It takes a little time to produce but its natural, warm, earthy colours make this a delightful enhancement well worth the effort, and something to keep.

MATERIALS

dried sunflower head
scissors
stub wires
small dried pomegranate
3 small pieces dried fungi
(graded in size)
3 slices dried orange
(graded in size)
silver stub wires
florist's tape
gift-wrapped present
raffia

1

Cut the sunflower to a stem length of 2.5 cm/1 in and double leg mount on a stub wire. Single leg mount the pomegranates on stub wire. Double leg mount the small pieces of fungi on stub wires and mount the orange slices on silver stub wires.

2

Wrap all the wired materials with tape, then attach the 3 orange slices to one side of the sunflower and pomegranate, then attach the 3 layers of fungi on the other side. Bind all these in place using the silver wire or reel wire if you prefer.

3

Trim the wire stems to a length of 5 cm/2 in and tape together with florist's tape. Tie the raffia around the present and push the wired stem of the decoration under the raffia knot. Secure in place with another stub wire or pieces of double-sided tape.

Dried Flowers as a Gift

This is a great way to present dried flowers as a gift. Treat them as you would a tied bouquet of cut fresh flowers, prettily wrapped in tissue paper and tied with a large bow.

The deep pink mixture of exotic and garden flowers – protea and amaranthus with peonies and larkspur – makes this a floral gift anyone would be thrilled to receive.

MATERIALS

10 small dried pink
Protea compacta *buds*
10 stems dried pink larkspur
10 stems dried pink peonies
10 stems dried green amaranthus
raffia
scissors
2 sheets blue tissue paper
pink ribbon

1

Lay out the dried materials so that they are all easily accessible. Start the bouquet with a dried protea held in your hand, add a stem of larkspur, a stem of peony and a stem of amaranthus, all the while turning the bunch with every addition.

2

Continue until all the dried materials have been used. Tie with raffia at the binding point – where the stems cross each other. Trim the stem ends so that their length is approximately one-third of the overall height of the finished bouquet.

3

Lay the sheets of tissue paper on a flat surface and place the bouquet diagonally across the tissue. Wrap the tissue paper around the flowers, overlapping it at the front. Tie securely at the binding point with a ribbon and form a large, floppy bow.

Leafy Pictures

Delicate skeletonized leaves come in such breathtakingly exquisite forms that they deserve to be shown off. Mount them on hand-made papers and frame them to make simple yet stunning natural collages.

MATERIALS

*wooden picture frame
sandpaper
paint
paintbrush
backing paper
pencil
scissors
skeletonized leaf
picture framer's wax gilt
hot glue gun and glue sticks
mounting paper*

1

Take the frame apart and sand it down to provide a key before painting. A translucent colourwash has been used for painting here, but any paint will do.

2

Allow the paint to dry, then sand the paint back so you're left with a wooden frame with shading in the mouldings, plus a veil of colour on the surface.

3

Use the hardboard back of the frame as a template for the backing paper. Draw around it with a pencil to form a cutting line.

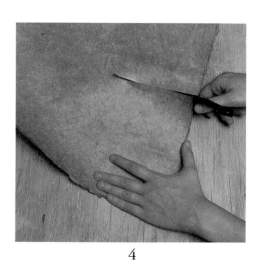

4

Cut the backing paper out.

5

Prepare the leaf by rubbing with picture framer's wax gilt. This does take a little time as the gilt has to be well worked in.

6

Stick the backing paper on the frame back, glue the mounting paper in the centre and attach the leaf on to that. Here, the leaf is centred with the stalk breaking the edge of the mounting paper. Finally, put the frame back together.

Spicy Pomander

Pomanders were originally nature's own air fresheners. The traditional orange pomanders are fairly tricky to do, because the critical drying process can so easily go wrong, leading to mouldy oranges. This one, made of cloves and cardamom pods offers none of those problems, and makes a refreshing change in soft muted colours.

MATERIALS

cloves
florist's dry foam ball,
about 7.5 cm / 3 in diameter
hot glue gun and glue sticks
green cardamom pods
raffia
florist's stub wire

1

Start by making a single line of cloves all around the circumference of the ball. Make another one in the other direction, so you have divided the ball into quarters.

2

Make a line of cloves on both sides of the original lines to make broad bands of cloves quartering the ball.

3

Starting at the top of the first quarter, glue cardamom pods over the foam, methodically working in rows to create a neat effect. Repeat on the other three quarters.

4

Tie a bow in the centre of a length of raffia. Pass a stub wire through the knot and twist the ends together.

5

Fix the bow to the top of the ball
using the stub wire.

6

Join the two loose ends in a knot
for hanging the pomander.

Tulip Pomander

In Elizabethan times pomanders were filled with herbs or scented flowers and carried to perfume the air. Today the pomander is more likely to be a bridesmaid's accessory.

The pomander illustrated does not boast exotic aromas but it does have a pleasing variety of surface textures, ranging from the spiky inner petals of double tulips through the beady black berries of myrtle to the softness of grey moss, all set against bands of smooth satin ribbon. It would be a charming alternative to the bridesmaid's traditional posy.

MATERIALS

plastic foam ball
ribbon
scissors
20 heads 'Appleblossom'
double tulips
bunch myrtle
stub wires
good handful
reindeer moss

1

Soak the foam ball in water. Tie the ribbon around the ball, starting at the top and crossing at the bottom, and then tying at the top to divide the ball into four equal segments. Make sure there is enough ribbon to tie into a bow.

2

Cut the tulips to a stem length of about 2.5 cm/1 in and push into the foam in vertical lines at the centre of each segment. Hold the tulip heads gently while positioning them on the foam ball to avoid the heads breaking off.

3

Push sprigs of myrtle into the foam to form lines on either side of each line of tulips.

4

Use bent stub wires to cover all remaining exposed areas of the foam ball with moss.

Cinnamon and Orange Ring

The warm colours, spicy smell and culinary content of this small decorated ring make it perfect for the wall of a kitchen. The display is not complicated to make but requires nimble fingers to handle the very small pieces of cinnamon used. These pieces have to be tightly packed together to achieve the right effect and attaching so much cinnamon to the plastic foam may cause it to collapse. To prevent this happening, you can glue the foam ring to a piece of card cut to the same outline before you begin.

MATERIALS

glue gun and glue sticks
5 dried oranges
plastic foam ring for
dried flowers, 13 cm /
5¼ in diameter
20 cinnamon sticks

1

Apply glue to the bases of the dried oranges and space them evenly around the foam ring. Break the cinnamon sticks into 2–4 cm /¾-1½ in pieces.

2

Apply glue to the bottom of the pieces of cinnamon and push them into the foam between the dried oranges, keeping them close together.

3

Glue a line of the cinnamon pieces around both the inside and outside edges of the ring to cover the plastic foam completely.

Classic Orange and Clove Pomander

This classic pomander starts as fresh material that, as you use it, dries into a beautiful old-fashioned decoration with a warm, spicy smell evocative of mulled wine and the festive season. Make several pomanders using different ribbons and display them in a bowl, hang them around the house, use them as Christmas decorations or even hang them in the airing-cupboard to perfume your sheets and towels.

MATERIALS

3 small firm oranges
3 types of ribbon
scissors
cloves

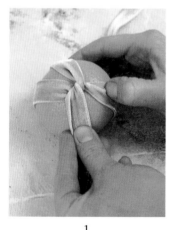

1

Tie a ribbon around an orange, crossing it over at the base so that it neatly quarters the orange.

2

Finish off at the top of the orange by tying the ribbon into a bow. Clip the ends of the ribbon to prevent it from fraying.

3

Starting at the edges of the areas, push the sharp ends of the exposed cloves into the orange and continue until it is completely covered.

Red Tied Sheaf

A tied sheaf of flowers arranged in the hand makes an attractive and informal wall decoration. To make a successful wall hanging, the sheaf must be made with a flat back, while at the same time it should have a profiled front to add visual interest. This richly coloured display would make a wonderful house-warming gift.

The demanding aspect of the construction of the sheaf is the technique of spiralling the materials in your hand. But this display is relatively small, which simplifies the task.

MATERIALS

50 stems *dried lavender*
10 stems **Protea** compacta
buds
10 stems *natural ti tree*
15 stems *dried red roses*
twine
scissors
satin ribbon, 5 cm / 2 in

1

Lay out the materials so that they are easily accessible and separate the lavender into 10 smaller groups. Hold the longest protea in your hand, and behind it add a slightly longer stem of ti tree, then hold rose stems to either side of the protea, both slightly shorter than the first. Continue adding materials in a regular repeating sequence to the growing bunch in your hand, spiralling the stems as you do so.

2

When all the materials have been used, tie the sheath with twine at the binding point. Trim the stems so that they make up about one-third of the overall length of the sheaf.

3

To finish the display make a separate ribbon bow and attach it to the sheaf at the binding point.

Rose and Clove Pomander

This pomander is a decadent display of rose heads massed in a ball. But it has a secret: cloves hidden between the rose heads, giving the pomander its lasting spicy perfume. It relies for its impact on the use of large quantities of tightly packed flowers, all of the same type and colour.

Almost profligate in its use of materials, this pomander is quick to make and would be a wonderful and very special gift.

1

Fold the ribbon in half and double leg mount its cut ends together with a stub wire. To form a ribbon handle, push the wires right through the plastic foam ball so that they come out the other end, and pull the projecting wires so that the double leg mounted part of the ribbon becomes firmly embedded in the plastic foam. Turn the excess wire back into the foam.

MATERIALS

*ribbon 40 × 2.5 cm /
16 × 1 in stub wire
plastic foam ball for dried
flowers, approximately
10 cm / 4 in diameter
scissors
100 stems dried roses
200 cloves*

2

Cut the stems of the dried rose heads to a length of approximately 2.5 cm / 1 in. Starting at the top of the plastic foam ball, push the stems of the dried rose heads into the foam to form a tightly packed circle around the base of the ribbon handle. As you work, push a clove into the plastic foam between each rose head. Continue forming concentric circles of rose heads and cloves around the plastic foam ball until it is completely covered.

Herbal Tablepiece

*Extremely strong-smelling herbs should be avoided for table centres because their
fragrance may overpower the flavour of the meal. However, gently scented herbs make a
delightful table decoration.*

MATERIALS

*shallow basket without handle
2 blocks florist's foam for dried
flowers
florist's wire
florist's tape
scissors
2 bunches cardoon thistles
3 large ivory candles
bunches of dried herbs, where
possible in flower, including oregano,
lavender, marjoram and fennel*

Caution: make sure that this arrangement
is never left unattended while the candles
are alight.

1

Fill the basket with foam, wedging it into
position. Group the cardoon heads into
3 positions in the foam. Make hairpins
from lengths of wire, and tape 3 hairpins
around the base of each candle. Place the
candles into the foam.

2

Wire small bunches of lavender and
marjoram, and spread evenly around the
arrangement. Place the fennel flower heads
in the arrangement singly or wired together
in groups, depending upon the space you
wish to fill.

Dried Herbal Topiary Tree

Topiary trees are an attractive way of displaying flowers and natural objects. This design includes small terracotta pots, which add to the textural interest in the top of the tree.

MATERIALS

large terracotta pot for the base
cement or plaster of Paris
piece of tree branch for the trunk
13 cm / 5 in ball of florist's foam for dried flowers
small pieces of similar foam
2 large bunches of glycerined copper beech foliage or other preserved foliage
scissors
heavy-gauge florist's wire
wire cutters
12 miniature terracotta pots
2 bunches golden rod
light florist's wire
hot glue gun (optional)
2 bunches poppy heads

1

Cover the hole in the large terracotta pot and half fill with wet cement or plaster of Paris. As the cement begins to harden, stand the branch in the pot to form the trunk. Leave to dry for at least 48 hours before proceeding to the next step.

2

Press the foam ball on to the trunk, making sure it is firmly in place, but not so far down that the trunk comes out the other side of the ball. Cover the cement in the base with pieces of foam.

3

Cover the ball and base with pieces of copper beech or other preserved foliage. Thread heavy-gauge wire through the holes in the small pots and make a stem so they can be attached to the tree and pressed into the foam.

4

Arrange the pots through the tree and base, and fill with small wired bunches of golden rod, trimming with scissors where needed. These can be glued into position if necessary. Finally, add the poppy heads.

Herbal Christmas Wreath

Orange slices can be dried on a wire rack in an oven at the lowest possible setting for several hours until they are crisp. They should then be carefully varnished with a clear, matt varnish so that they cannot reabsorb moisture from the atmosphere.

MATERIALS

*few stems fresh holly
2 sprays fresh conifer
scissors
hot glue gun
wreath ring, approximately 23 cm /
9 in in diameter
gold spray paint
5 cm / 2 in terracotta pot
broken pieces of terracotta pot
7 ears of wheat, sprayed gold
small bunch dried sage
small bunch oregano
florist's wire
3 dried orange slices*

1

Attach the holly and conifer to the ring using the hot glue gun. Cover approximately half the ring.

2

In a well-ventilated area, spray a little gold paint on to the pot and pieces of pot and glue them to the design. Add the ears of wheat. Make small bunches of sage and tuck those among the pieces of broken pot.

3

Make a chunky bunch of the dried oregano, wiring it together. Glue into the main pot in the centre of the design. Cut the orange slices into quarters and glue those into the arrangement. The fresh ingredients will dry on the wreath and look most attractive.

Dried Herbal Posy

This posy could be given as a present or to say 'thank you'. It would also make a very pretty dressing table decoration. The ingredients are dried, so it can be made well in advance or you could make a few to have ready to give to guests.

MATERIALS

small bunch dried red roses
florist's wire
small bunch alchemilla
small bunch marjoram
cotton posy frill, deep pink
3 sprays dried bay
hot glue gun
florist's tape
scissors
ribbon, as preferred

1

Start with a small cluster of red roses, binding them with wire to form a centre. Add some alchemilla, binding gently but firmly in the same spot.

2

Bind in some marjoram and then more red roses and alchemilla, until you are happy with the size of the posy. Carefully push the stems of the paper posy through the centre of the posy frill.

3

Separate the bay leaves from the stems and glue them in, one at a time, through the arrangement and around the edge as a border.

4

Push the posy frill up towards the flowers and fasten with tape. Tie ribbon around the stem of the posy and make a bow.

Bath Bags

These are much more fun than putting commercial bubble bath into the water. Tie them over the taps and make sure the hot running water is going through them — this will release lovely herbal scents that relax and comfort you.

INGREDIENTS

3 × 23 cm / 9 in diameter circles of
muslin
6 tbsp bran
1 tbsp lavender flowers
1 tbsp chamomile flowers
1 tbsp rosemary tips
3 small rubber bands
3 m / 3 yd narrow ribbon or twine

1

Place 2 tbsp bran in the centre of each
circle of muslin. Add the lavender to one
bag, the chamomile to a second and the
rosemary to the third, mixing the herbs
through the bran.

2

Gather each circle of material up and close
with a rubber band. Then tie a reasonable
length of ribbon or twine around each bag
to make a loop so that the bag can be hung
from the hot tap in the stream of water.

Herb Corsages

Making your own buttonhole or corsage is easy. Tiny posy frills are obtainable from specialist floral suppliers or you could use the centre of a small paper doily.

MATERIALS

medium-sized flower
sprig of any herb with attractive leaves
thin florist's wire
miniature posy frill or cut-down doily
florist's tape

1

For a centrepiece, you could use a rose or small spray carnation. wrap some herb foliage around it – fresh green parsley would look good – and then bind it tightly with thin wire.

2

Push the stems through the centre of the frill and tape them together, covering the stems all the way down. Other combinations could include rosemary, sage, lavender or box.

Scented Valentine Heart

Valentine gifts in the shape of a heart are always popular. This heart-shaped gift box with dried flower and herb decoration on the lid is accompanied by a matching wreath made with fresh leaves and flowers that remain attractive when they dry.

MATERIALS

heart-shaped box
broad and narrow ribbon
hot glue gun
5 dried roses
dried bay leaves
bunch of dried goldenrod
heart-shaped wreath form
houttuynia leaves
'Minuet' roses
sprig of fresh lavender

1

Start decorating the gift box by making a large bow with broad ribbon. Then glue the dried ingredients onto the box to resemble a bunch of flowers. Stick the bow on top.

2

Wrap some narrow ribbon around the wreath form and secure with glue. Add a few houttuynia leaves (this variety is *H. cordata*), some 'Minuet' roses and fresh lavender. These could be attached with wire instead of glue if you prefer.

Herb-decorated Crackers

Home-made touches are important at Christmas, as they add the final touch to a family celebration. These crackers are easy to decorate and could be made by adults and children together. Buy ready-decorated crackers and remove the commercial trimming.

MATERIALS

crackers
narrow ribbon, as preferred
scissors
small sprigs of various herbs
pretzels, gilded rosehips
hot glue gun or general-purpose
adhesive

1

Tie the ends of the crackers with ribbon, making attractive bows.

2

Make small posies of herbs and glue them to the central part of the crackers. Add pretzels and gilded rosehips.

379

Scented Pressed Herb Diary

A notebook or diary can be scented by placing it in a box with a strong lavender sachet, or a cotton-wool ball sprinkled with a few drops of essential oil. Leave it in the sealed box for a month or so to impart a sweet, lingering fragrance. Try to find a very plain diary or notebook which does not have lettering or decoration on the cover, as these would spoil the design. Use a plastic film made for covering books.

MATERIALS

*pressed leaves and flowers, such as
borage flowers, alchemilla flowers
and small leaves, daisies, single roses
and forget-me-nots
plain diary or notebook
tweezers
large tapestry needle
white latex adhesive
clear plastic film
iron and cloth pad (optional)*

1

Start by arranging a selection of pressed leaves on the front of the diary or notebook, using the tweezers for positioning.

2

Continue to build up your design by adding the pressed flower heads.

3

Once you are happy with the design stick it down, using a large tapestry needle and latex adhesive. Slide the needle into the glue and then, without moving the design, place a small amount of glue under each leaf and petal so that they are secure. Cover with clear film. Some kinds of film needs heating, and you should iron gently with a cloth pad between the film and the iron.

Pressed Herb Cards

A home-made card is always one that will be treasured long after the occasion has passed. Although it takes time and trouble to make your own cards, it is always worth the effort to give someone something with your personal touch.

MATERIALS

*pressed herbs and flowers, such as
blue cornflower, ivy, rosemary and
borage
blank greetings card
large tapestry needle
white latex adhesive
clear plastic film
iron and cloth pad (optional)*

1

Arrange a selection of pressed herbs and flowers on the front of the card, using tweezers to position them.

2

When the design is complete, stick it down. Using a large tapestry needle, slide small dabs of adhesive beneath the herbs and flowers without altering their position. Cover with a clear film. If the film needs heating, iron gently with a cloth pad between the film and the iron.

Bath-time Bottle

Recycle a glass bottle containing home-made lotion and decorate it with corrugated card in gem-like colours for a real impact.

MATERIALS

*scissors
coloured corrugated card
flower-water bottle
hot glue gun and glue sticks
coloured raffia*

1

Cut the corrugated card to size, and then glue in position around the bottle. Tie with raffia.

2

Make a matching label from corrugated card, and tie it on using raffia.

Bath-time Treat Jar

Decorate a jar of lotion to complement the bottle, using brilliantly coloured fine corrugated card. Royal blue and emerald green make a rich combination that could be used for both men and women.

MATERIALS

*scissors
coloured corrugated card
baby-food jar
hot glue gun and glue sticks
twine*

1

Cut the corrugated card to size, and then glue in place around the jar. Tie the twine around the jar.

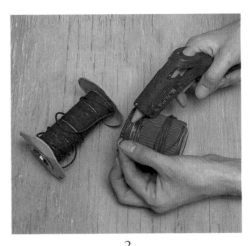

2

Cut a piece of corrugated card to fit the top of the lid and glue it in place. Glue twine to cover the side of the lid.

Chamomile and Honey Mask

Although this mask makes you look a little strange while it is on your face, it smooths and softens skin beautifully. Chamomile flowers are usually easy to obtain from a health food shop as they are often used for making chamomile tea.

INGREDIENTS

1 tbsp dried chamomile flowers
175 ml / 6 fl oz boiling water
2 tbsp bran
1 tsp clear honey, warmed

1

Pour the boiling water over the chamomile flowers and allow them to stand for 30 minutes. Then strain the infusion and discard the chamomile flowers.

2

Mix 3 tbsp of the liquid with the bran and honey and rub this mixture over your face. Leave for at least 10 minutes, then rinse off with warm water.

Tansy Skin Tonic

Tansy leaves smell fairly strong, but this tonic will invigorate your skin, especially if you keep the bottle in the refrigerator. Splash on this cool herbal liquid to start the day.

INGREDIENTS

*large handful tansy leaves
150 ml / ¼ pint water
150 ml / ¼ pint milk*

1

Put the leaves, water and milk in a small pan and bring to the boil. Simmer for 15 minutes, then allow to cool in the pan.

2

Strain the tonic into a bottle. Keep the mixture in the refrigerator, and apply cold to the skin as a soothing toner or tonic.

Feverfew Complexion Milk

Feverfew grows prolifically in the garden, self-seeding all over the herb beds, and this is a welcome use for some of this over-enthusiastic plant. The milk will moisturize dry skin, help to fade blemishes and discourage blackheads.

Feverfew can be cultivated easily; it is especially pretty grown in tubs and pots in the greenhouse or conservatory.

Hang bunches of flowers upside down and leave to air dry; use as a decorative addition to dried flower arrangements.

INGREDIENTS

large handful feverfew leaves
300 ml / ½ pint milk

1

Put the leaves and milk in a small saucepan and simmer for 20 minutes.

2

Allow the mixture to cool in the pan then strain into a bottle. Keep it in the refrigerator.

Fennel Cleanser

Fennel is another herb that self-seeds all over the garden, so once you have planted it supplies will be no problem. The leaves have an aniseed aroma. This mixture gently but thoroughly cleanses the day's grime away.

The tall, graceful heads of fennel seeds add height to a cottage herb garden. The seeds are valued for their distinctive aroma. In Victorian times the seeds came to symbolize the virtue of strength.

At one time, fennel seeds were combined with those of dill and caraway in little sacks or purses, to be chewed at prayer meetings to quell hunger pangs: they were known as 'meeting seeds'.

INGREDIENTS

1 tbsp fennel seed
250 ml / 8 fl oz boiling water
1 tsp honey
2 tbsp buttermilk

1

Lightly crush the fennel seeds, pour on the boiling water and allow to infuse for about 30 minutes.

2

Strain the cooled liquid into a small bowl and add the honey and buttermilk. Transfer to a clean bottle and keep the mixture refrigerated.

Parsley Hair Tonic

Parsley stimulates the scalp and gets the circulation going, which aids hair growth and adds shine. Parsley is cultivated in the garden in numerous forms, including curly, plain and turnip-rooted. It is one of the most versatile herbs, and no herb garden should be without at least one plant.

*large handful parsley sprigs
2 tbsp water*

1

Place the parsley sprigs and water in a food processor.

2

Process until ground to a smooth purée. Apply the green lotion to the scalp, then wrap your head in a warm towel and leave for about 1 hour before shampooing as normal.

Lemon Verbena Hair Rinse

Add a delicious fragrance to your hair with this rinse. It will also stimulate the pores and circulation. Lemon verbena is worth growing in the garden, if only so that you can walk past and pick a wonderfully scented leaf.

INGREDIENTS

*handful lemon verbena leaves
250 ml / 8 fl oz boiling water*

1

Pour the boiling water over the lemon verbena leaves and leave to soak for 1 hour.

2

Strain the mixture and discard the leaves. Pour this rinse over your hair after conditioning.

Chamomile Conditioning Rinse

Chamomile flowers help to keep blonde hair a bright, clear colour. They will not lift the colour in hair that is medium to dark, but will help to brighten naturally fair hair, as well as leaving a pleasant fragrance.

INGREDIENTS

125 ml / 4 fl oz chamomile flowers
600 ml / 1 pint water
handful scented geranium leaves

1

Place the flowers and water in a saucepan and bring to the boil. Simmer for approximately 15 minutes.

2

While the liquid is still hot, strain on to the scented geranium leaves. Leave to soak for 30–40 minutes. Strain again, this time into a bottle. Use the mixture after shampooing.

Rosemary Hair Tonic

Rosemary is an excellent substitute for mildly medicated shampoos, and this tonic also helps to control greasy hair and enhances the shine and natural colour.

INGREDIENTS

250 ml / 8 fl oz fresh rosemary tips
1.2 litres / 2 pints bottled water

1

Put the ingredients in a saucepan and bring to the boil. Simmer for approximately 20 minutes, then allow to cool in the pan.

2

Strain the mixture and store it in a clean bottle. Use after shampooing the hair.

Dill Aftershave

Most recipes are for fragrances for women, so here is one for men. It is best kept in the refrigerator so that the cool liquid has a bracing effect as well as smelling good.

50 g / 2 oz dill seed
1 tbsp honey
600 ml / 1 pint bottled water
1 tbsp distilled witch hazel

1

2

Place the dill seed, honey and water in a small saucepan and bring to the boil. Simmer for about 20 minutes.

Allow to cool in the pan, then add the witch hazel. Strain the cooled mixture into a bottle and refrigerate.

Lavender Bubble Bath

There is no need to buy commercially made bubble baths again. This fragrance is quite delicious and so simple to make that you can make some spares as gifts for friends and family – you will be in great demand!

INGREDIENTS

bunch lavender
clean wide-necked jar, with screw top
large bottle clear organic shampoo
5 drops oil of lavender

1

Place the bunch of lavender head downwards in the jar. If the stalks are longer than the jar cut them down, as it is the flowers that do the work. Add the shampoo and the lavender oil.

2

Close the jar and place on a sunny window sill for 2–3 weeks, shaking occasionally.

3

Strain the liquid and re-bottle. Use about 1 tbsp in a bath.

Lemon Grass, Coriander and Clove Bath

If you are suffering from stiff limbs after excessive exercise, this bath will help stimulate the circulation and relieve suffering in joints and muscles.

*2 tbsp almond oil
2 drops lemon grass oil
2 drops coriander oil
2 drops clove oil*

1

Carefully measure the almond oil into a small dish.

2

Slowly drop in the other essential oils. Mix all the ingredients and pour into the bath while the water is running.

Lavender and Marjoram Bath

This bath mixture has the added bonus of moisturizing the skin while it gently soothes away cares and troubles. The essential oils induce sleep. To enhance the effect, you could add a bath bag containing fresh lavender and marjoram to the water.

Lavender oil is the most useful of all the essential oils, and perhaps the safest. Allergic reaction is virtually unknown and, unlike many of the other essential oils, it is safe to apply it directly to the skin.

It can help to promote sleep – sprinkle a few drops on to the pillow, or on to a handkerchief placed on the pillow, for adults and children to enjoy untroubled rest.

It is also excellent for treating burns, stings, scalds and minor wounds. Deter flying insects by rubbing the essential oil into uncovered parts of the body, such as hands and feet, on a warm evening when sitting outside.

*2 tbsp almond oil
7 drops lavender oil
3 drops marjoram oil*

1

Measure out all the ingredients into a small dish or bowl.

2

Mix all the ingredients together and pour them into the bath while the water is running, then have a long soothing soak.

Gifts from the Pantry

....

Make the most of seasonal fruits and vegetables, by making jams, jellies and preserves to enjoy the year round, or to give as gifts. Country favourites include strawberry jam, apple or mint jelly, or piccalilli.

Apple and Mint Jelly

This jelly is delicious served with garden peas, as well as the more traditional rich roasted meat such as lamb.

INGREDIENTS

*900 g / 2 lb Bramley
cooking apples
granulated sugar
45 ml / 3 tbsp chopped fresh mint*

Makes 3 × 450 g / 1 lb jars

1

Chop the apples roughly and put them
in a preserving pan.

2

Add enough water to cover. Simmer until
the fruit is soft.

3

Pour through a jelly bag, allowing it
to drip overnight. Do not squeeze the bag
or the jelly will become cloudy.

4

Measure the amount of juice. To every
600 ml / 1 pint / 2½ cups of juice, add
500 g / 1¼ lb / 2¾ cups granulated sugar.

5

Place the juice and sugar in a large pan and
heat gently. Dissolve the sugar and then
bring to the boil. Test for setting,
by pouring about 15 ml / 1 tbsp into a saucer
and leaving to cool slightly. If a wrinkle
forms on the surface when pushed with a
fingertip, the jelly will set. When a set is
reached, leave to cool.

6

Stir in the mint and pot into sterilized jars.
Seal each jar with a waxed disc and a tightly
fitting cellophane top. Store in a cool,
dark place. The jelly will keep unopened
for up to a year. Once opened, keep in the
fridge and consume within a week.

Lemon and Lime Curd

Serve this creamy, tangy spread with toast or muffins,
instead of jam, for a delightful change.

INGREDIENTS

115 g / 4 oz / ½ cup   grated rind and juice of 2 lemons
unsalted butter   grated rind and juice of 2 limes
3 eggs   225 g / 8 oz / 1⅛ cups caster sugar

Makes 2 × 450 g / 1 lb jars

1

Set a heatproof mixing bowl over a large pan
of simmering water. Add the butter.

2

Lightly beat the eggs and add them
to the butter.

3

Add the lemon and lime rinds and juices,
then add the sugar.

4

Stir the mixture constantly until it thickens.
Pour into sterilized jars. Seal each jar with a
waxed disc and a tightly fitting cellophane top.
Store in a cool, dark place. The curd will
keep unopened for up to a month.
Once opened, keep in the fridge and
consume within a week.

Poached Spiced Plums in Brandy

Bottling spiced fruit is a great way to preserve summer flavours for eating in winter. Serve these with whipped cream as a dessert.

600 ml / 1 pint / 2½ cups brandy
rind of 1 lemon, peeled in a
long strip
350 g / 12 oz / 1⅔ cups
caster sugar
1 cinnamon stick
900 g / 2 lb fresh plums

Makes 900 g / 2 lb

1

Put the brandy, lemon rind, sugar and
cinnamon stick in a large pan and heat gently
to dissolve the sugar. Add the plums and
poach for 15 minutes, or until soft.
Remove with a slotted spoon.

2

Reduce the syrup by a third by rapid boiling.
Strain it over the plums. Bottle the plums
in large sterilized jars. Seal tightly and store
for up to 6 months in a cool, dark place.

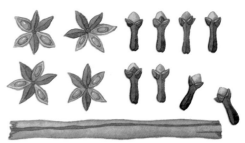

Spiced Pickled Pears

These delicious pears are the perfect accompaniment for cooked ham or cold meat salads.

INGREDIENTS

900 g / 2 lb pears
600 ml / 1 pint / 2½ cups
white-wine vinegar
225 g / 8 oz / 1⅛ cups caster sugar
1 cinnamon stick
5 star anise
10 whole cloves

Makes 900 g / 2 lb

1

Peel the pears, keeping them whole
and leaving on the stalks. Heat the vinegar
and sugar together until the sugar has melted.
Pour over the pears and poach for 15 minutes.

2

Add the cinnamon, star anise and cloves
and simmer for 10 minutes. Remove the
pears and pack tightly into sterilized jars.
Simmer the syrup for a further 15 minutes
and pour it over the pears. Seal the jars
tightly and store in a cool, dark place. The
pears will keep for up to a year unopened.
Once opened, store in the fridge and
consume within a week.

Tomato Chutney

*This spicy chutney is delicious with a selection of cheeses and biscuits,
or with cold meats.*

INGREDIENTS

900 g / 2 lb tomatoes, skinned
225 g / 8 oz / 1⅓ cups raisins
225 g / 8 oz onions, chopped

225 g / 8 oz / 1⅛ cups caster sugar
600 ml / 1 pint / 2½ cups
malt vinegar

Makes 4 × 450 g / 1 lb jars

1

Chop the tomatoes roughly. Put them in
a preserving pan.

2

Add the raisins, onions and caster sugar.

3

Pour over the vinegar. Bring to the boil
and let it simmer for 2 hours, uncovered.
Pot into sterilized jars. Seal with a waxed disc
and cover with a tightly fitting cellophane
top. Store in a cool, dark place. The chutney
will keep unopened for up to a year. Once
opened, store in the fridge and consume
within a week.

Strawberry Jam

This classic recipe is always popular. Make sure the jam is allowed to cool before pouring into jars so the fruit doesn't float to the top.

INGREDIENTS

1.5 kg / 3–3½ lb strawberries
juice of ½ lemon
1.5 kg / 3–3½ lb granulated sugar

Makes about 2.25 kg / 5 lb

1

Hull the strawberries.

2

Put the strawberries in a pan with the lemon juice. Mash a few of the strawberries. Let the fruit simmer for 20 minutes or until softened.

3

Add the sugar and let it dissolve slowly over a gentle heat. Then let the jam boil rapidly until a setting point is reached.

4

Leave to stand until the strawberries are well distributed through the jam. Pot into sterilized jars. Seal each jar with a waxed disc and cover with a tightly fitting cellophane top. Store in a cool dark place. The jam may be kept unopened for up to a year. Once opened, keep in the fridge and consume within a week.

Three-fruit Marmalade

Home-made marmalade may be time-consuming but the results are incomparably better than store-bought varieties.

INGREDIENTS

350 g / 12 oz oranges
350 g / 12 oz lemons
700 g / 1½ lb grapefruit
2.5 litres / 4½ pints / 10¼ cups water
2.75 kg / 6 lb granulated sugar
Makes 6 × 450 g / 1 lb jars

1

Rinse and dry the fruit.

2

Put the fruit in a preserving pan. Add the water and let it simmer for about 2 hours.

3

Quarter the fruit, remove the pulp and add it to the pan with the cooking liquid.

4

Cut the rinds into slivers, and add to the pan. Add the sugar. Gently heat until the sugar has dissolved. Bring to the boil and cook until a setting point is reached. Leave to stand for 1 hour to allow the peel to settle. Pour into sterilized jars. Seal each jar with a waxed disc and a tightly fitting cellophane top. Store in a cool, dark place.

Piccalilli

The piquancy of this relish partners well with sausages, bacon or ham.

INGREDIENTS

675 g / 1½ lb cauliflower
450 g / 1 lb small onions
350 g / 12 oz French beans
5 ml / 1 tsp ground turmeric

5 ml / 1 tsp dry mustard powder
10 ml / 2 tsp cornflour
600 ml / 1 pint / 2½ cups vinegar

Makes 3 × 450g / 1 lb jars

1

Cut the cauliflower into tiny florets.

2

Peel the onions and top and tail
the French beans.

3

In a small saucepan, measure in the turmeric,
mustard powder and cornflour, and pour
over the vinegar. Stir well and simmer
for 10 minutes.

4

Pour the vinegar mixture over the vegetables
in a pan, mix well and simmer
for 45 minutes.

5

Pour into sterilized jars. Seal each jar with a
waxed disc and a tightly fitting cellophane
top. Store in a cool dark place. The piccalilli
will keep unopened for up to a year. Once
opened store in the fridge and consume
within a week.

Rosemary-flavoured Oil

This pungent oil is ideal drizzled over meat or vegetables before grilling.

INGREDIENTS

600 ml / 1 pint / 2½ cups olive oil
5 fresh rosemary sprigs

Makes 600 ml / 1 pint / 2½ cups

1

Heat the oil until warm but not too hot.

2

Add four rosemary sprigs and heat gently.
Put the reserved rosemary sprig in a clean
bottle. Strain the oil, pour in the bottle and
seal tightly. Allow to cool and store in a
cool, dark place. Use within a week.

Thyme-flavoured Vinegar

This vinegar is delicious sprinkled over salmon intended for poaching.

INGREDIENTS

600 ml / 1 pint / 2½ cups
white-wine vinegar
5 fresh thyme sprigs
3 garlic cloves, peeled

Makes 600 ml / 1 pint / 2½ cups

1

Warm the vinegar.

2

Add four thyme sprigs and the garlic and
heat gently. Put the reserved thyme sprig in
a clean bottle, strain the vinegar, and add to
the bottle. Seal tightly, allow to cool and
store in a cool, dark place. The vinegar
may be kept unopened for up to 3 months.

COUNTRY
Cooking

Spring Recipes

Spring brings the first of the year's tender young vegetables, and there are plenty of tempting recipes to make the most of seasonal produce. Treat yourself to a zesty lemon cake or an Easter plait studded with fruit and spices, for an Easter tea.

Warm Chicken Salad with Sesame and Coriander

INGREDIENTS

4 medium chicken breasts, boned and
skinned
225 g / 8 oz mange-tout
2 heads decorative lettuce
3 carrots, peeled and julienned
170 g / 6 oz button mushrooms, sliced
6 rashers of bacon, fried

For the dressing
115 ml / 4 fl oz lemon juice
2 tbsp wholegrain mustard
250 ml / 8 fl oz olive oil
65 ml / 2½ fl oz sesame oil
1 tsp coriander seeds, crushed
1 tbsp fresh coriander leaves
chopped, to garnish

Serves 6

1

Mix all the dressing ingredients in a bowl.
Place the chicken in a dish and pour on
half the dressing. Refrigerate overnight.

2

Cook the mange-tout for 2 minutes in
boiling water, then cool under running
cold water to stop them cooking any
further. Tear the lettuces into small pieces
and mix all the other salad ingredients and
the chopped bacon together.

3

Grill the chicken breasts until cooked
through, then slice them on the diagonal
into quite thin pieces. Divide between the
bowls of salad, and add some dressing to
each dish. Combine quickly and scatter
some fresh coriander over each bowl.

Spinach and Roquefort Pancakes

INGREDIENTS

115 g / 4 oz plain flour
2 eggs
5 tbsp sunflower oil
a little salt
250 ml / 8 fl oz milk
45 g / 1½ oz / 3 tbsp butter for frying

For the filling
1 kg / 2 lb frozen spinach, thawed
225 g / 8 oz cream cheese
225 g / 8 oz Roquefort cheese
2 tbsp chopped walnuts
2 tsp chervil

For the sauce
50 g / 2 oz / 4 tbsp butter
50 g / 2 oz flour
600 ml / 1 pint milk
1 tsp wholegrain mustard
170 g / 6 oz Roquefort cheese
1 tbsp finely chopped walnuts
1 tbsp fresh chopped chervil, to garnish

Makes 16

1

Process the flour, eggs, oil and salt, slowly
adding milk until the mixture has the
consistency of single cream. (You may not
need to add all the milk.) Let the batter
rest in the refrigerator for 1 hour. Put 1 tsp
of the butter into a frying pan, and once it
has melted swirl it around to coat the
surface of the pan.

3

Cook the spinach over a low heat for about
15 minutes. Strain off the water and let the
spinach cool. Process in a food processor
with the cream cheese and Roquefort until
smooth. Turn into a bowl and add half the
walnuts and chervil.

2

Drop a large tablespoonful of batter into
the pan and tilt to spread it around evenly.
Cook until golden brown on the bottom,
then turn and cook briefly on the other
side. Lay the pancake on a wire rack. Cook
the others in the same way.

4

Preheat the oven to 190°C / 375°F / Gas
Mark 5. Fill all the pancakes and place in a
shallow ovenproof dish, rolled tightly and
in rows. Make the sauce by melting the
butter, adding the flour and cooking for a
minute or two. Add the milk and stir
constantly until the sauce comes to the
boil. Stir in all the other ingredients except
the chervil. Pour the sauce over the
pancakes and bake for 20 minutes. Serve
immediately, garnished with chervil and
the remaining walnuts.

Leek and Monkfish with Thyme Sauce

Monkfish is a well-known fish now, thanks to its excellent flavour and firm texture.

INGREDIENTS

1 kg / 2 lb monkfish, cubed
salt and pepper
75 g / 3 oz/generous ⅓ cup butter
4 leeks, sliced
1 tbsp flour
150 ml / ¼ pint/ ⅔ cup fish or
vegetable stock
2 tsp finely chopped fresh thyme,
plus more to garnish
juice of 1 lemon
150 ml / ¼ pint/ ⅔ cup single cream
radicchio, to garnish

Serves 4

1

Season the fish to taste. Melt about a third of the butter in a pan, and fry the fish for a short time. Put to one side.

2

Fry the leeks in the pan with another third of the butter until they have softened. Put these to one side with the fish.

3

In a saucepan, melt the rest of the butter, add the butter from the pan, stir in the flour, and add the stock. As the sauce thickens, add the thyme and lemon juice.

4

Return the leeks and monkfish to the pan and cook gently for a few minutes. Add the cream and season to taste. Serve immediately garnished with thyme and radicchio leaves.

Fish Stew with Calvados, Parsley and Dill

This rustic stew harbours all sorts of interesting flavours and will please and intrigue.
Many varieties of fish can be used, just choose the freshest and best.

INGREDIENTS

1 kg / 2 lb assorted white fish
1 tbsp chopped parsley, plus a few
leaves to garnish
225 g / 8 oz mushrooms
225 g / 8 oz can of tomatoes
salt and pepper
2 tsp flour
15 g / ½ oz / 1 tbsp butter
450 ml / ¾ pint cider
45 ml / 3 tbsp Calvados
1 large bunch fresh dill sprigs,
reserving 4 fronds to garnish

Serves 4

1

Chop the fish roughly and place it in a casserole or stewing pot with the parsley, mushrooms and tomatoes, adding salt and pepper to taste.

2

Preheat the oven to 180°C/350°F/Gas Mark 4. Work the flour into the butter. Heat the cider and stir in the flour and butter mixture a little at a time. Cook, stirring, until it has thickened slightly.

3

Add the cider mixture and the remaining ingredients to the fish and mix gently. Cover and bake for about 30 minutes. Serve garnished with sprigs of dill and parsley leaves.

Lamb and Leeks with Mint and Spring Onions

If you do not have any home-made chicken stock, use a good
quality ready-made stock rather than a stock cube.

INGREDIENTS

2 tbsp sunflower oil
2 kg / 4 lb lamb (fillet or boned leg)
10 spring onions, thickly sliced
3 leeks, thickly sliced
1 tbsp flour
150 ml / ¼ pint white wine
300 ml / ½ pint chicken stock
1 tbsp tomato purée
1 tbsp sugar
salt and pepper
2 tbsp fresh mint leaves, finely
chopped, plus a few more to garnish
115 g / 4 oz dried pears
1 kg / 2 lb potatoes, peeled and sliced
30 g / 1¼ oz melted butter

Serves 6

1

Heat the oil and fry the cubed lamb to seal it. Transfer to a casserole. Preheat the oven to 180°C/350°F/Gas Mark 4.

2

Fry the onions and leeks for 1 minute, stir in the flour and cook for another minute. Add the wine and stock and bring to the boil. Add the tomato purée, sugar, salt and pepper with the mint and chopped pears and pour into the casserole. Stir the mixture. Arrange the sliced potatoes on top and brush with the melted butter.

3

Cover and bake for 1½ hours. Then increase the temperature to 200°C/400°F/Gas Mark 6, cook for a further 30 minutes, uncovered, to brown the potatoes. Garnish with mint leaves.

Stuffed Parsleyed Onions

Although devised as a vegetarian dish, these stuffed onions make a wonderful accompaniment to meat dishes, or an appetizing supper dish with crusty bread and a salad.

INGREDIENTS

4 large onions
4 tbsp cooked rice
4 tsp finely chopped fresh parsley,
plus extra to garnish
4 tbsp strong Cheddar cheese, finely
grated
salt and pepper
2 tbsp olive oil
1 tbsp white wine, to moisten

Serves 4

1

Cut a slice from the top of each onion and scoop out the centre to leave a thick shell.

2

Combine all the remaining ingredients, moistening with enough wine to mix well. Preheat the oven to 180°C/350°F/ Gas Mark 4.

3

Fill the onions and bake in the oven for 45 minutes. Serve garnished with parsley.

Lamb Pie with Pear, Ginger and Mint Sauce

Cooking lamb with fruit is an idea taken from traditional Persian cuisine.

INGREDIENTS

*1 boned mid-loin of lamb, 1 kg / 2 lb
after boning
salt and pepper
8 large sheets filo pastry
25 g / 1 oz / scant 2 tbsp butter*

*For the stuffing
1 tbsp butter
1 small onion, chopped
115 g / 4 oz wholemeal breadcrumbs
grated rind of 1 lemon
170 g / 6 oz drained canned pears from*

*a 400 g / 14 oz can (rest
of can, and juice, used for sauce)
¼ tsp ground ginger
1 small egg, beaten
skewers, string and large needle to
make roll*

*For the sauce
rest of can of pears, including juice
2 tsp finely chopped fresh mint*

Serves 6

1

Prepare the stuffing. Melt the butter in a pan and add the onion, cooking until soft. Preheat the oven to 180°C/350°F/Gas Mark 4. Put the butter and onion into a mixing bowl and add the breadcrumbs, lemon rind, pears and ginger. Season lightly and add enough beaten egg to bind.

2

Spread the loin out flat, fat side down, and season. Place the stuffing along the middle of the loin and roll carefully, holding with skewers while you sew it together with string. Heat a large baking pan in the oven and brown the loin slowly on all sides. This will take 20–30 minutes. Leave to cool, and store in the refrigerator until needed.

3

Preheat the oven to 200°C/400°F/Gas Mark 6. Take two sheets of filo pastry and brush with melted butter. Overlap by about 13 cm/5 in to make a square. Place the next two sheets on top and brush with butter. Continue until all the pastry has been used.

4

Place the roll of lamb diagonally across one corner of the pastry, without overlapping the sides. Fold the corner over the lamb, fold in the sides, and brush the pastry well with melted butter. Roll to the far corner of the sheet. Place join side down on a buttered baking sheet and brush all over with the rest of the melted butter. Bake for about 30 minutes or until golden brown.

5

Blend the remaining pears with their juice and the mint, and serve with the lamb.

Steak and Kidney Pie, with Mustard and Bay Gravy

This is a sharpened-up, bay-flavoured version of a traditional favourite. The fragrant mustard, bay and parsley perfectly complement the flavour of the beef.

INGREDIENTS

450 g / 1 lb puff pastry
2½ tbsp flour
salt and pepper
750 g / 1½ lb rump steak, cubed
170 g / 6 oz pig's or lamb's kidney
25 g / 1 oz / scant 2 tbsp butter
1 medium onion, chopped
1 tbsp made English mustard
2 bay leaves
1 tbsp chopped parsley
150 ml / 5 fl oz beef stock
1 egg, beaten

Serves 4

1

Roll out two-thirds of the pastry on a floured surface to about 3 mm / ⅛ in thick. Line a 1.5 litre / 2½ pint pie dish. Place a pie funnel in the middle.

2

Put the flour, salt and pepper in a bowl and toss the cubes of steak in the mixture. Remove all fat and skin from the kidneys, and slice thickly. Add to the steak cubes and toss well. Melt the butter in a pan and fry the chopped onion until soft, then add the mustard, bay leaves, parsley and stock and stir well.

3

Preheat the oven to 190°C / 375°F / Gas Mark 5. Place the steak and kidney in the pie and add the stock mixture. Roll out the remaining pastry to a thickness of 3 mm / ⅛ in. Brush the edges of the pastry forming the lower half of the pie with beaten egg and cover with the second piece of pastry. Press the pieces of pastry together to seal the edges, then trim. Use the trimmings to decorate the top with a pattern of leaves.

4

Brush the whole pie with beaten egg and make a small hole over the top of the funnel. Bake for about 1 hour until the pastry is golden brown.

Spring Roasted Chicken with Fresh Herbs and Garlic

A smaller chicken or four poussins can also be roasted in this way.

INGREDIENTS

*1.75 kg / 4½ lb free-range chicken
or 4 small poussins
finely grated rind and
juice of 1 lemon
1 garlic clove, crushed
30 ml / 2 tbsp olive oil
2 fresh thyme sprigs
2 fresh sage sprigs
75 g / 3 oz / 6 tbsp unsalted butter,
softened
salt and freshly ground
black pepper*

Serves 4

1

Season the chicken or poussins well.
Mix the lemon rind and juice, garlic and
olive oil together and pour them over the
chicken. Leave to marinate for at least
2 hours in a non-metallic dish.
When the chicken has marinated preheat
the oven to 230°C / 450°F / Gas Mark 8.

2

Place the herbs in the cavity of the bird and
smear the butter over the skin. Season well.
Roast the chicken for 10 minutes, then turn
the oven down to 190°C / 375°F / Gas Mark 5.
Baste the chicken well, and then roast for a
further 1 hour 30 minutes, until the juices run
clear when the thigh is pierced with a skewer.
Leave to rest for 15 minutes before carving.

Lemon and Rosemary Lamb Chops

*Spring lamb is delicious with the fresh flavour of lemon. Garnish with sprigs of
fresh rosemary – the aroma is irresistible.*

INGREDIENTS

*12 lamb cutlets
45 ml / 3 tbsp olive oil
2 large rosemary sprigs
juice of 1 lemon
3 garlic cloves, sliced
salt and freshly ground
black pepper*

Serves 4

1

Trim the excess fat from the cutlets.
Mix the oil, rosemary, lemon juice and
garlic together and season well.

2

Pour over the chops in a shallow dish and
marinate for 30 minutes. Remove from the
marinade, and blot the excess with kitchen
paper and grill for 10 minutes on each side.

Carrot and Coriander Soufflés

Use tender young carrots for this light-as-air dish.

INGREDIENTS

450 g / 1 lb carrots
30 ml / 2 tbsp fresh chopped
coriander
4 eggs, separated
salt and freshly ground
black pepper

Serves 4

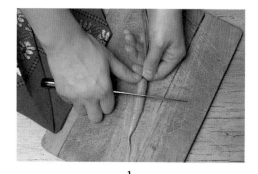

1

Peel the carrots.

2

Cook in boiling salted water for 20 minutes or until tender. Drain, and process until smooth in a food processor.

3

Preheat the oven to 200°C / 400°F / Gas Mark 6. Season the puréed carrots well, and stir in the chopped coriander.

4

Fold the egg yolks into the carrot mixture.

5

In a separate bowl, whisk the egg whites until stiff.

6

Fold the egg whites into the carrot mixture and pour into four greased ramekins. Bake for about 20 minutes or until risen and golden. Serve immediately.

Leeks with Ham and Cheese Sauce

A tasty teatime or supper dish: use a strong cheese for best results.

4 leeks
4 slices ham

For the sauce
25 g / 1 oz / 2 tbsp unsalted butter
25 g / 1 oz / 1 tbsp plain flour
300 ml / ½ pint / 1¼ cups milk
½ tsp French mustard
115 g / 4 oz hard cheese, grated
salt and freshly ground
black pepper

Serves 4

1

Preheat the oven to 190°C / 375°F /
Gas Mark 5. Trim the leeks to 2 cm / 1 in of
the white and cook in salted water for about
20 minutes until soft. Drain thoroughly.
Wrap the leeks in the ham slices.

2

To make the sauce, melt the butter in a
saucepan. Add the flour and cook for a few
minutes. Remove from the heat and
gradually add the milk, whisking well with
each addition. Return to the heat and whisk
until the sauce thickens. Stir in the mustard
and 75 g / 3 oz of the cheese and season well.
Lay the leeks in a shallow ovenproof dish and
pour over the sauce. Scatter the extra cheese
on top and bake for 20 minutes.

Baked Eggs with Double Cream and Chives

This is a rich dish best served with Melba toast: it's very easy and quick to make.

15 g / ½ oz / 1 tbsp unsalted
butter, softened
60 ml / 4 tbsp double cream
15 ml / 1 tbsp snipped fresh chives
4 eggs
50 g / 2 oz Gruyère cheese,
finely grated
salt and freshly ground
black pepper

Serves 2

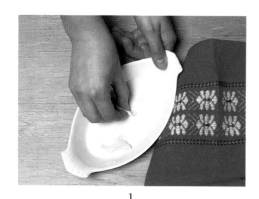

1

Preheat the oven to 180°C / 350°F /
Gas Mark 4. Grease two individual gratin
dishes. Mix the cream with the chives,
and season with salt and pepper.

2

Break the eggs into each dish and top with
the cream mixture. Sprinkle the cheese
around the edges of the dishes and bake in
the oven for 15–20 minutes. When cooked,
brown the tops under the grill for a minute.

Lemon Drizzle Cake

*You can also make this recipe using a large orange instead of the lemons;
either way, it makes a zesty treat for afternoon tea.*

INGREDIENTS

finely grated rind of 2 lemons
175 g / 6 oz / 12 tbsp caster sugar
225 g / 8 oz / 1 cup unsalted
butter, softened
4 eggs
225 g / 8 oz / 2 cups self-raising
flour
5 ml / 1 tsp baking powder
¼ tsp salt
shredded rind of 1 lemon,
to decorate

For the syrup
juice of 1 lemon
150 g / 5 oz / ¾ cup caster sugar

Serves 6

1

Preheat the oven to 160°C / 325°F /
Gas Mark 3. Grease a 1 kg / 2 lb loaf tin or
18–20 cm / 7–8 in round cake tin and line it
with greaseproof paper or baking parchment.
Mix the lemon rind and caster sugar together.

2

Cream the butter with the lemon and sugar
mixture. Add the eggs and mix until
smooth. Sift the flour, baking powder and
salt into a bowl and fold a third at a time into
the mixture. Turn the batter into the tin,
smooth the top and bake for 1½ hours or
until golden brown and springy to the touch.

3

To make the syrup, slowly heat the juice
with the sugar and dissolve it gently. Make
several slashes in the top of the cake and pour
over the syrup. Sprinkle the shredded lemon
rind and 5 ml / 1 tsp granulated sugar on top
and leave to cool.

Wholemeal Bread

Home-made bread creates one of the most evocative smells in country cooking.
Eat this on the day of making, to enjoy the superb fresh taste.

INGREDIENTS

20 g / ¾ oz fresh yeast
300 ml / ½ pint / 1¼ cups
lukewarm milk
5 ml / 1 tsp caster sugar
225 g / 8 oz / 1½ cups strong
wholemeal flour, sifted
225 g / 8 oz / 2 cups strong
white flour, sifted
5 ml / 1 tsp salt
50 g / 2 oz / 4 tbsp butter,
chilled and cubed
1 egg, lightly beaten
30 ml / 2 tbsp mixed seeds

Makes 4 rounds or 2 loaves

1

Gently dissolve the yeast with a little of the milk and the sugar to make a paste. Place both the flours plus any bran from the sieve and the salt in a large warmed mixing bowl. Rub in the butter until the mixture resembles breadcrumbs.

2

Add the yeast mixture, remaining milk and egg and mix into a fairly soft dough. Knead on a floured board for 15 minutes. Lightly grease the mixing bowl and put the dough back in the bowl, covering it with a piece of greased cling film. Leave to double in size in a warm place (this should take at least an hour).

3

Knock the dough back and knead it for a further 10 minutes. Preheat the oven to 200°C / 400°F / Gas Mark 6. To make round loaves, divide the dough into four pieces and shape them into flattish rounds. Place them on a floured baking sheet and leave to rise for a further 15 minutes. Sprinkle the loaves with the mixed seeds. Bake for about 20 minutes until golden and firm.

NOTE

For tin-shaped loaves, put the knocked-back dough into two greased loaf tins instead. Leave to rise for a further 45 minutes and then bake for about 45 minutes, until the loaf sounds hollow when turned out of the tin and knocked on the base.

Easter Plait

Serve this delicious plait sliced with butter and jam.
It is also very good toasted on the day after you made it.

INGREDIENTS

200 ml / 7 fl oz / ⅞ cup milk
2 eggs, lightly beaten
450 g / 1 lb / 4 cups plain flour
½ tsp salt
10 ml / 2 tsp ground mixed spice
75 g / 3 oz / 6 tbsp butter
20 g / ¾ oz dried yeast
75 g / 3 oz / 6 tbsp caster sugar

175 g / 6 oz / 1¼ cups currants
25 g / 1 oz / ¼ cup candied mixed
peel, chopped
a little sweetened milk, to glaze
25 g / 1 oz / 1½ tbsp glacé
cherries, chopped
15 g / ½ oz / 1 tbsp angelica,
chopped

Serves 8

1

Warm the milk to lukewarm, add two-thirds of it to the eggs and mix well.

2

Sift the flour, salt and mixed spice together. Rub in the butter, then add the sugar and dried yeast. Make a well in the centre, and add the milk mixture, adding more milk as necessary to make a sticky dough.

3

Knead on a well-floured surface and then knead in the currants and mixed peel, reserving 15 ml / 1 tbsp for the topping. Put the dough in a lightly greased bowl and cover it with a damp tea towel. Leave to double its size. Preheat the oven to 220°C / 425°F / Gas Mark 7.

4

Turn the dough out on to a floured surface and knead again for 2–3 minutes. Divide the dough into three even pieces. Roll each piece into a sausage shape roughly 20 cm / 8 in long. Plait the three pieces together, turning under and pinching each end. Place on a floured baking sheet and leave to rise for 15 minutes.

5

Brush the top with sweetened milk and scatter with roughly chopped cherries, strips of angelica and the reserved mixed peel. Bake in the preheated oven for 45 minutes or until the bread sounds hollow when tapped on the bottom. Cool slightly on a wire rack.

Orange-blossom Jelly

A fresh orange jelly makes a delightful dessert: the natural fruit flavour combined with the smooth jelly has a cleansing quality that is especially welcome after a rich main course. This is delicious served with thin, crisp langues de chat *biscuits.*

INGREDIENTS

65 g / 2½ oz / 5 tbsp caster sugar
150 ml / ¼ pint / ⅔ cup water
2 sachets of gelatine
(about 25 g / 1 oz)
600 ml / 1 pint / 2½ cups freshly
squeezed orange juice
30 ml / 2 tbsp orange-flower water

Serves 4–6

1

Place the caster sugar and water in a small saucepan and gently heat to dissolve the sugar. Leave to cool.

2

Sprinkle over the gelatine, ensuring it is completely submerged in the water. Leave to stand until the gelatine has absorbed all the liquid and is solid.

3

Gently melt the gelatine over a bowl of simmering water until it becomes clear and transparent. Leave to cool. When the gelatine is cold, mix it with the orange juice and orange-flower water.

4

Wet a jelly mould and pour in the jelly. Chill in the refrigerator for at least 2 hours, or until set. Turn out to serve.

Rhubarb and Orange Crumble

The almonds give this crumble topping a nutty taste and crunchy texture.
This crumble is extra-delicious with home-made custard.

900 g / 2 lb rhubarb, cut in
5 cm / 2 in lengths
75 g / 3 oz / 6 tbsp caster sugar
finely grated rind and juice
of 2 oranges

115 g / 4 oz / 1 cup plain flour
115 g / 4 oz / ½ cup unsalted
butter, chilled and cubed
75 g / 3 oz / 6 tbsp demerara sugar
115 g / 4 oz / 1¼ cups ground almonds

Serves 6

1

Preheat the oven to 180°C / 350°F /
Gas Mark 4. Place the rhubarb in a shallow
ovenproof dish.

2

Sprinkle over the caster sugar and add the
orange rind and juice.

3

Sift the flour into a mixing bowl and add the
butter. Rub the butter into the flour until
the mixture resembles breadcrumbs.

4

Add the demerara sugar and ground almonds
and mix well.

5

Spoon the crumble mixture over the fruit to
cover it completely. Bake for 40 minutes,
until the top is browned and the fruit is
cooked. Serve warm.

Summer Recipes

....

*The warm, lazy days and long nights of summer
provide the perfect excuse for outdoor dining
with friends and family. Try Mediterranean quiche
or a glorious garden salad with nasturtium flowers.
Cooling treats include strawberry fool, or
home-made mint ice cream.*

Herb and Chilli Gazpacho

Gazpacho is a lovely soup, set off perfectly by the addition of a few herbs.

INGREDIENTS

1.2 kg / 2½ lb ripe tomatoes
225 g / 8 oz onions
2 green peppers
1 green chilli
1 large cucumber
30 ml / 2 tbsp red wine vinegar
15 ml / 1 tbsp balsamic vinegar
30 ml / 2 tbsp olive oil
1 clove of garlic, peeled and crushed
300 ml / ½ pint tomato juice
30 ml / 2 tbsp tomato purée
salt and pepper
2 tbsp finely chopped mixed fresh
herbs, plus some extra to garnish

Serves 6

1

Keep back about a quarter of all the fresh vegetables, except the green chilli, and place all the remaining ingredients in a food processor and season to taste. Process finely and chill in the refrigerator.

2

Chop all the remaining vegetables and serve in a separate bowl to sprinkle over the soup. Crush some ice cubes and add to the centre of each bowl and garnish with fresh herbs. Serve with bread rolls.

Pear and Watercress Soup with Stilton Croûtons

Pears and Stilton taste very good when you eat them together after the main course —
here, for a change, they are served as a starter.

INGREDIENTS

1 bunch watercress
4 medium pears, sliced
900 ml / 1½ pints chicken stock,
preferably home-made
salt and pepper
120 ml / 4 fl oz double cream
juice of 1 lime

For the croûtons
25 g / 1 oz butter
30 ml / 1 tbsp olive oil
200 g / 7 oz cubed stale bread
140 g / 5 oz chopped Stilton cheese

Serves 6

1

Keep back about a third of the watercress leaves. Place all the rest of the watercress leaves and stalks in a pan with the pears, stock and a little seasoning. Simmer for about 15–20 minutes.

2

Reserving some watercress leaves for garnishing, add the rest of the leaves and immediately blend in a food processor until smooth.

3

Put the mixture into a bowl and stir in the cream and lime juice to mix the flavours thoroughly. Season again to taste. Pour all the soup back into a pan and reheat, stirring gently until warmed through.

4

To make the croûtons, melt the butter and oil and fry the bread cubes until golden brown. Drain on kitchen paper. Put the cheese on top and heat under a hot grill until bubbling. Reheat the soup and pour into bowls. Divide the croûtons and remaining watercress between the bowls.

Herbed Halibut Mille-feuille

The herbs add their own special flavours to the creamy fish.

INGREDIENTS

250 g / 9 oz puff pastry
butter for baking sheet
1 egg, beaten
1 small onion
1 tbsp fresh ginger, grated
7 ml / 1½ tbsp oil
150 ml / ¼ pint / ⅔ cup fish stock
15 ml / 1 tbsp dry sherry
350 g / 12 oz halibut, cooked and
flaked
225 g / 8 oz crab meat
salt and pepper
1 avocado
juice of 1 lime
1 mango
1 tbsp chopped mixed parsley, thyme
and chives, to garnish

Serves 2

1

Roll the pastry out into a square
25 × 25 cm /10 × 10 in, trim the edges
and place on a buttered baking sheet. Prick
with a fork, then rest it in the refrigerator
for at least 30 minutes. Preheat the oven to
230°C/450°F/Gas Mark 8. Brush the
top with beaten egg, and bake for
10–15 minutes or until golden.

3

Fry the onion and ginger in the oil until
tender. Add the fish stock and sherry, and
simmer for 5 minutes. Add the halibut and
crab meat, and season to taste. Peel and
chop the avocado and toss in the lime
juice. Peel and chop the mango reserving a
few slices for garnishing. Add the avocado
and the mango to the fish.

2

Let the pastry cool for a few minutes, then
cut it twice across in one direction and
once in the other to make six pieces. Leave
to cool completely.

4

Build up alternate layers of fish and pastry,
starting and finishing with a piece of pastry.
Serve garnished with herbs and mango slices.

Salmon and Ginger Pie

This exceptional pie is highly
recommended. This recipe uses
salmon's special flavour to the full.

INGREDIENTS

800 g / 1¾ lb middle cut of salmon
45 ml / 3 tbsp walnut oil
15 ml / 1 tbsp lime juice
2 tsp chopped fresh lemon thyme
30 ml / 2 tbsp white wine
salt and pepper
40 0g / 14 oz puff pastry
50 g / 2 oz / ½ cup flaked almonds
3–4 pieces stem ginger in syrup,
chopped

Serves 4–6

1

Split the salmon in half, remove all the
bones and skin and divide into 4 fillets.
Mix the oil, lime juice, thyme, wine and
pepper, and pour over the fish. Leave to
marinate overnight in the refrigerator.

2

Divide the pastry into 2 pieces, one slightly
larger than the other, and roll out – the
smaller piece should be large enough to take
2 of the salmon fillets and the second piece
about 5 cm/2 in larger all round.

3

Drain the fillets. Discard the marinade.
Preheat the oven to 190°C/375°F/Gas
Mark 5. Place 2 of the fillets on the smaller
piece of pastry, and season. Add the
almonds and ginger and cover with the
other 2 fillets.

4

Season again, cover with the second piece
of pastry and seal well. Brush with beaten
egg and decorate with any leftover pastry.
Bake for 40 minutes.

Mackerel with Roasted Blueberries

Fresh blueberries burst with flavour when roasted, and their sharpness
complements the rich flesh of mackerel very well.

INGREDIENTS

15 g / ½ oz / 2 tsp plain flour
4 small cooked, smoked mackerel
fillets
50 g / 2 oz / 4 tbsp unsalted butter
juice of ½ lemon
salt and freshly ground
black pepper

For the roasted blueberries
450 g / 1 lb blueberries
25 g / 1 oz / 2 tbsp caster sugar
15 g / ½ oz / 1 tbsp unsalted butter
salt and freshly ground
black pepper

Serves 4

1

Preheat the oven to 200°C / 400°F /
Gas Mark 6. Season the flour. Dip each fish
fillet into the flour to coat it well.

2

Dot the butter on the fillets and bake in the
oven for 20 minutes.

3

Place the blueberries, sugar, butter and
seasoning in a separate small roasting tin
and roast them, basting them occasionally,
for 15 minutes. To serve, drizzle the
lemon juice over the roasted mackerel,
accompanied by the roasted blueberries.

Griddled Trout with Bacon

This dish can also be cooked on the barbecue.

INGREDIENTS

25 g / 1 oz / 1 tbsp plain flour
4 trout, cleaned and gutted
75 g / 3 oz streaky bacon
50 g / 2 oz / 4 tbsp butter
15 ml / 1 tbsp olive oil
juice of ½ lemon
salt and freshly ground
black pepper

Serves 4

1

Pat the trout dry with kitchen roll and
mix the flour and seasoning together.

2

Roll the trout in the seasoned flour mixture
and wrap tightly in the streaky bacon.
Heat a heavy frying pan. Heat the butter and
oil in the pan and fry the trout for 5 minutes
on each side. Serve immediately, with the
lemon juice drizzled on top.

Cod, Basil and Tomato with a Potato Thatch

With a green salad, this makes an ideal dish for lunch or a family supper.

INGREDIENTS

1 kg / 2 lb smoked cod
1 kg / 2 lb white cod
600 ml / 1 pint milk
2 sprigs basil
1 sprig lemon thyme
75 g / 3 oz butter
1 onion, peeled and chopped
75 g / 3 oz flour
30 ml / 2 tbsp tomato purée
2 tbsp chopped basil
12 medium-sized old potatoes
50 g / 2 oz butter
300 ml / ½ pint milk
salt and pepper
1 tbsp chopped parsley

Serves 8

1

Place both kinds of fish in a roasting pan with the milk, 1.2 litres / 2 pints water and herbs. Simmer for about 3–4 minutes. Leave to cool in the liquid for about 20 minutes. Drain the fish, reserving the liquid for use in the sauce. Flake the fish, taking care to remove any skin and bone, which should be discarded.

2

Melt the butter in a pan, add the onion and cook for about 4 minutes until tender but not browned. Add the flour, tomato purée and half the basil. Gradually add the reserved fish stock, adding a little more milk if necessary to make a fairly thin sauce. Bring this to the boil, season with salt and pepper, and add the remaining basil. Add the fish carefully and stir gently. Pour into an ovenproof dish.

3

Preheat the oven to 180°C/350°F/Gas Mark 4. Boil the potatoes until tender. Add the butter and milk, and mash well. Add salt and pepper to taste and cover the fish, forking to create a pattern. If you like, you can freeze the pie at this stage. Bake for 30 minutes. Serve with chopped parsley.

Lamb with Mint and Lemon

Lamb has been served with mint for many years – it is a great combination.

INGREDIENTS

8 lamb steaks, 225 g / 8 oz each
grated rind and juice of 1 lemon
2 cloves garlic, peeled and crushed
2 spring onions, finely chopped
2 tsp finely chopped fresh mint
leaves, plus some leaves for
garnishing
4 tbsp extra virgin olive oil
salt and black pepper

Serves 8

1

Make a marinade for the lamb by mixing all the other ingredients and seasoning to taste. Place the lamb steaks in a shallow dish and cover with the marinade. Refrigerate overnight.

2

Grill the lamb under a high heat until just cooked, basting with the marinade occasionally during cooking. Turn once during cooking. Serve garnished with fresh mint leaves.

Mediterranean Quiche

The strong Mediterranean flavours of tomatoes, peppers and anchovies complement beautifully the cheesy pastry in this unusual quiche.

INGREDIENTS

For the pastry
225 g / 8 oz / 2 cups plain flour
pinch of salt
pinch of dry mustard
115 g / 4 oz / ½ cup butter,
chilled and cubed
50 g / 2 oz Gruyère cheese, grated

For the filling
50 g / 2 oz can of anchovies in oil,
drained
50 ml / 2 fl oz / ¼ cup milk
30 ml / 2 tbsp French mustard
45 ml / 3 tbsp olive oil
2 large Spanish onions, sliced
1 red pepper, seeded and
very finely sliced
3 egg yolks
350 ml / 12 fl oz / 1½ cups
double cream
1 garlic clove, crushed
175 g / 6 oz mature Cheddar
cheese, grated
2 large tomatoes, thickly sliced
salt and freshly ground
black pepper
30 ml / 2 tbsp chopped fresh basil,
to garnish

Serves 8

1

First make the pastry. Place the flour, salt and mustard powder in a food processor, add the butter and process the mixture until it resembles breadcrumbs.

2

Add the cheese and process again briefly. Add enough iced water to make a stiff dough: it will be ready when the dough forms a ball. Wrap with cling film and chill for 30 minutes.

3

Meanwhile, make the filling. Soak the anchovies in the milk for 20 minutes. Drain away the milk.

4

Roll out the chilled pastry and line a 23 cm / 9 in loose-based flan tin. Spread over the mustard and chill for a further 15 minutes.

5

Preheat the oven to 200°C / 400°F / Gas Mark 6. Heat the oil in a frying pan and cook the onions and red pepper until soft. In a separate bowl, beat the egg yolks, cream, garlic and Cheddar cheese together; season well. Arrange the tomatoes in a single layer in the pastry case. Top with the onion and pepper mixture and the anchovy fillets. Pour over the egg mixture. Bake for 30–35 minutes. Sprinkle over the basil and serve.

New Potato Salad

Potatoes freshly dug up from the garden are the best. Always leave the skins on: just wash the dirt away thoroughly. If you add the mayonnaise and other ingredients when the potatoes are hot, the flavours will develop as the potatoes cool.

INGREDIENTS

900 g / 2 lb baby new potatoes
2 green apples, cored and chopped
4 spring onions, chopped
3 celery sticks, finely chopped
150 ml / ¼ pint / ⅔ cup mayonnaise
salt and freshly ground black pepper

Serves 6

1

Cook the potatoes in salted, boiling water for about 20 minutes, or until they are very tender.

2

Drain the potatoes well and immediately add the remaining ingredients and stir until well mixed. Leave to cool and serve cold.

French Bean Salad

The secret of this recipe is to dress the beans while still hot.

INGREDIENTS

175 g / 6 oz cherry tomatoes, halved
5 ml / 1 tsp sugar
450 g / 1 lb French beans, topped and tailed
175 g / 6 oz feta cheese, cubed
salt and freshly ground black pepper

For the dressing
90 ml / 6 tbsp olive oil
45 ml / 3 tbsp white-wine vinegar
¼ tsp Dijon mustard
2 garlic cloves, crushed
salt and freshly ground black pepper

Serves 6

1

Preheat the oven to 230°C / 450°F / Gas Mark 8. Put the cherry tomatoes on a baking sheet and sprinkle over the sugar, salt and pepper. Roast for 10 minutes, then leave to cool. Meanwhile, cook the beans in boiling, salted water for 10 minutes.

2

Make the dressing by whisking together the oil, vinegar, mustard, garlic and seasoning. Drain the beans and immediately pour over the vinaigrette and mix well. When cool, stir in the roasted tomatoes and the feta cheese. Serve chilled.

Squash à la Greque

A traditional French-style dish that is usually made with mushrooms.
Make sure that you cook the baby squash until they are quite tender,
so they can fully absorb the delicious flavours of the marinade.

175 g / 6 oz patty-pan squash
250 ml / 8 fl oz / 1 cup white wine
juice of 2 lemons
fresh thyme sprig
bay leaf
small bunch of fresh chervil,
roughly chopped
¼ tsp coriander seeds, crushed
¼ tsp black peppercorns, crushed
75 ml / 5 tbsp olive oil

Serves 4

1

Blanch the patty-pan squash in boiling
water for 3 minutes, and then refresh them
in cold water.

2

Place all the remaining ingredients in a pan,
add 150 ml / ½ pint / ⅔ cup of water and
simmer for 10 minutes, covered. Add the
patty-pans and cook for 10 minutes. Remove
with a slotted spoon when they are cooked
and tender to the bite.

3

Reduce the liquid by boiling hard for
10 minutes. Strain it and pour it over the
squashes. Leave until cool for the flavours to
be absorbed. Serve cold.

Garden Salad

You can use any fresh, edible flowers from your garden for this beautiful salad.

INGREDIENTS

1 cos lettuce
175 g / 6 oz rocket
1 small frisée lettuce
fresh chervil and tarragon sprigs
15 ml / 1 tbsp snipped fresh chives
handful of mixed edible flower
heads, such as nasturtiums
or marigolds

For the dressing
45 ml / 3 tbsp olive oil
15 ml / 1 tbsp white-wine vinegar
½ tsp French mustard
1 garlic clove, crushed
pinch of sugar

Serves 4

1

Mix the cos, rocket and frisée leaves
and herbs together.

2

Make the dressing by whisking all the
ingredients together in a large bowl. Toss the
salad leaves in the bowl with the dressing,
add the flower heads and serve at once.

Smoked Salmon, Lemon and Dill Pasta

This has been tried and tested as both a main-dish salad and a starter, and the only preference stated was that as a main dish you got a larger portion.

INGREDIENTS

salt
350 g / 12 oz pasta twists
6 large sprigs fresh dill, chopped, plus more sprigs to garnish
30 ml / 2 tbsp extra virgin olive oil
15 ml / 1 tbsp white wine vinegar
300 ml / ½ pint double cream
pepper
170 g / 6 oz smoked salmon

Serves 2 as a main course

1

Boil the pasta in salted water until it is just cooked. Drain and run under the cold tap until completely cooled. Make the dressing by combining all the remaining ingredients, apart from the smoked salmon and reserved dill, in the bowl of a food processor and blend well. Season to taste.

2

Slice the salmon into small strips. Place the cooled pasta and the smoked salmon, in a mixing bowl. Pour on the dressing and toss carefully. Transfer to a serving bowl and garnish with the dill sprigs.

Avocado and Pasta Salad with Coriander

Served as one of a variety of salads or alone, this tasty combination is sure to please.

INGREDIENTS

115 g / 4 oz pasta shells or bows
900 ml / 1½ pints chicken stock
4 sticks celery, finely chopped
2 avocados, chopped
1 clove garlic, peeled and chopped
1 tbsp finely chopped fresh coriander, plus some whole leaves to garnish
115 g / 4 oz grated mature Cheddar cheese

For the dressing
150 ml / ¼ pint extra virgin olive oil
15 ml / 1 tbsp cider vinegar
30 ml / 2 tbsp lemon juice
grated rind of 1 lemon
5 ml / 1 tsp French mustard
1 tbsp chopped fresh coriander
salt and pepper

Serves 4

1

Bring the chicken stock to the boil, add the pasta, and simmer for about 10 minutes until just cooked. Drain and cool under cold running water.

2

Mix the celery, avocados, garlic and chopped coriander in a bowl and add the cooled pasta. Sprinkle with the grated Cheddar.

3

Place all the ingredients for the dressing in a food processor and mix until the coriander is finely chopped. Serve separately or pour over the salad and toss before serving. Garnish with coriander leaves.

Country Strawberry Fool

Make this delicious fool on the day you want to eat it, and chill it well,
for the best strawberry taste.

INGREDIENTS

300 ml / ½ pint / 1 ¼ cups milk
2 egg yolks
90 g / 3 ½ oz / scant ½ cup
caster sugar
few drops of vanilla essence
900 g / 2 lb ripe strawberries
juice of ½ lemon
300 ml / ½ pint / 1 ¼ cups double
cream

To decorate
12 small strawberries
4 fresh mint sprigs

Serves 4

1

First make the custard. Whisk 30 ml / 2 tbsp
milk with the egg yolks, 15 ml / 1 tbsp caster
sugar and the vanilla essence.

2

Heat the remaining milk until it is just
below boiling point.

3

Stir the milk into the egg mixture. Rinse
the pan out and return the mixture to it.

4

Gently heat and whisk until the mixture
thickens (it should be thick enough to coat
the back of a spoon). Lay a wet piece of
greaseproof paper on top of the custard and
leave it to cool.

5

Purée the strawberries in a food processor or
blender with the lemon juice and the
remaining sugar.

6

Lightly whip the cream and fold in the fruit
purée and custard. Pour into glass dishes and
decorate with the whole strawberries and
sprigs of mint.

Mint Ice Cream

*This ice cream is best served slightly softened, so take it out
of the freezer 20 minutes before you want to serve it. For a special occasion,
this looks spectacular served in an ice bowl.*

INGREDIENTS

*8 egg yolks
75 g / 3 oz / 6 tbsp caster sugar
600 ml / 1 pint / 2½ cups single
cream
1 vanilla pod
60 ml / 4 tbsp chopped fresh mint*

Serves 8

1

Beat the egg yolks and sugar until they are
pale and light using a hand-held electric
beater or a balloon whisk. Transfer to a
small saucepan.

2

In a separate saucepan, bring the cream to
the boil with the vanilla pod.

3

Remove the vanilla pod and pour the hot cream
on to the egg mixture, whisking briskly.

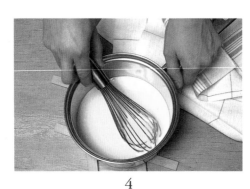

4

Continue whisking to ensure the eggs
are mixed into the cream.

5

Gently heat the mixture until the custard
thickens enough to coat the back of a
wooden spoon. Leave to cool.

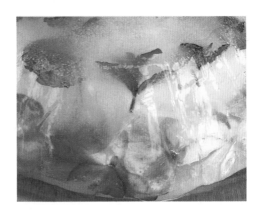

6

Stir in the mint and place in an ice-cream
maker to churn, about 3–4 hours. If you
don't have an ice-cream maker, freeze the
ice cream until mushy and then whisk it well
again, to break down the ice crystals. Freeze
for another 3 hours until it is softly frozen
and whisk again. Finally freeze until hard:
at least 6 hours.

Mixed Berry Tart

The orange-flavoured pastry is delicious with the fresh fruits of summer.
Serve this with some extra shreds of orange rind scattered on top.

INGREDIENTS

For the pastry
225 g / 8 oz / 2 cups plain flour
*115 g / 4 oz / ½ cup unsalted
butter*
*finely grated rind of 1 orange,
plus extra to decorate*

For the filling
*300 ml / ½ pint / 1¼ cups
crème fraîche*
finely grated rind of 1 lemon
10 ml / 2 tsp icing sugar
*675 g / 1½ lb mixed
summer berries*

Serves 8

1

To make the pastry, put the flour and butter in a large bowl. Rub in the butter until the mixture resembles breadcrumbs.

2

Add the orange rind and enough cold water to make a soft dough.

3

Roll into a ball and chill for at least 30 minutes. Roll out the pastry on a lightly floured surface.

4

Line a 23 cm / 9 in loose-based flan tin with the pastry. Chill for 30 minutes. Preheat the oven to 200°C / 400°F / Gas Mark 6 and place a baking sheet in the oven to heat up. Line the tin with greaseproof paper and baking beans and bake blind on the baking sheet for 15 minutes. Remove the paper and beans and bake for 10 minutes more, until the pastry is golden. Allow to cool completely. To make the filling, whisk the crème fraîche, lemon rind and sugar together and pour into the pastry case. Top with fruit, sprinkle with orange rind and serve sliced.

Summer Fruit Gâteau with Heartsease

No one could resist the appeal of little heartsease pansies. This cake would be lovely for a sentimental summer occasion in the garden.

INGREDIENTS

100 g / 3½ oz / scant ½ cup soft margarine, plus more to grease mould
100 g / 3¾ oz / scant ½ cup sugar
10 ml / 2 tsp clear honey
150 g / 5 oz / 1¼ cups self-raising flour
3 ml / ½ tsp baking powder
30 ml / 2 tbsp milk
2 eggs, plus white of one more for crystallizing
15 ml / 1 tbsp rosewater
15 ml / 1 tbsp Cointreau
16 heartsease flowers
caster sugar, as required, to crystallize
icing sugar, to decorate
500 g / 1 lb strawberries
strawberry leaves, to decorate

Serves 6–8

1

Crystallize the heartsease pansies by painting them with lightly beaten egg white and sprinkling with caster sugar. Leave to dry.

2

Preheat the oven to 190°C/375°F/ Gas Mark 5. Grease and lightly flour a ring mould.

3

Take a large mixing bowl and add the soft margarine, sugar, honey, flour, baking powder, milk and 2 eggs to the mixing bowl and beat well for 1 minute. Add the rosewater and the Cointreau and mix well.

4

Pour the mixture into the pan and bake for 40 minutes. Allow to stand for a few minutes and then turn out on to the plate that you wish to serve it on.

5

Sift icing sugar over the cake. Fill the centre of the ring with strawberries. Decorate with crystallized heartsease flowers and some strawberry leaves.

Borage, Mint and Lemon Balm Sorbet

Borage has such a pretty flower head that it is worth growing just to make this recipe, and to float the flowers in summer drinks. The sorbet itself has a very refreshing, delicate taste, perfect for a hot afternoon.

INGREDIENTS

500 g / 1 lb / 2⅛ cups sugar
500 ml / 17 fl oz / 2⅛ cups water
6 sprigs mint, plus more to decorate
6 lemon balm leaves
250 ml / 8 fl oz / 1 cup white wine
30 ml / 2 tbsp lemon juice
borage sprigs, to decorate

Serves 6–8

1

Place the sugar and water in a saucepan with the washed herbs. Bring to a boil. Remove from the heat and add the wine. Cover and cool. Chill for several hours, then add the lemon juice. Freeze and as soon as the mixture begins to freeze, stir briskly and replace in the freezer. Repeat every 15 minutes for at least 3 hours.

3

Place a small freezer-proof bowl inside each larger bowl and put inside a heavy weight such as a metal weight from some scales. Fill with more cooled boiled water, float more herbs in this and freeze.

2

To make the small ice bowls, pour about 1 cm/½ in cold, boiled water into small freezer-proof bowls about 600 ml/ 1 pint/1¼ US pints in capacity, and arrange some herbs in the water. Freeze, then add a little more water to cover the herbs.

4

To release the ice bowls, warm the inner bowl with a small amount of very hot water and twist it out. Warm the outer bowl by standing it in very hot water for a few seconds then tip out the ice bowl. Spoon the sorbet into the ice bowls and decorate with sprigs of mint and borage.

Lemon Meringue Bombe with Mint Chocolate

*This easy ice cream will cause a sensation at a dinner party – it is unusual but quite the
most delicious combination of tastes that you can imagine.*

INGREDIENTS

*2 large lemons
150 g / 5 oz granulated sugar
3 small sprigs fresh mint
150 ml / ¼ pint whipping cream
600 ml / 1 pint natural yogurt
2 large meringues
225 g / 8 oz good-quality mint
chocolate, grated*

Serves 6–8

1

Slice the rind off the lemons with a potato
peeler, then squeeze them for juice. Place the
lemon rind and sugar in a food processor
and blend finely. Add the cream, yogurt and
lemon juice and process thoroughly. Pour
the mixture into a mixing bowl and add the
meringues, roughly crushed.

3

When the ice cream has frozen, scoop out
the middle and pour in the grated mint
chocolate. Replace the ice cream to cover
the chocolate and refreeze.

2

Reserve one of the mint sprigs and chop
the rest finely. Add to the mixture. Pour
into a 1.2 litre / 2 pint glass bowl and freeze
for 4 hours.

4

To turn out, dip the basin in very hot
water for a few seconds to loosen the ice
cream, then turn the basin upside down
over the serving plate. Decorate with grated
chocolate and a sprig of mint.

Apple Mint and Pink Grapefruit Fool

Apple mint can easily run riot in the herb garden; this is an excellent
way of using up an abundant crop.

INGREDIENTS

500 g / 1 lb tart apples, peeled, cored
and sliced
225 g / 8 oz pink grapefruit segments
45 ml / 3 tbsp clear honey
30 ml / 2 tbsp water
6 large sprigs apple mint, plus more
to garnish
150 ml / ¼ pint double cream
300 ml / ½ pint custard

Serves 4–6

1

Place the apples, grapefruit, honey, water
and apple mint in a pan, cover and simmer
for 10 minutes until soft. Leave in the pan
to cool, then discard the apple mint. Purée
the mixture in a food processor.

2

Whip the cream until it forms soft peaks,
and fold into the custard, keeping 2 tbsp to
decorate. Carefully fold the cream into the
fruit mixture. Serve chilled and decorated
with swirls of cream and sprigs of mint.

Autumn Recipes

....

*Reap the benefits of the autumn harvest with this
collection of recipes; wild mushroom tart,
thyme-roasted onions and duck and chestnut casserole
all make the most of autumn produce.
Warming desserts such as steamed ginger and
syrup pudding or poached pears, are guaranteed to
keep away the autumn chill.*

Wild Mushroom Tart

The flavour of wild mushrooms makes this tart really rich: use as wide a variety
of mushrooms as you can get.

INGREDIENTS

For the pastry
225 g / 8 oz / 2 cups plain flour
50 g / 2 oz / 4 tbsp hard white fat
10 ml / 2 tsp lemon juice
about 150 ml / ¼ pint / ⅔ cup
ice-cold water
115 g / 4 oz / ½ cup butter,
chilled and cubed
1 egg, beaten, to glaze

For the filling
150 g / 5 oz / 10 tbsp butter
2 shallots, finely chopped
2 garlic cloves, crushed
450 g / 1 lb mixed wild
mushrooms, sliced
45 ml / 3 tbsp chopped fresh parsley
30 ml / 2 tbsp double cream
salt and freshly ground
black pepper

Serves 6

1

To make the pastry, sieve the flour and
½ tsp salt together into a large bowl.
Add the white fat and rub into the mixture
until it resembles breadcrumbs.

2

Add the lemon juice and enough iced water
to make a soft but not sticky dough.
Cover and chill for 20 minutes.

3

Roll the pastry out into a rectangle on a
lightly floured surface. Mark the dough into
three equal strips and arrange half the butter
cubes over two-thirds of the dough.

4

Fold the outer two-thirds over, folding over
the uncovered third last. Seal the edges with
a rolling pin. Give the dough a quarter turn
and roll it out again. Mark it into thirds and
dot with the remaining butter cubes
in the same way.

5

Chill the pastry for 20 minutes. Repeat the
process of marking into thirds, folding over,
giving a quarter turn and rolling out three
times, chilling for 20 minutes in between
each time. To make the filling, melt
50 g / 2 oz / 4 tbsp butter and fry the shallots
and garlic until soft but not browned. Add
the remaining butter and the mushrooms
and cook for 35–40 minutes. Drain off any
excess liquid and stir in the remaining
ingredients. Leave to cool. Preheat the oven
to 220°C / 450°F / Gas Mark 7.

6

Divide the pastry in two. Roll out one half
into a 22 cm / 9 in round, cutting around a
plate to make a neat shape. Pile the filling
into the centre. Roll out the remaining
pastry large enough to cover the base. Brush
the edges of the base with water and then lay
the second pastry circle on top. Press the
edges together to seal and brush the top with
a little beaten egg. Bake for 45 minutes,
or until the pastry is risen, golden and flaky.

Mushroom and Parsley Soup

*Thickened with bread, this rich mushroom soup will warm you up
on cold autumn days. It makes a terrific hearty lunch.*

INGREDIENTS

75 g / 3 oz / 6 tbsp unsalted butter
900 g / 2 lb field mushrooms,
sliced
2 onions, roughly chopped
600 ml / 1 pint / 2½ cups milk
8 slices white bread
60 ml / 4 tbsp chopped fresh parsley
300 ml / ½ pint / 1¼ cups
double cream
salt and freshly ground
black pepper

Serves 8

1

Melt the butter and sauté the mushrooms
and onions until soft but not coloured –
about 10 minutes. Add the milk.

2

Tear the bread into pieces, drop them into
the soup and leave the bread to soak for
15 minutes. Purée the soup and return it to
the pan. Add the parsley, cream and seasoning.
Re-heat, but do not allow the soup to boil.
Serve at once.

Thyme-roasted Onions

*These slowly roasted onions develop a delicious, sweet flavour which is perfect
with roast meat. You could prepare par-boiled new potatoes in the same way.*

INGREDIENTS

75 ml / 5 tbsp olive oil
50 g / 2 oz / 4 tbsp unsalted butter
900 g / 2 lb small onions
30 ml / 2 tbsp chopped fresh thyme
salt and freshly ground
black pepper

Serves 4

1

Preheat the oven to 220°C / 425°F /
Gas Mark 7. Heat the oil and butter in a
large roasting tin. Add the onions and toss
them in the oil and butter mixture.

2

Add the thyme and seasoning and roast for
45 minutes, basting regularly.

Spinach, Cognac, Garlic and Chicken Pâté

INGREDIENTS

12 slices streaky bacon
2 tbsp butter
1 onion, peeled and chopped
1 clove garlic, peeled and crushed
285 g / 10 oz frozen spinach, thawed
50 g / 2 oz wholemeal breadcrumbs
30 ml / 2 tbsp Cognac
500 g / 1 lb minced chicken
(dark and light meat)
500 g / 1 lb minced pork
2 eggs, beaten
2 tbsp chopped mixed fresh herbs,
such as parsley, sage and dill
salt and pepper

Serves 12

1

Fry the bacon in a pan until it is only just done, then arrange it round the sides of a 900 ml / 1½ pints dish, if possible leaving a couple of slices to garnish.

3

Preheat the oven to 180°C / 350°F / Gas Mark 4. Combine all the remaining ingredients, apart from any remaining bacon strips, in a bowl and mix well to blend. Spoon the pâté into the loaf tin and cover with any remaining bacon.

2

Melt the butter in a pan. Fry the onion and garlic until soft. Squeeze the spinach to remove as much water as possible, then add to the pan, stirring until the spinach is dry.

4

Cover the tin with a double thickness of foil and set it in a baking pan. Pour 2.5 cm / 1 in boiling water into the baking pan. Bake for about 1¼ hours. Remove the pâté and let it cool. Place a heavy weight on top of the pâté and refrigerate overnight.

Beef, Celeriac and Horseradish Pâté

INGREDIENTS

500 g / 1 lb topside of beef, cubed
350 ml / 12 fl oz red wine
85 ml / 3 fl oz Madeira
250 ml / 8 fl oz beef or chicken stock
2 tbsp finely chopped celeriac
15 ml / 1 tbsp horseradish cream
salt and pepper
2 bay leaves
2 tbsp brandy
170 g / 6 oz butter, melted

Serves 4

1

Preheat the oven to 130°C / 250°F / Gas Mark ½. Place the beef in a casserole. Mix all the other ingredients together except the brandy and butter, and pour them over the beef. Cover tightly and cook for 2 hours.

3

Melt the remaining butter, skim any foam off the top and pour over the top of the beef, leaving any residue at the bottom of the pan. Cover the pâté and refrigerate overnight.

2

Remove and drain. Strain the liquid and reduce to about 45 ml / 3 tbsp. Slice and roughly chop the meat and put it with the reduced liquid in the food processor. Blend until fairly smooth. Add the brandy and a third of the butter. Turn into a pâté dish and leave to cool.

Chicken Stew with Blackberries and Lemon Balm

INGREDIENTS

4 chicken breasts, partly boned
salt and pepper
25 g / 1oz / scant 2 tbsp butter
15 ml / 1 tbsp sunflower oil
25 g / 1 oz / 4 tbsp flour
150 ml / ¼ pint / ⅔ cup red wine
150 ml / ¼ pint / ⅔ cup chicken stock
grated rind of half an orange plus
15 ml / 1 tbsp juice
3 sprigs lemon balm, finely chopped,
plus 1 sprig to garnish
150 ml / ¼ pint / ⅔ cup double cream
1 egg yolk
100 g / 4 oz / ⅔ cup fresh blackberries,
plus 50 g / 2 oz / ⅓ cup to garnish

Serves 4

1

Remove any skin from the chicken, and season the meat. Heat the butter and oil in a pan, fry the chicken to seal it, then transfer to a casserole dish. Stir the flour into the pan, then add wine and stock and bring to the boil. Add the orange rind and juice, and also the chopped lemon balm. Pour over the chicken.

2

Preheat the oven to 180°C / 350°F / Gas Mark 4. Cover the casserole and cook in the oven for about 40 minutes.

3

Blend the cream with the egg yolk, add some of the liquid from the casserole and stir back into the dish with the blackberries (reserving those for the garnish). Cover and cook for another 10–15 minutes. Serve garnished with the rest of the blackberries and lemon balm.

Pork and Mushrooms with Sage and Mango Chutney

INGREDIENTS

25 g / 1 oz / scant 2 tbsp butter
1 tbsp sunflower oil
750 g / 1½ lb cubed pork
175 g / 6 oz onion, peeled and
chopped
2 tbsp flour
450 ml / ¾ pint / 1⅞ cups stock
60 ml / 4 tbsp white wine
salt and pepper
225 g / 8 oz mushrooms, sliced
6 fresh sage leaves, finely chopped
2 tbsp mango chutney
1 fresh mango, peeled and sliced, to
garnish

Serves 4

1

Heat the butter and oil and fry the pork in a pan to seal it. Transfer to a casserole. Fry the onion in the pan, stir in the flour and cook for 1 minute. Preheat the oven to 180°C / 350°F / Gas Mark 4.

2

Gradually add the stock and white wine to the onion and bring to the boil. Season well and add the mushrooms, sage leaves and mango chutney. Pour the sauce mixture over the pork and cover the casserole. Cook in the oven for about 1 hour, depending on the cut of pork, until tender. Check the seasoning, garnish with mango slices, and serve with rice.

Chicken with Sloe Gin and Juniper

Juniper is used in the manufacture of gin, and this dish is flavoured with both sloe gin and juniper. Sloe gin is easy to make and has a wonderful flavour, but it can also be bought ready-made.

INGREDIENTS

2 tbsp butter
30 ml / 2 tbsp sunflower oil
8 chicken breast fillets, skinned
350 g / 12 oz carrots, cooked
1 clove garlic, peeled and crushed
1 tbsp finely chopped parsley
60 ml / 2 fl oz / ¼ cup chicken stock
60 ml / 2 fl oz / ¼ cup red wine
60 ml / 2 fl oz / ¼ cup sloe gin
1 tsp crushed juniper berries
salt and pepper
1 bunch basil, to garnish

Serves 8

1

Melt the butter with the oil in a pan, and sauté the chicken fillets until they are browned on all sides.

2

In a food processor, combine all the remaining ingredients except the basil, and blend to a smooth purée. If the mixture seems too thick add a little more red wine or water until a thinner consistency is reached.

3

Put the chicken breasts in a pan, pour the sauce over the top and cook until the chicken is cooked through, which should take about 15 minutes. Adjust the seasoning and serve garnished with chopped fresh basil leaves.

Spicy Duck Breasts with Red Plums

Duck breasts can be bought separately, which makes this dish very easy to prepare.

INGREDIENTS

*4 duck breasts, 175 g / 6 oz
each, skinned
salt
2 tsp stick cinnamon, crushed
50 g / 2 oz butter
1 tbsp plum brandy (or Cognac)
250 ml / 8 fl oz chicken stock
250 ml / 8 fl oz double cream
pepper
6 fresh red plums, stoned and sliced
6 sprigs coriander leaves, plus some
extra to garnish*

Serves 4

1

Preheat the oven to 190°C/375°F/Gas Mark 5. Score the duck breasts and sprinkle with salt. Press the crushed cinnamon on to both sides of the duck breasts. Melt half the butter in a pan and fry them on both sides to seal, then place in an ovenproof dish with the butter and bake for 6–7 minutes.

2

Remove the dish from the oven and return the contents to the pan. Add the brandy and set it alight. When the flames have died down, remove from the pan and keep warm. Add the stock and cream to the pan and simmer gently until reduced and thick. Adjust the seasoning.

3

Reserve a few plum slices for garnishing. In a pan, melt the other half of the butter and fry the plums and coriander, just enough to cook the fruit through. Slice the duck breasts and pour some sauce around each one, then garnish with slices of plum and chopped coriander.

Stuffed Tomatoes, with Wild Rice, Corn and Coriander

These tomatoes could be served as a light meal or as an accompaniment for meat or fish.

INGREDIENTS

8 medium tomatoes
50g / 2oz sweetcorn kernels
2 tbsp white wine
50g / 2oz cooked wild rice
1 clove garlic
50g / 2oz grated Cheddar cheese
1 tbsp chopped fresh coriander
salt and pepper
1 tbsp olive oil

Serves 4

1

Cut the tops off the tomatoes and remove the seeds with a small teaspoon. Scoop out all the flesh and chop finely – remember to chop the tops as well.

2

Preheat the oven to 180°C/350°F/Gas Mark 4. Put the chopped tomato in a pan. Add the sweetcorn and the white wine. Cover with a close-fitting lid and simmer until tender. Drain the excess liquid.

3

Mix together all the remaining ingredients except the olive oil, adding salt and pepper to taste. Carefully spoon the mixture into the tomatoes, piling it higher in the centre. Sprinkle the oil over the top, arrange the tomatoes in an ovenproof dish and bake at 180°C/350°F/Gas Mark 4 for 15–20 minutes until cooked through.

Spinach, Walnut and Gruyère Lasagne with Basil

This nutty lasagne is a delicious combination of flavours that easily equals the traditional meat and tomato version.

INGREDIENTS

350 g / 12 oz spinach lasagne (quick cooking)

For the walnut and tomato sauce
45 ml / 3 tbsp walnut oil
1 large onion, chopped
225 g / 8 oz celeriac, finely chopped
400g / 14oz can chopped tomatoes
1 large clove garlic, finely chopped
½ tsp sugar
115 g / 4 oz / ⅔ cup chopped walnuts
150 ml / ¼ pint / ⅔ cup Dubonnet

For the spinach and Gruyère sauce
75 g / 3 oz / ⅓ cup butter
30 ml / 2 tbsp walnut oil
1 medium onion, chopped
75 g / 3 oz / ⅔ cup flour
1 tsp mustard powder
1.2 litres / 2 pints / 5 cups milk
225 g / 8 oz / 2 cups grated Gruyère cheese
salt and pepper
ground nutmeg
500 g / 1 lb frozen spinach, thawed and puréed
2 tbsp basil, chopped

Serves 8

2

To make the spinach and Gruyère sauce, melt the butter with the walnut oil and add the onion. Cook for 5 minutes, then stir in the flour. Cook for another minute and add the mustard powder and milk, stirring vigorously. When the sauce has come to the boil, take off the heat and add three-quarters of the grated Gruyère. Season to taste with salt, pepper and nutmeg. Finally add the puréed spinach.

1

First make the walnut and tomato sauce. Heat the walnut oil and sauté the onion and celeriac. Cook for about 8–10 minutes. Meanwhile purée the tomatoes in a food processor. Add the garlic to the pan and cook for about 1 minute, then add the sugar, walnuts, tomatoes and Dubonnet. Season to taste. Simmer, uncovered, for 25 minutes.

3

Preheat the oven to 180°C/350°F/Gas Mark 4. Layer the lasagne in an ovenproof dish. Start with a layer of the spinach and Gruyère sauce, then add a little walnut and tomato sauce, then a layer of lasagne, and continue until the dish is full, ending with a layer of either sauce. Sprinkle the remaining Gruyère over the top of the dish, followed by the basil. Bake for 45 minutes.

Duck and Chestnut Casserole

Serve this casserole with a mixture of mashed potatoes and celeriac,
to soak up the rich duck juices.

INGREDIENTS

1.75 kg / 4½ lb duck
45 ml / 3 tbsp olive oil
175 g / 6 oz small onions
50 g / 2 oz field mushrooms
50 g / 2 oz shiitake mushrooms
300 ml / ½ pint / 1¼ cups
red wine
300 ml / ½ pint / 1¼ cups
beef stock
225 g / 8 oz canned, peeled,
unsweetened chestnuts, drained
salt and freshly ground
black pepper

Serves 4–6

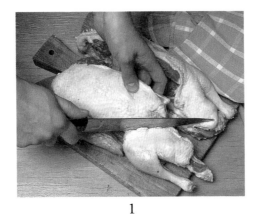

1

Joint the duck into eight pieces. Heat the oil in a large frying pan and brown the duck pieces. Remove from the frying pan.

2

Add the onions to the pan and brown them well for 10 minutes.

3

Add the mushrooms and cook for a few minutes more. Deglaze the pan with the red wine and boil to reduce the volume by half. Meanwhile, preheat the oven to 180°C / 350°F / Gas Mark 4.

4

Pour the wine and the stock into a casserole. Replace the duck, add the chestnuts, season well and cook in the oven for 1½ hours.

Cheese Scones

These delicious scones make a good tea-time treat. They are best served fresh and still slightly warm.

INGREDIENTS

*225 g / 8 oz / 2 cups plain flour
12 ml / 2½ tsp baking powder
½ tsp dry mustard powder
½ tsp salt
50 g / 2 oz / 4 tbsp butter, chilled
75 g / 3 oz Cheddar cheese, grated
150 ml / ¼ pint / ⅔ cup milk
1 egg, beaten*

Makes 12

1

Preheat the oven to 230°C / 450°F / Gas Mark 8. Sift the flour, baking powder, mustard powder and salt into a mixing bowl. Add the butter and rub it into the flour mixture until the mixture resembles breadcrumbs. Stir in 50 g / 2 oz of the cheese.

2

Make a well in the centre and add the milk and egg. Mix gently and then turn the dough out on to a lightly floured surface. Roll it out and cut it into triangles or squares. Brush lightly with milk and sprinkle with the remaining cheese. Leave to rest for 15 minutes, then bake them for 15 minutes, or until well risen.

Oatcakes

These are very simple to make and are an excellent addition to a cheese board.

INGREDIENTS

*225 g / 8 oz / 1⅔ cups medium oatmeal
75 g / 3 oz / ¾ cup plain flour
¼ tsp bicarbonate of soda
5 ml / 1 tsp salt
25 g / 1 oz / 2 tbsp hard white vegetable fat
25 g / 1 oz / 2 tbsp butter*

Makes 24

1

Preheat the oven to 220°C / 425°F / Gas Mark 7. Place the oatmeal, flour, soda and salt in a large bowl. Gently melt the two fats together in a pan.

2

Add the melted fat and enough boiling water to make a soft dough. Turn out on to a surface scattered with a little oatmeal. Roll out the dough thinly and cut it into circles. Bake the oatcakes on ungreased baking trays for 15 minutes, until crisp.

Blackberry Charlotte

A classic pudding, perfect for cold days. Serve with lightly whipped cream or home-made custard.

INGREDIENTS

65 g / 2½ oz / 5 tbsp unsalted butter
175 g / 6 oz / 3 cups fresh white breadcrumbs
50 g / 2 oz / 4 tbsp soft brown sugar
60 ml / 4 tbsp golden syrup
finely grated rind and juice of 2 lemons
50 g / 2 oz walnut halves
450 g / 1 lb blackberries
450 g / 1 lb cooking apples, peeled, cored and finely sliced

Serves 4

1

Preheat the oven to 180°C / 350°F / Gas Mark 4. Grease a 450 ml / ¾ pint / 2 cup dish with 15 g / ½ oz / 1 tbsp of the butter. Melt the remaining butter and add the breadcrumbs. Sauté them for 5–7 minutes, until the crumbs are a little crisp and golden. Leave to cool slightly.

2

Place the sugar, syrup, lemon rind and juice in a small saucepan and gently warm them. Add the crumbs.

3

Process the walnuts until they are finely ground.

4

Arrange a thin layer of blackberries on the dish. Top with a thin layer of crumbs.

5

Add a thin layer of apple, topping it with another thin layer of crumbs. Repeat the process with another layer of blackberries, followed by a layer of crumbs. Continue until you have used up all the ingredients, finishing with a layer of crumbs.

The mixture should be piled well above the top edge of the dish, because it shrinks during cooking. Bake for 30 minutes, until the crumbs are golden and the fruit is soft.

Poached Pears

Serve warm with clotted cream and crisp shortbread fingers.

INGREDIENTS

6 medium pears
350 g / 12 oz / 1¾ cups caster
sugar
75 ml / 5 tbsp runny honey
1 vanilla pod
600 ml / 1 pint / 2½ cups red wine
5 ml / 1 tsp whole cloves
7 cm / 3 in cinnamon stick

Serves 4

__1__

Peel the pears but leave them whole,
keeping the stalks as well.

__2__

Put the sugar, honey, vanilla pod, wine,
cloves and cinnamon stick in a large pan.

__3__

Add the pears and poach until soft, about
30 minutes. When the pears are tender,
remove them with a slotted spoon and keep
them warm. Remove the vanilla pod, cloves
and cinnamon stick and boil the liquid
until it is reduced by half. Serve spooned
over the pears.

Steamed Ginger and Cinnamon Syrup Pudding

A traditional and comforting steamed pudding, best served with custard.

INGREDIENTS

120 g / 4½ oz / 9 tbsp softened butter
45 ml / 3 tbsp golden syrup
115 g / 4 oz / ½ cup caster sugar
2 eggs, lightly beaten
115 g / 4 oz / 1 cup plain flour
5 ml / 1 tsp baking powder
5 ml / 1 tsp ground cinnamon
25 g / 1 oz stem ginger, finely chopped
30 ml / 2 tbsp milk

Serves 4

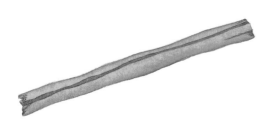

1

Set a full steamer or saucepan of water on to boil. Lightly grease a 600 ml / 1 pint / 2½ cup pudding basin with 15 g / ½ oz / 1 tbsp butter. Place the golden syrup in the basin.

2

Cream the remaining butter and sugar together until light and fluffy. Gradually add the eggs until the mixture is glossy. Sift the flour, baking powder and cinnamon together and fold them into the mixture, with the stem ginger. Add the milk to make a soft, dropping consistency.

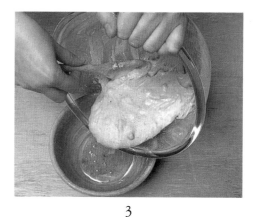

3

Spoon the batter into the basin and smooth the top. Cover with a pleated piece of greaseproof paper, to allow for expansion during cooking. Tie securely with string and steam for 1½–2 hours, making sure that the water level is kept topped up, to ensure a good flow of steam to cook the pudding. Turn the pudding out to serve it.

French Apple Tart

For added flavour, scatter some toasted, flaked almonds over the top of this classic tart.

INGREDIENTS

For the pastry
*115 g / 4 oz / ½ cup unsalted
butter, softened
50 g / 2 oz / 4 tbsp vanilla sugar
1 egg
225 g / 8 oz / 2 cups plain flour*

For the filling
*50 g / 2 oz / 4 tbsp unsalted butter
5 large tart apples, peeled, cored
and sliced
juice of ½ lemon
300 ml / ½ pint / 1¼ cups double
cream
2 egg yolks
25 g / 1 oz / 2 tbsp vanilla sugar
50 g / 2 oz / ⅔ cup ground
almonds, toasted
25 g / 1 oz / 2 tbsp flaked almonds,
toasted, to garnish*

Serves 8

1

Place the butter and sugar in a food processor and process them well together. Add the egg and process to mix it in well.

2

Add the flour and process till you have a soft dough. Wrap the dough in cling film and chill it for 30 minutes.

3

Roll the pastry out on a lightly floured surface to about 22–25 cm / 9–10 in diameter.

4

Line a flan tin with the pastry and chill it for a further 30 minutes. Preheat the oven to 220°C / 425°F / Gas Mark 7 and place a baking sheet in the oven to heat up. Line the pastry case with greaseproof paper and baking beans and bake blind on the baking sheet for 10 minutes. Then remove the beans and paper and cook for a further 5 minutes.

5

Turn the oven down to 190°C / 375°F / Gas Mark 5. To make the filling, melt the butter in a frying pan and lightly sauté the apples for 5–7 minutes. Sprinkle the apples with lemon juice.

6

Beat the cream and egg yolks with the sugar. Stir in the toasted ground almonds. Arrange the apple slices on top of the warm pastry and pour over the cream mixture. Bake for 25 minutes, or until the cream is just about set – it tastes better if the cream is still slightly runny in the centre. Serve hot or cold, scattered with flaked almonds.

Winter Recipes

....

*With the nights drawing in, we all need something
substantial and warming to keep out the cold.
Try roast beef with roasted peppers, or raised
country pie. Scotch pancakes or cranberry muffins
are a perfect fire-side treat, and rich Christmas
pudding is the perfect way to round off the year.*

Roast Beef with Porcini and Roasted Sweet Peppers

A substantial and warming dish for cold, dark evenings.

INGREDIENTS

1.5 kg / 3–3½ lb piece of sirloin
15 ml / 1 tbsp olive oil
450 g / 1 lb small red peppers
115 g / 4 oz mushrooms
*175 g / 6 oz thick-sliced pancetta
or smoked bacon, cubed*
50 g / 2 oz / 2 tbsp plain flour
*150 ml / ¼ pint / ⅔ cup full-
bodied red wine*
300 ml / ½ pint / 1¼ cups beef stock
30 ml / 2 tbsp Marsala
*10 ml / 2 tsp dried mixed herbs
salt and freshly ground
black pepper*

Serves 8

1

Preheat the oven to 190°C / 375°F /
Gas Mark 5. Season the meat well. Heat the
olive oil in a large frying pan. When very
hot, brown the meat on all sides. Place in a
large roasting tin and cook for 1¼ hours.

2

Put the red peppers in the oven to roast for
20 minutes, if small ones are available, or
45 minutes if large ones are used.

3

Near the end of the meat's cooking time,
prepare the gravy. Roughly chop the
mushroom caps and stems.

4

Heat the frying pan again and add the
pancetta or bacon. Cook until the fat runs
freely from the meat. Add the flour and cook
for a few minutes until browned.

5

Gradually stir in the red wine and the stock.
Bring to the boil, stirring. Lower the heat
and add the Marsala, herbs and seasoning.

6

Add the mushrooms to the pan and heat
through. Remove the sirloin from the oven
and leave to stand for 10 minutes before
carving it. Serve with the roasted peppers
and the hot gravy.

Bacon and Lentil Soup

Serve this hearty soup with chunks of warm, crusty bread.

INGREDIENTS

450 g / 1 lb thick-sliced
bacon, cubed
1 onion, roughly chopped
1 small turnip, roughly chopped
1 celery stick, chopped
1 carrot, sliced
1 potato, peeled and
roughly chopped
75 g / 3 oz / ½ cup lentils
1 bouquet garni
freshly ground black pepper

Serves 4

1

Heat a large pan and add the bacon. Cook for a few minutes, allowing the fat to run out.

2

Add all the vegetables and cook for 4 minutes.

3

Add the lentils, bouquet garni, seasoning and enough water to cover. Bring to the boil and simmer for 1 hour, or until the lentils are tender.

Creamy Layered Potatoes

Cook the potatoes on the hob first to help the dish to bake more quickly.

INGREDIENTS

*1.5 kg / 3–3 ½ lb large potatoes,
peeled and sliced
2 large onions, sliced
75 g / 3 oz / 6 tbsp unsalted butter
300 ml / ½ pint / 1 ¼ cups double
cream
salt and freshly ground
black pepper*

Serves 6

1

Preheat the oven to 200°C / 400°F /
Gas Mark 6. Blanch the sliced potatoes for 2
minutes, and drain well. Place the potatoes,
onions, butter and cream in a large pan,
stir well and cook for about 15 minutes.

2

Transfer to an ovenproof dish, season and
bake for 1 hour, until the potatoes are tender.

Traditional Beef Stew and Dumplings

This dish can cook in the oven while you go for a wintery walk to work up an appetite.

INGREDIENTS

25 g / 1 oz / 1 tbsp plain flour
1.2 kg / 2½ lb stewing steak,
cubed
30 ml / 2 tbsp olive oil
2 large onions, sliced
450 g / 1 lb carrots, sliced
300 ml / ½ pint / 1¼ cups
Guinness or dark beer
3 bay leaves
10 ml / 2 tsp brown sugar
3 fresh thyme sprigs
5 ml / 1 tsp cider vinegar
salt and freshly ground
black pepper

For the dumplings
115 g / 4 oz / ½ cup grated hard
white fat
225 g / 8 oz / 2 cups self-raising
flour
30 ml / 2 tbsp chopped mixed
fresh herbs
about 150 ml / ¼ pint / ⅔ cup
water

Serves 6

1

Preheat the oven to 160°C / 325°F /
Gas Mark 3. Season the flour and sprinkle
over the meat, tossing to coat.

2

Heat the oil in a large casserole and lightly
sauté the onions and carrots. Remove the
vegetables with a slotted spoon and
reserve them.

3

Brown the meat well in batches
in the casserole.

4

Return all the vegetables to the casserole and
add any leftover seasoned flour. Add the
Guinness or beer, bay leaves, sugar and
thyme. Bring the liquid to the boil and then
transfer to the oven. Leave the meat to cook
for 1 hour and 40 minutes, before making
the dumplings.

5

Mix the grated fat, flour and herbs together.
Add enough water to make a soft
sticky dough.

6

Form the dough into small balls with floured
hands. Add the cider vinegar to the meat and
spoon the dumplings on top. Cook for a
further 20 minutes, until the dumplings
have cooked through, and serve hot.

Country Pie

*A classic raised pie. It takes quite a long time to make,
but is a perfect winter treat.*

INGREDIENTS

1 small duck
1 small chicken
350 g / 12 oz pork belly, minced
1 egg, lightly beaten
2 shallots, finely chopped
½ tsp ground cinnamon
½ tsp grated nutmeg
5 ml / 1 tsp Worcestershire sauce
finely grated rind of 1 lemon
½ tsp freshly ground black pepper
150 ml / ¼ pint / ⅔ cup red wine
175 g / 6 oz ham, cut into cubes
salt and freshly ground
black pepper

For the jelly
all the meat bones and trimmings
2 carrots
1 onion
2 celery sticks
15 ml / 1 tbsp red wine
1 bay leaf
1 whole clove
1 sachet of gelatine
(about 15 g / 1 oz)

For the pastry
225 g / 8 oz / 1 cup hard white fat
300 ml / ½ pint / 1¼ cups boiling
water
675 g / 1½ lb / 6 cups plain flour
1 egg, lightly beaten with a
pinch of salt

Serves 12

1

Cut as much meat from the raw duck and
chicken as possible, removing the skin and
sinews. Cut the duck and chicken breasts
into cubes and set them aside.

2

Mix the rest of the duck and chicken meat
with the minced pork, egg, shallots, spices,
Worcestershire sauce, lemon rind and salt
and pepper. Add the red wine and leave for
about 15 minutes for the flavours to develop.

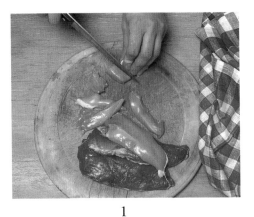

3

To make the jelly, place the meat bones and
trimmings, carrots, onion, celery, wine, bay
leaf and clove in a large pan and cover with
2.75 litres / 5 pints / 12½ cups of water.
Bring to the boil, skimming off any scum,
and simmer gently for 2½ hours.

4

To make the pastry, place the fat and water
in a pan and bring to the boil. Sieve the flour
and a pinch of salt into a bowl and pour on the
liquid. Mix with a wooden spoon, and,
when the dough is cool enough to handle,
knead it well and let it sit in a warm place,
covered with a cloth, for 20–30 minutes or
until you are ready to use it. Preheat the
oven to 200°C / 400°F / Gas Mark 6.

5

Grease a 25 cm / 10 in loose-based deep cake tin. Roll out about two-thirds of the pastry thinly enough to line the cake tin. Make sure there are no holes and allow enough pastry to leave a little hanging over the top. Fill the pie with a layer of half the minced-pork mixture; then top this with a layer of the cubed duck and chicken breast-meat and cubes of ham. Top with the remaining minced pork. Brush the overhanging edges of pastry with water and cover with the remaining rolled-out pastry. Seal the edges well. Make two large holes in the top and decorate with any pastry trimmings.

6

Bake the pie for 30 minutes. Brush the top with the egg and salt mixture. Turn down the oven to 180°C / 350°F / Gas Mark 4. After 30 minutes loosely cover the pie with foil to prevent the top getting too brown, and bake it for a further 1 hour.

7

Strain the stock after 2½ hours. Let it cool and remove the solidified layer of fat from the surface. Measure 600 ml / 1 pint / 2½ cups of stock. Heat it gently to just below boiling point and whisk the gelatine into it until no lumps are left. Add the remaining strained stock and leave to cool.

8

When the pie is cool, place a funnel through one of the holes and pour in as much of the stock as possible, letting it come up to the holes in the crust. Leave to set for at least 24 hours before slicing and serving.

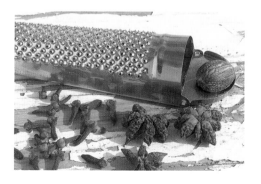

Leek and Onion Tart

This unusual recipe isn't a normal tart with pastry, but an all-in-one savoury
slice that is excellent served as an accompaniment to roast meat.

INGREDIENTS

50 g / 2 oz / 4 tbsp unsalted butter
350 g / 12 oz leeks, sliced thinly
225 g / 8 oz / 2 cups self-raising
flour
115 g / 4 oz / ½ cup grated hard
white fat
150 ml / ¼ pint / ⅔ cup water
salt and freshly ground
black pepper

Serves 4

1

Preheat the oven to 200°C / 400°F /
Gas Mark 6. Melt the butter in a pan
and sauté the leeks until soft. Season well.

2

Mix the flour, fat and water together in a
bowl to make a soft but sticky dough.
Mix into the leek mixture in the pan. Place
in a greased shallow ovenproof dish and bake
for 30 minutes, or until brown and crispy.
Serve sliced, as a vegetable accompaniment.

Orange Shortbread Fingers

These are a real tea-time treat. The fingers will keep in an airtight tin for up to two weeks.

115 g / 4 oz / ½ cup unsalted
butter, softened
50 g / 2 oz / 4 tbsp caster sugar,
plus a little extra
finely grated rind of 2 oranges
175 g / 6 oz / 1½ cups plain flour

Makes 18

1

Preheat the oven to 190°C / 375°F /
Gas Mark 5. Beat the butter and sugar
together until they are soft and creamy.
Beat in the orange rind.

2

Gradually add the flour and gently pull the
dough together to form a soft ball. Roll the
dough out on a lightly floured surface until
about 1 cm / ½ in thick. Cut it into fingers,
sprinkle over a little extra caster sugar,
prick with a fork and bake for about
20 minutes, or until the fingers are a
light golden colour.

Cranberry Muffins

A tea or breakfast dish that is not too sweet.

INGREDIENTS

3 cups all-purpose flour
1 tsp baking powder
pinch of salt
1/2 cup superfine sugar
2 eggs
2/3 cup milk
4 tbsp corn oil
finely grated rind of 1 orange
5 oz cranberries

Makes 12

1

Preheat the oven to 375°F. Line a muffin pan with paper cases. Mix the flour, baking powder, salt and superfine sugar together.

2

Lightly beat the eggs with the milk and oil. Add them to the dry ingredients and blend to make a smooth batter. Stir in the orange rind and cranberries. Divide the mixture between the muffin cases and bake for 25 minutes until risen and golden. Let cool in the pan for a few minutes, and serve warm or cold.

Country Pancakes

Serve these hot with butter and maple syrup or jam.

INGREDIENTS

2 cups self-rising flour
4 tbsp superfine sugar
4 tbsp butter, melted
1 egg
1 1/4 cups milk
1 tbsp corn oil or margarine

Makes 24

1

Mix the flour and sugar together. Add the melted butter and egg with two-thirds of the milk. Mix to a smooth batter – it should be thin enough to find its own level.

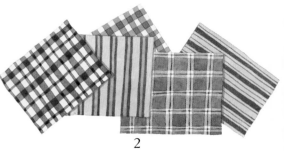

2

Heat a griddle or a heavy-based frying pan and wipe it with a little oil or margarine. When hot, drop spoonfuls of the mixture on to the hot griddle or pan. When bubbles come to the surface of the pancakes, flip them over to cook until golden on the other side. Keep the pancakes warm wrapped in a dish towel while cooking the rest of the mixture. Serve as soon as possible.

Christmas Pudding

The classic Christmas dessert. Wrap it in muslin and store it in an airtight container for up to a year for the flavours to develop.

INGREDIENTS

115 g / 4 oz / 1 cup plain flour
pinch of salt
5 ml / 1 tsp ground mixed spice
½ tsp ground cinnamon
¼ tsp freshly grated nutmeg
225 g / 8 oz / 1 cup grated hard white fat
1 dessert apple, grated
225 g / 8 oz / 2 cups fresh white breadcrumbs
350 g / 12 oz / 1⅞ cups soft brown sugar
50 g / 2 oz flaked almonds
225 g / 8 oz / 1½ cups seedless raisins
225 g / 8 oz / 1½ cups currants
225 g / 8 oz / 1½ cups sultanas
115 g / 4 oz ready-to-eat dried apricots
115 g / 4 oz / ¾ cup chopped mixed peel
finely grated rind and juice of 1 lemon
30 ml / 2 tbsp black treacle
3 eggs
300 ml / ½ pint / 1¼ cups milk
30 ml / 2 tbsp rum

Serves 8

1

Sieve the flour, salt and spices into a large bowl.

2

Add the fat, apple and other dry ingredients, including the grated lemon rind.

3

Heat the treacle until warm and runny and pour into the dry ingredients.

4

Mix together the eggs, milk, rum and lemon juice.

5

Stir the liquid into the dry mixture.

6

Spoon the mixture into two 1.2 litre / 2 pint / 5 cup basins. Overwrap the puddings with pieces of greaseproof paper, pleated to allow for expansion, and tie with string. Steam the puddings in a steamer or saucepan of boiling water. Each pudding needs 10 hours' cooking and 3 hours' reheating. Remember to keep the water level topped up to keep the pans from boiling dry. Serve decorated with holly.

Index

Acorn and Oak-leaf Border 30–31
Aftershave, Dill 392
All-foliage Arrangement 232
Alphabet Cot Quilt 105–6
Amish:
Amish Bag 116
Amish Sewing Box 80
anchovies: Mediterranean Quiche 448
apples:
Apple and Mint Jelly 398
Apple Mint and Pink Grapefruit Fool
465
French Apple Tart 488
Peony and Apple Table Arrangement
278–9
appliqué:
Appliqué T-shirt 128
Appliqué Wool Scarf 119
Baby's Appliqué Pillow 152
Heart Appliqué Pillowslip 131
Quilted Appliqué Cushion Cover
108–10
Apron, Kitchen 178
Artichoke Pinholder Display 288
Arum Lily Vase 251
Autumn Candle Display 244–5
Autumn Crocus Trug 242
Autumn Fruitfulness 264
Autumn Gold 265
Autumn Leaf Shoe Bag 129
Autumnal Orange Display 306
Avocado and Pasta Salad with Coriander
454

baby:
Baby Birth Gift 346
Baby's Appliqué Pillow 152
Planted Basket for Baby 347
bacon:
Bacon and Lentil Soup 494
Griddled Trout with Bacon 445
bags:
Amish Bag 116
Autumn Leaf Shoe Bag 129
Embroidered Laundry Bag 188
Lavender Bag 334
Toy Bag 134
Baked Eggs with Double Cream and
Chives 430
basil:
Cod, Basil and Tomato with a Potato
Thatch 446
Spinach, Walnut and Gruyère Lasagne
with Basil 479

baskets:
Edging Basket in Blue 290
Everlasting Basket 319
Fruit and Fungi Basket Rim Decoration
305
Hydrangea Basket Edging 240
Lavender Basket 310
Pink Basket Display 308–9
Planted Basket for Baby 347
Summer Basket Display 237
bath:
Bath-bags 376
Bath-time Bottle 382
Bath-time Treat Jar 382
Herb Bath-bag 348–9
Lavender and Marjoram Bath 394
Lavender Bubble Bath 393
Lemon Grass, Coriander and Clove Bath
394
Bathroom Display 294–5
Bay Gravy, Steak and Kidney Pie with
Mustard and 425
Bean Salad, French 450
Bear's Paw Quilt 102–4
beef:
Beef, Celeriac and Horseradish Pâté 472
Roast Beef with Porcini and Roasted
Sweet Peppers 492
Traditional Beef Stew and Dumplings
496
Birth Keepsake 344
blackberries:
Blackberry Charlotte 484
Chicken Stew with Blackberries and
Lemon Balm 474
blue:
Blue and Yellow Arrangement in a
Pitcher 246
Blue and Yellow Bud Vases 236
Edging Basket in Blue 290
Massed Arrangement in Blue and
Yellow 286
Blueberries, Mackerel with Roasted 444
Bolster Cushion 122
Bombe, Lemon Meringue, with Mint
Chocolate 464
Book, Rag 126
Bootees, Crazy Patchwork 148
Borage, Mint and Lemon Balm Sorbet 462
border:
Acorn and Oak-leaf Border 30–31
Stencilled Border 18–19
Bottle, Bath-time 382
Bowl, Hyacinth Bulb 226

boxes:
Herb Box and Pot Stand 198–9
Shaker Box 164
Shell Box 351
Utensil Box 167
Brandy, Poached Spiced Plums in 402
bread:
Easter Plait 434
Wholemeal Bread 433
Bread Bin, French 72–3
Brushed-out Colour Glaze 16
Bubble Bath, Lavender 393
Bud Vases, Blue and Yellow 236
bulbs:
Autumn Crocus Trug 242
Hyacinth Bulb Bowl 226
Hyacinth Bulb Vases 220

cakes:
Lemon Drizzle Cake 432
Summer Fruit Gâteau with Heartsease
462
Calico Rag Doll 124
Calla Lilies, Decorated Vase with 254
Calvados, Fish Stew with, Parsley and Dill
421
Candleholder Display, Small 289
candles:
Autumn Candle Display 244–5
Candle Ring 231
Peony and Globe Thistle Candle
Decoration 292
Shell Candle Centrepiece 352
Candlesticks, Wooden 62–3
Canvas Floorcloth, Painted 32–3
cards:
Greetings Card 341
Patchwork Cards 338
Pressed Herb Cards 380
Carrot and Coriander Soufflés 428
cases:
Handkerchief Case 342
Nightdress Case 192
casseroles and stews:
Chicken Stew with Blackberries and
Lemon Balm 474
Duck and Chestnut Casserole 480
Fish Stew with Calvados, Parsley and
Dill 421
Traditional Beef Stew and Dumplings
496
Celeriac and Horseradish Pâté, Beef 472
centrepieces:
Shell Candle Centrepiece 352

Vegetable Centrepiece 261
Chair, Painted and Lined Country 46–7
chamomile:
    Bath Bags 376
    Chamomile and Honey Mask 384
    Chamomile Conditioning Rinse 390
Charlotte, Blackberry 484
cheese:
    Cheese Scones 482
    Leeks with Ham and Cheese Sauce 430
    Pear and Watercress Soup with Stilton
        Croûtons 441
    Spinach and Roquefort Pancakes 418
    Spinach, Walnut and Gruyère Lasagne
        with Basil 479
Cherry Basket Patchwork Cushion 146
Chest, Painted 40–41
Chestnut Casserole, Duck and 480
chicken:
    Chicken Stew with Blackberries and
        Lemon Balm 474
    Chicken with Sloe Gin and Juniper 476
    Country Pie 498–9
    Spinach, Cognac, Garlic and Chicken
        Pâté 472
    Spring Roasted Chicken with Fresh
        Herbs and Garlic 426
    Warm Chicken Salad with Sesame and
        Coriander 418
Child's Strip Patchwork Rucksack 132
Child's Strip Patchwork Skirt 137
Child's Strip Patchwork Waistcoat 136
Child's Suffolk Puff Waistcoat 158
Chilli Gazpacho, Herb and 440
Chives, Baked Eggs with Double Cream
    and 430
Christmas:
    Christmas Pudding 505
    Everlasting Christmas Tree 316
    Herbal Christmas Wreath 374
chutney:
    Pork and Mushrooms with Sage and
        Mango Chutney 474
    Tomato Chutney 404
cinnamon:
    Cinnamon and Orange Ring 368
    Steamed Ginger and Cinnamon Syrup
        Pudding 487
Circlet, Hydrangea 303
Cleanser, Fennel 387
clove:
    Lemon Grass, Coriander and Clove Bath
        394
    Orange and Clove Pomander 369

Rose and Clove Pomander 371
Coathanger, Embroidered 202
Cod, Basil and Tomato with a Potato
    Thatch 446
Cognac, Garlic and Chicken Pâté, Spinach
    472
Colour Glaze, Brushed-out 16
Complexion Milk, Feverfew 386
Conditioning Rinse, Chamomile 390
coriander:
    Avocado and Pasta Salad with Coriander
        454
    Carrot and Coriander Soufflés 428
    Lemon Grass, Coriander and Clove Bath
        394
    Stuffed Tomatoes with Wild Rice, Corn
        and Coriander 478
    Warm Chicken Salad with Sesame and
        Coriander 418
Cork-tile Chequer-board Floor 29
Corn and Coriander, Stuffed Tomatoes with
    Wild Rice 478
Corsages, Herb 377
Cot Quilt, Alphabet 105–6
Country Pie 498–9
Country Strawberry Fool 456
Country Throw 114
Country Wreath Cushion 123
Country-style Motifs and Patterns 36–7
Cow, Folk Art 185
Crackers, Herb-decorated 379
Cranberry Muffins 502
Crazy Patchwork Bootees 148
Cream, Double, and Chives, Baked Eggs
    with 430
Creamy Layered Potatoes 495
Crocus Trug, Autumn 242
Cross Stitch Pincushion 204–5
Crumble, Rhubarb and Orange 436
Cube, Patchwork 153
Cupboard, Pie-safe 48–9
Curd, Lemon and Lime 400
Curtain Pelmet 171
Curtain-pole Hanging Display 78
cushion covers:
    Bolster Cushion 122
    Cherry Basket Patchwork Cushion 146
    Country Wreath Cushion 123
    Dresden Plate Herb Cushion 142
    Oak Leaf Seat Cushion 154
    Patchwork Cushion 176
    Pieced Cushion Cover 111–13
    Quilted Appliqué Cushion Cover
        108–10

Dahlia Arrangement, Large 247
Decorated Vase with Calla Lilies 254
Découpage Tray 59–60
Dhurrie, Hardboard Floor with Trompe-
    l'oeil 26–8
Diamond-in-a-Square Quilt 144
Diary, Scented Pressed Herb 380
dill:
    Dill Aftershave 392
    Fish Stew with Calvados, Parsley and
        Dill 421
    Smoked Salmon, Lemon and Dill Pasta
        454
distressed plaster effect 17
Doll, Calico Rag 124
Dresden Plate Herb Cushion 142
Dresser, Painted 52–3
dried flowers
    Dried Fireplace Arrangement 302
    Dried Flower Gift-wrap 360
    Dried-flower Pot 318
    Dried Flowers as a Gift 361
    Dried-herb Wreath 320
    Dried Herbal Posy 375
    Dried Herbal Topiary Tree 373
    Dried Mantelpiece Display 300
    Flower Topiary 312
duck:
    Country Pie 498–9
    Duck and Chestnut Casserole 480
    Spicy Duck Breasts with Red Plums
        477
Dummy Board, Rabbit 74–5
Dumplings, Traditional Beef Stew and 496

Easter Plait 434
Edging Basket in Blue 290
Edging, Hydrangea Basket 240
Egg Cosy, Patchwork Tea and 140
Eggs, Baked, with Double Cream and
    Chives 430
Embroidered Coathanger 202
Embroidered Laundry Bag 188
Embroidered Pelmet 79
Embroidered Sheet and Pillow Case 200
Everlasting Basket 319
Everlasting Christmas Tree 316

Fan, Hanging 157
Fennel Cleanser 387
Feverfew Complexion Milk 386
Filigree Leaf Wrap 356
Fireplace Arrangement 250
Fireplace Arrangement, Dried 302

fish:
    Cod, Basil and Tomato with a Potato
       Thatch 446
    Fish Stew with Calvados, Parsley and
       Dill 421
    Herbed Halibut Mille-feuille 442
    Leek and Monkfish with Thyme Sauce
       420
    Mackerel with Roasted Blueberries
       444
    Salmon and Ginger Pie 442
    Smoked Salmon, Lemon and Dill Pasta
       454
Floorboards, Limed 24
floors:
    Cork-tile Chequer-board Floor 29
    Hardboard Floor with Trompe-l'oeil
       Dhurrie 26–8
    Painted Canvas Floorcloth 32–3
Floral Tie-backs 196
Flower Topiary 312
Foam-block Painting 22–3
Folk Art Cow 185
fools:
    Apple Mint and Pink Grapefruit Fool
       465
    Country Strawberry Fool 456
frames:
    Patchwork Frame 118
    Photo Frame 339
Free-hand Frieze with Half-gloss to Dado
    Height 20–21
French Apple Tart 488
French Bean Salad 450
French Bread Bin 72–3
Fresh-flower Fruit Bowl 260
Fresh Herbal Wreath 222
Frieze, Free-hand, with Half-gloss to Dado
    Height 20–21
fruit:
    Autumn Fruitfulness 264
    Fresh-flower Fruit Bowl 260
    Fruit and Flower Swag 228
    Fruit and Foliage Gift-wrap 356
    Fruit and Fungi Basket Rim Decoration
       305
    Mixed Berry Tart 460
    Summer Fruit Gâteau with Heartsease
       462
Fruity Tree 317

Game Board 172
Garden Salad 453
Garland, Springtime 266–7

garlic:
    Spinach, Cognac, Garlic and Chicken
       Pâté 472
    Spring Roasted Chicken with Fresh
       Herbs and Garlic 426
Gâteau, Summer Fruit, with Heartsease
    462
Gazpacho, Herb and Chilli 440
Gift Tag 340
gifts:
    Baby Birth Gift 346
    Dried Flowers as a Gift 361
gift-wraps:
    Dried Flower Gift-wrap 360
    Filigree Leaf Wrap 356
    Fruit and Foliage Gift-wrap 356
    Lavender Tissue Gift-wrap 358
    Tissue Rosette Gift-wrap 358
ginger:
    Lamb Pie with Pear, Ginger and Mint
       Sauce 424
    Salmon and Ginger Pie 442
    Steamed Ginger and Cinnamon Syrup
       Pudding 487
Gingham, Lace and, Shelf Trimming 70
glass:
    Painted Glass 84
    Red Display in a Glass Cube 298
Glaze, Brushed-out Colour 16
globe thistle:
    Globe Thistle and Mussel Shell Ring
       287
    Peony and Globe Thistle Candle
       Decoration 292
grapefruit:
    Apple Mint and Pink Grapefruit Fool
       465
    Three-fruit Marmalade 408
Greetings Card 341
Griddled Trout with Bacon 445
Guest Towel 184

hair:
    Chamomile Conditioning Rinse 390
    Lemon Verbena Hair Rinse 388
    Parsley Hair Tonic 388
    Rosemary Hair Tonic 391
Halibut Mille-feuille, Herbed 442
Ham and Cheese Sauce, Leeks with 430
Hand Towel 179
Handkerchief Case 342
hanging decorations:
    Curtain-pole Hanging Display 78
    Hanging Fan 157

Hanging Heart Sachet 130
Hanging Hearts 156
Hanging Salt Box 86
Provençal Herb Hanging 258
Shelf with Hanging Hooks 50–51
Wall Hanging Sheaf 297
Hardboard Floor with Trompe-l'oeil
    Dhurrie 26–8
hearts:
    Hanging Heart Sachet 130
    Hanging Hearts 156
    Heart Appliqué Pillowslip 131
    Heart Vine Wreath 168
    Lacy Lavender Heart 332–3
    Scented Valentine Heart 378
herbs (cosmetic):
    Bath-bags 376
    Chamomile Conditioning Rinse 390
    Herb Bath-bag 348–9
    Lavender and Marjoram Bath 394
    Lavender Bubble Bath 393
    Lemon Grass, Coriander and Clove Bath
       394
    Lemon Verbena Hair Rinse 388
    Parsley Hair Tonic 388
    Rosemary Hair Tonic 391
    Tansy Skin Tonic 385
herbs (culinary):
    Baked Eggs with Double Cream and
       Chives 430
    Carrot and Coriander Soufflés 428
    Herb and Chilli Gazpacho 440
    Herbed Halibut Mille-feuille 442
    Lemon and Rosemary Lamb Chops 426
    Mushroom and Parsley Soup 470
    Rosemary-flavoured Oil 412
    Spring Roasted Chicken with Fresh
       Herbs and Garlic 426
    Thyme-flavoured Vinegar 412
    Thyme-roasted Onions 470
herbs (decorative):
    Dresden Plate Herb Cushion 142
    Dried-herb Wreath 320
    Dried Herbal Posy 375
    Dried Herbal Topiary Tree 373
    Fresh Herbal Wreath 222
    Herb Box and Pot Stand 198–9
    Herb Corsages 377
    Herb Decoration 175
    Herb Obelisk 256
    Herb Pot-mat 328
    Herb-decorated Crackers 379
    Herbal Christmas Wreath 374
    Herbal Tablepiece 372

Herbs on a Rope 186
Pressed Herb Cards 380
Provençal Herb Hanging 258
Scented Pressed Herb Diary 380
Tussie Mussie 269
Hexagon Pincushion 147
Honey Mask, Chamomile and 384
Horse, Party 182
Horseradish Pâté, Beef, Celeriac and 472
Hyacinth Bulb Bowl 226
Hyacinth Bulb Vases 220
hydrangeas:
Everlasting Basket 319
Hydrangea Basket Edging 240
Hydrangea Circlet 303
Hydrangea Pot 314

Ice Cream, Mint 458

Jam, Strawberry 406
Jelly, Apple and Mint 398
Juniper, Chicken with Sloe Gin
and 476

Key Ring, Little House 336
Kitchen Apron 178

Lace and Gingham Shelf Trimming 70
Lacy Lavender Heart 332–3
lamb:
Lamb and Leeks with Mint and Spring
Onions 422
Lamb Pie with Pear, Ginger and Mint
Sauce 424
Lamb with Mint and Lemon 447
Lemon and Rosemary Lamb Chops 426
Large Dahlia Arrangement 247
Lasagne with Basil, Spinach, Walnut and
Gruyère 479
Laundry Bag, Embroidered 188
lavender:
Bath Bags 376
Dried-flower Pot 318
Lacy Lavender Heart 332–3
Lavender and Marjoram Bath 394
Lavender Bag 334
Lavender Basket 310
Lavender Bubble Bath 393
Lavender Sachets 330
Lavender Tissue Gift-wrap 358
Tussie Mussie 269
Leaf and Petal Decoration 313
Leaf Wrap, Filigree 356
Leafy Pictures 362–3

Leather-edged Shelf Trimming 69
leeks:
Lamb and Leeks with Mint and Spring
Onions 422
Leek and Monkfish with Thyme Sauce
420
Leek and Onion Tart 500
Leeks with Ham and Cheese Sauce 430
lemon:
Lamb with Mint and Lemon 447
Lemon and Lime Curd 400
Lemon and Rosemary Lamb
Chops 426
Lemon Drizzle Cake 432
Lemon Meringue Bombe with Mint
Chocolate 464
Smoked Salmon, Lemon and Dill Pasta
454
Three-fruit Marmalade 408
lemon balm:
Borage, Mint and Lemon Balm Sorbet
462
Chicken Stew with Blackberries and
Lemon Balm 474
Lemon Grass, Coriander and Clove
Bath 394
Lemon Verbena Hair Rinse 388
Lentil Soup, Bacon and 494
Lime Curd, Lemon and 400
Limed Floorboards 24
Little House Key Ring 336
Log Cabin Throw 138

Mackerel with Roasted Blueberries 444
Mango Chutney, Pork and Mushrooms
with Sage and 474
Mantelpiece Arrangement 248
Mantelpiece Display, Dried 300
Marjoram Bath, Lavender and 394
Marmalade, Three-fruit 408
Mask, Chamomile and Honey 384
Massed Arrangement in Blue and Yellow
286
Massed Star-shaped Decoration 304
Mediterranean Quiche 448
Mille-feuille, Herbed Halibut 442
mint:
Apple and Mint Jelly 398
Borage, Mint and Lemon Balm Sorbet
462
Lamb and Leeks with Mint and Spring
Onions 422
Lamb Pie with Pear, Ginger and Mint
Sauce 424

Lamb with Mint and Lemon 447
Lemon Meringue Bombe with Mint
Chocolate 464
Mint Ice Cream 458
Mirror, Shell 354
Mixed Berry Tart 460
Mobile, Wooden Spoon 180
Monkfish with Thyme Sauce, Leek and
420
Motifs and Patterns, Country-style
36–7
Muffins, Cranberry 502
mushrooms:
Fruit and Fungi Basket Rim Decoration
305
Mushroom and Parsley Soup 470
Pork and Mushrooms with Sage and
Mango Chutney 474
Roast Beef with Porcini and Roasted
Sweet Peppers 492
Wild Mushroom Tart 468
Mussel Shell Ring, Globe Thistle and
287
Mustard and Bay Gravy, Steak and Kidney
Pie with 425

napkins:
Napkin 174
Napkin and Napkin Ring 141
Napkin Tie 227
Spring Napkin Decoration 221
Tablecloth and Napkin 194–5
New Potato Salad 450
Nightdress Case 192
Nine Star Picture 166

Oak Leaf Seat Cushion 154
Oatcakes 482
Obelisk, Herb 256
Oil, Rosemary-flavoured 412
Old-fashioned Garden Rose Arrangement
234
onions:
Leek and Onion Tart 500
Stuffed Parsleyed Onions 423
Thyme-roasted Onions 470
Orange Display, Autumnal 306
oranges:
Cinnamon and Orange Ring 368
Orange and Clove Pomander 369
Orange Arrangement 252–3
Orange Shortbread Fingers 501
Rhubarb and Orange Crumble 436
Three-fruit Marmalade 408

Paint Finish for Walls, Powdery 17
paint, mixing 14
Painted and Lined Country Chair 46–7
Painted Bench 42
Painted Canvas Floorcloth 32–3
Painted Chest 40–41
Painted Dresser 52–3
Painted Glass 84
Painted Picture Frame 82
Painted Table 38–9
Painted Tin or Toleware 76–7
Painting, Foam-block 22–3
pancakes:
    Scotch Pancakes 502
    Spinach and Roquefort Pancakes 418
parsley:
    Fish Stew with Calvados, Parsley and
        Dill 421
    Mushroom and Parsley Soup 470
    Parsley Hair Tonic 388
    Stuffed Parsleyed Onions 423
Party Horse 182
pasta:
    Avocado and Pasta Salad with Coriander
        454
    Smoked Salmon, Lemon and Dill Pasta
        454
patchwork:
    Cherry Basket Patchwork Cushion 146
    Hanging Fan 157
    Hanging Hearts 156
    Patchwork Cards 338
    Patchwork Cube 153
    Patchwork Cushion 176
    Patchwork Frame 118
    Patchwork Tea and Egg Cosies 140
    Woollen Patchwork Throw 64–5
pâté:
    Beef, Celeriac and Horseradish Pâté 472
    Spinach, Cognac, Garlic and Chicken
        Pâté 472
pears:
    Lamb Pie with Pear, Ginger and Mint
        Sauce 424
    Pear and Watercress Soup with Stilton
        Croûtons 441
    Poached Pears 486
    Spiced Pickled Pears 403
Peg Rail, Shaker-inspired 44–5
pelmets:
    Curtain Pelmet 171
    Embroidered Pelmet 79
Peony and Apple Table Arrangement
    278–9

Peony and Globe Thistle Candle
    Decoration 292
Peony and Shell Display 281
peppers:
    Mediterranean Quiche 448
    Roast Beef with Porcini and Roasted
        Sweet Peppers 492
Petal Decoration, Leaf and 313
Photo Frame 339
Piccalilli 410
Pickled Pears, Spiced 403
Picture Frame, Painted 82
pictures:
    Folk Art Cow 185
    Leafy Pictures 362–3
    Nine Star Picture 166
pies:
    Lamb Pie with Pear, Ginger and Mint
        Sauce 424
    Salmon and Ginger Pie 442
    Steak and Kidney Pie with Mustard and
        Bay Gravy 425
Pie-safe Cupboard 48–9
Pieced Cushion Cover 111–13
pillows:
    Baby's Appliqué Pillow 152
    Embroidered Sheet and Pillow Case
        200
    Heart Appliqué Pillowslip 131
    Sleep Pillow 144–5
pincushions:
    Cross Stitch Pincushion 204–5
    Hexagon Pincushion 147
Pinholder Display, Artichoke 288
Pink Basket Display 308–9
Pink Phlox Arrangement in a Pitcher 230
pitchers:
    Blue and Yellow Arrangement in a
        Pitcher 246
    Pink Phlox Arrangement in a Pitcher
        230
Plaited 'Rag-rug' Tie-backs 66
Planted Basket for Baby 347
plums:
    Poached Spiced Plums in Brandy 402
    Spicy Duck Breasts with Red Plums
        477
Poached Pears 486
Poached Spiced Plums in Brandy 402
pomanders:
    Orange and Clove Pomander 369
    Rose and Clove Pomander 371
    Spicy Pomander 364–5
    Tulip Pomander 366

Pork and Mushrooms with Sage and
    Mango Chutney 474
posies:
    Dried Herbal Posy 375
    Tied Posy 268
pot pourri:
    Pot Pourri Sachet 190
    Summer Pot Pourri 293
Pot Stand, Herb Box and 198–9
pots:
    Hydrangea Pot 314
    Shell Pot 350
    Spice Pots 314
Pot-mat, Herb 328
potatoes:
    Cod, Basil and Tomato with a Potato
        Thatch 446
    Creamy Layered Potatoes 495
    New Potato Salad 450
Powdery Paint Finish for Walls 17
pressed herbs:
    Pressed Herb Cards 380
    Scented Pressed Herb Diary 380
Provençal Herb Hanging 258
puddings:
    Blackberry Charlotte 484
    Christmas Pudding 505
    Rhubarb and Orange Crumble 436
    Steamed Ginger and Cinnamon Syrup
        Pudding 487

Quiche, Mediterranean 448
quilts:
    Alphabet Cot Quilt 105–6
    Bear's Paw Quilt 102–4
    Diamond-in-a-Square Quilt 144
    Small Quilt 150
Quilted Appliqué Cushion Cover 108–10
Quilted Tie-backs 68

Rabbit Dummy Board 74–5
Rag Book 126
Rag Doll, Calico 124
Red Display in a Glass Cube 298
Red Tied Sheaf 370
Rhubarb and Orange Crumble 436
Rice, Wild, Corn and Coriander, Stuffed
    Tomatoes with 478
Ring, Candle 231
rings see wreaths and rings
Roast Beef with Porcini and Roasted Sweet
    Peppers 492
Rose and Clove Pomander 371
Rose and Starfish Wreath 280

rosemary:
Bath Bags 376
Lemon and Rosemary Lamb Chops 426
Rosemary Hair Tonic 391
Rosemary-flavoured Oil 412
roses:
Massed Star-shaped Decoration 304
Old-fashioned Garden Rose
Arrangement 234
Rucksack, Child's Strip Patchwork 132

sachets:
Hanging Heart Sachet 130
Lavender Sachets 330
Pot Pourri Sachet 190
Sage and Mango Chutney, Pork and
Mushrooms with 474
salads:
Avocado and Pasta Salad with Coriander
454
French Bean Salad 450
Garden Salad 453
New Potato Salad 450
Warm Chicken Salad with Sesame and
Coriander 418
salmon:
Salmon and Ginger Pie 442
Smoked Salmon, Lemon and Dill Pasta
454
Salt Box, Hanging 86
Sampler 206
Scarf, Appliqué Wool 119
Scented Pressed Herb Diary 380
Scented Valentine Heart 378
Sconce, Wall 58
Scones, Cheese 482
Scotch Pancakes 502
Sesame and Coriander, Warm Chicken
Salad with 418
Sewing Box, Amish 80
Shaker Box 164
Shaker-inspired Peg Rail 44–5
sheaves:
Red Tied Sheaf 370
Wall Hanging Sheaf 297
Sheet and Pillow Case, Embroidered 200
Shelf Edging, Sunflower 120
shelf trimming:
Lace and Gingham Shelf Trimming 70
Leather-edged Shelf Trimming 69
Shelf with Hanging Hooks 50–51
shells:
Peony and Shell Display 281
Shell Box 351

Shell Candle Centrepiece 352
Shell Mirror 354
Shell Pot 350
Shoe Bag, Autumn Leaf 129
Shortbread Fingers, Orange 501
Skin Tonic, Tansy 385
Skirt, Child's Strip Patchwork 137
Sleep Pillow 144–5
Sloe Gin and Juniper, Chicken with 476
Small Candleholder Display 289
Small Quilt 150
Smoked Salmon, Lemon and Dill Pasta
454
Sorbet, Borage, Mint and Lemon Balm
462
Soufflés, Carrot and Coriander 428
soups:
Bacon and Lentil Soup 494
Herb and Chilli Gazpacho 440
Mushroom and Parsley Soup 470
Pear and Watercress Soup with Stilton
Croûtons 441
Spice Pots 314
Spiced Pickled Pears 403
Spiced Plums in Brandy, Poached 402
Spicy Duck Breasts with Red Plums 477
Spicy Pomander 364–5
Spinach and Roquefort Pancakes 418
Spinach, Cognac, Garlic and Chicken Pâté
472
Spinach, Walnut and Gruyère Lasagne
with Basil 479
Spring Blossom Urn 224
Spring Napkin Decoration 221
Spring Onions, Lamb and Leeks with Mint
and 422
Spring Roasted Chicken with Fresh Herbs
and Garlic 426
Springtime Garland 266–7
Squash à la Greque 452
Star-shaped Decoration, Massed 304
starfish:
Bathroom Display 294–5
Rose and Starfish Wreath 280
Steak and Kidney Pie with Mustard and
Bay Gravy 425
Steamed Ginger and Cinnamon Syrup
Pudding 487
Stencilled Border 18–19
strawberry:
Country Strawberry Fool 456
Strawberry Jam 406
strip patchwork:
Child's Strip Patchwork Rucksack 132

Child's Strip Patchwork Skirt 137
Child's Strip Patchwork Waistcoat 136
Stuffed Parsleyed Onions 423
Stuffed Tomatoes with Wild Rice, Corn
and Coriander 478
Summer Basket Display 237
Summer Displays 282
Summer Fruit Gâteau with Heartsease 462
Summer Pot Pourri 293
Summer Table Display 284–5
Sunflower Shelf Edging 120
Swag, Fruit and Flower 228

Table, Painted 38–9
Tablecloth and Napkin 194–5
Tablepiece, Herbal 372
Tag, Gift 340
Tansy Skin Tonic 385
tarts:
French Apple Tart 488
Leek and Onion Tart 500
Mixed Berry Tart 460
Wild Mushroom Tart 468
Tea and Egg Cosies, Patchwork 140
Textured Foliage Ring 296
Three-fruit Marmalade 408
throws:
Country Throw 114
Log Cabin Throw 138
Woollen Patchwork Throw 64–5
thyme:
Leek and Monkfish with Thyme Sauce
420
Thyme-flavoured Vinegar 412
Thyme-roasted Onions 470
tie-backs:
Floral Tie-backs 196
Plaited 'Rag-rug' Tie-backs 66
Quilted Tie-backs 68
Tied Posy 268
Tin or Toleware, Painted 76–7
Tissue Rosette Gift-wrap 358
Toleware 76–7
tomatoes:
Cod, Basil and Tomato with a Potato
Thatch 446
Mediterranean Quiche 448
Stuffed Tomatoes with Wild Rice, Corn
and Coriander 478
Tomato Chutney 404
tonics:
Parsley Hair Tonic 388
Rosemary Hair Tonic 391
Tansy Skin Tonic 385

topiary:
Dried Herbal Topiary Tree 373
Flower Topiary 312
Tulip Topiary Tree 238
towels:
Guest Towel 184
Hand Towel 179
Toy Bag 134
Traditional Beef Stew and Dumplings
496
Tray Cloth 170
Tray, Découpage 59–60
Treat Jar, Bath-time 382
tree:
Dried Herbal Topiary Tree 373
Tulip Topiary Tree 238
Trout with Bacon, Griddled 445
Trug, Autumn Crocus 242
T-shirt, Appliqué 128
Tulip Pomander 366
Tulip Topiary Tree 238
Tussie Mussie 269

Urn, Spring Blossom 224
Utensil Box 167

Valentine Heart, Scented 378
vases:
Arum Lily Vase 251
Blue and Yellow Bud Vases 236
Decorated Vase with Calla Lilies 254
Hyacinth Bulb Vases 220
Vegetable Centrepiece 261
Vine Wreath, Hearth 168
Vinegar, Thyme-flavoured 412

waistcoats:
Child's Strip Patchwork Waistcoat 136
Child's Suffolk Puff Waistcoat 158
Wall Hanging Sheaf 297
Wall Sconce 58
Walls, Powdery Paint Finish for 17
walnuts:
Spinach and Roquefort Pancakes 418
Spinach, Walnut and Gruyère Lasagne
with Basil 479
Warm Chicken Salad with Sesame and
Coriander 418
Watercress Soup, Pear and, with Stilton
Croûtons 441
Wholemeal Bread 433

Wild at Heart 262
Wild Mushroom Tart 468
Winter Twigs Arrangement 255
Wooden Candlesticks 56, 62–3
Wooden Spoon Mobile 180
Woollen Patchwork Throw 64–5
wreaths and rings:
Candle Ring 231
Cinnamon and Orange Ring 368
Fresh Herbal Wreath 222
Globe Thistle and Mussel Shell Ring
287
Heart Vine Wreath 168
Herbal Christmas Wreath 374
Rose and Starfish Wreath 280
Textured Foliage Ring 296

yellow:
Blue and Yellow Arrangement in a
Pitcher 246
Blue and Yellow Bud Vases 236
Massed Arrangement in Blue and
Yellow 286

Acknowledgements

Appalachia: The Folk Art Shop
14a George Street
St Albans
Herts AL3 4ER
(tel: 01727 836796; fax: 01992 467560)

Brats
281 King's Road
London SW3 5EW
(tel: 0171 351 7674)
also
624c Fulham Road
London SW6 5RS
(tel: 0171 731 6915)
Suppliers of Mediterranean palette paints

Farrow & Ball Ltd
Madens Trading Estate
Wimborne
Dorset BH21 7NL
(tel: 01202 876141; fax: 01202 873793)
Suppliers of National Trust paints

Hill Farm Herbs
Park Walk
Brigstock
Northants NN14 3HH
(tel: 01536 373694; fax: 01536 373246)
Suppliers of potted fresh herbs, dried herbs
and flowers, dried flower decorations

Manic Botanic
34 Juer Street
London SW11 4RF
(tel: 0171 978 4505)
Suppliers of made-to-order floral
decorations

Paint Magic
79 Shepperton Road
London N1 3DF
(tel: 0171 354 9696; fax: 0171 226 7760)
Suppliers of paints and varnishes

Shaker Ltd
25 Harcourt Street
London W1H 1DT
also
322 King's Road
London SW3 5UH
Mail order enquiries to Harcourt Street
address or by telephone on 0171 742 7672

Somerset House of Iron
779 Fulham Road
London SW6 5HR
(tel: 0171 371 0436)

Robert Young Antiques
68 Battersea Bridge Road
London SW11 3AG
(tel: 0171 228 7847)